Concepts *of* Pattern Grading

Techniques for Manual and Computer Grading

Carolyn L. Moore
Assistant Professor
Radford University

Kathy K. Mullet
Associate Professor
Radford University

Margaret Prevatt Young
Designer
Wolff Fording & Company

Fairchild Publications, Inc.

New York

Executive Director: **Olga Kontzias**
Production Editor: **Joann Muscolo**
Editorial Assistant: **Beth Applebome**
Copy Editor: **Frances Koblin**
Art Director: **Nataliya Gurshman**
Production Manager: **Priscilla Taguer**
Cover Design & Illustration: **Nataliya Gurshman**

Library of Congress Catalog Card Number: 00-30155

ISBN: 1-56367-210-3

GST R 133004424

Printed in the United States of America

Contents

Extended Contents

List of Tables

Preface

Pattern grading is the process of systematically increasing and decreasing the size of a master pattern to create a range of sizes. *Concepts of Pattern Grading: Techniques for Manual and Computer Grading* is a comprehensive textbook that focuses on pattern grading using the Cartesian graph. Concepts are presented with a mix of theory and practice to facilitate the learning process.

Chapter 1 surveys the history of anthropometric studies and the development of sizing specifications and grade guides. Appendexes A through C are provided to allow the more advanced student to understand how grade guides are developed. Chapter 1 and the Appendexes are theory-based for the student who is seriously interested in the development of grading systems that result in optimal fit of apparel in a range of sizes.

Chapters 2 through 4 cover the concepts and principles of pattern grading. Since computerized grading incorporates the Cartesian graph orientation, the grading concepts introduced in these chapters are based on using the graph. These chapters guide the student through manually marking and grading a basic pattern block. The differences and similarities of manual and computerized grading are discussed.

Grading problems are introduced in Chapters 5, 6, and 7. The examples presented are representative of basic garment designs. In these chapters the student learns how a grade is distributed through different garment patterns and begins writing grade rules. Grade distributions are presented in a grade rule table format to facilitate the learning process. This format also facilitates the transition to computerized grading.

Chapters 8 through 11 contain more advanced grading problems and require a thorough understanding of the grading principles. Chapter 8 discusses the use of alternative reference axes for more complex pattern designs. Grading stretch fabric garments is explained in Chapter 9, and grading from garment specifications is discussed in Chapter 10. Chapter 11 focuses on converting a numerical sizing chart to an alphanumeric sizing chart. Completion of the exercises in these chapters will result in a valuable reference book that can be useful in the workplace.

The grading system used in this text is derived from the PS 42-70 Grade Guide because it is based on the most recent data available and contains sufficient information to develop both complex and simplified grading systems. The disadvantage of using the PS 42-70 Grade Guide is that the size nomenclature does not reflect the comparable sizes in most ready-to-wear. For example, the PS 42-70 size12 is generally closer to ready-to-wear size 8 as defined in the American Society for Testing and Materials (ASTM) Standard Table of Body Measurements for Adult Female Misses

Figure Type, Sizes 2–20 (D 5585-95). However, the advantage is that other anthropometric data can be substituted in the simplified system because the developmental method used to create grade guides is the same regardless of the body dimensions used.

The fewer sizes there are in the size range, the better the fit will be in the extreme sizes when using the simplified system. The authors therefore recommend the use of more than one sample-size pattern for a size range of six or more sizes. However, the problems in this book use a wide range to give students the experience of grading across the 1-inch, the 1 1/2-inch, and the 2-inch grades.

ACKNOWLEDGMENTS

The authors wish to thank the following people for their cooperation and aid: the students who have been enrolled in the pattern grading course at Radford University as we wrote the book. They have endured our trials and failures and most of all provided valuable input. Our colleagues and former colleagues at Radford University, Baylor University, and Wolff Fording and Company gave us encouragement, input, and support for this project. We thank Alan Young for his proofreading expertise and the fortitude to read our text out of the kindness of his heart. The reviewers selected by the publisher were very helpful. They include Susan Suarez, Fashion Careers of California; Bonnie Belleau, Louisiana State University; Elizabeth Bye, University of Minnesota; Ann Stemm, Illinois State University; Mary Farahnakian, Brigham Young University; Mela Hoyt-Heydon, Fullerton College; and Nancy Staples, Clemson University.

Concepts *of* Pattern Grading

Pattern Grading

Fundamentals

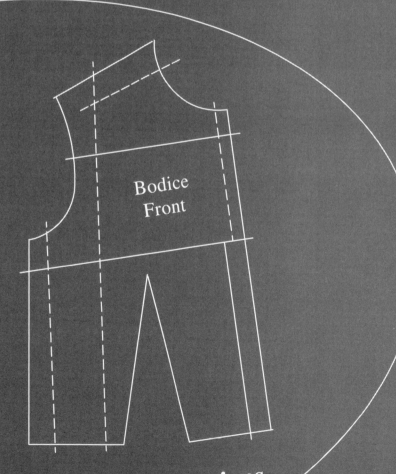

Grading System

Grade Guide

Size	6-8	8-10	10-12	12-14
Bust	1"	1"	11/2"	11/2"
Waist	1"	1"	11/2"	11/2"
Hip	1"	1"	11/2"	11/2"

Bodice Front

Grade Guide

Grade Distributions

Introduction

Pattern grading is the process of systematically increasing and decreasing the dimensions of a **master pattern** into a range of sizes for production. Due to cost constraints, one **sample-size pattern** is developed and fitted, then other sizes are graded from this master pattern. The purpose is to achieve a good fit in each size without changing the **style sense** (proportion and balance) of the garment **design** from the master pattern (Solinger, 1988).

Grading systems are developed to translate the body changes from size to size to corresponding pattern pieces. The procedure used to develop a grading system is (1) collect anthropometrical data from individuals within a target population; (2) statistically analyze the collected data to determine sizing specifications and standards; and (3) distribute the dimensions from the **size specifications** across the body, to replicate the body shape changes from size to size. This systematic increasing and decreasing of the body dimensions between sizes is fundamental to developing a grading system.

This chapter provides a brief review of available anthropometric studies and the development of sizing specifications which are basic to pattern grading. The development of the grading system used in this text is also discussed.

Anthropometric Surveys

The transition from custom-made clothing to ready-to-wear apparel was in progress by the beginning of the 20th century and has escalated with each decade since. Custom-made clothing is sized specifically to fit the wearer, whereas ready-to-wear apparel is sized according to **body types**. The ready-to-wear size is based on the statistical averages of many people. Therefore, it is impossible for ready-to-wear to fit every single wearer. Initially, manufacturers subjectively determined the dimensions for each size in their size range and made fit improvements as needed by trial and error.

USDA Survey

The first **anthropometric survey** of women in the United States was sponsored by the U.S. Department of Agriculture (USDA) in 1940 for the purpose of developing sizing standards for women's patterns and apparel (O'Brien & Shelton, 1941). The project provided **anthropometric data** (body measurements) that represented the female population across the United States. Measurements were taken in 60 locations on the body with a sample of more than 10,000 women participating. The sample data were divided into four subgroups or body types based upon key length and **circumference (girth) measurements**. The subgroups were designated as juniors, misses, half-sizes, and women's, with each of these groups subdivided into a range of seven to ten sizes, depending upon the subgroup. Statistical averages from each specific size group were used to derive a set of size specifications to fit a segment of the population with similar **body dimensions**.

The Mail Order Association of American requested that the USDA publish the sizing specifications based on 1941 USDA survey data to aid in consistent sizing of women's apparel. The goal was to provide a standard classification of body types, size designation, and body measurements for each size so that the information could be used by manufacturers, retailers, and consumers (O'Brien & Shelton, 1941). Commercial Standard CS 215-58, *Body Measurements for the Sizing of Women's Patterns and Apparel* was published in 1958 by The Department of Commerce. The same mail-order organization requested an update of the standard in 1968 that more accurately reflected the female population. **The PS 42-70, *Voluntary Product Standard: Body Measurements for the Sizing of Women's Patterns and Apparel*** was published by the Department of Commerce National Bureau of Standards (National Bureau of Standards, 1971). This **voluntary sizing standard** expanded the body types from four to seven to include junior petite, misses petite, and misses tall in order to improve the fit for a greater number of segments in the population.

Military Surveys

The 1941 anthropometric data are still being used as the foundation for most domestic apparel sizing, even though the size nomenclature has changed. However, other studies have had an impact on sizing specifications. The increase of the female population in the armed forces has prompted a number of military surveys in recent decades. Among them were anthropometric surveys of U.S. Army women, completed in 1977, and U.S. Air Force women, in 1978 (Churchill, Churchill, McConville & White, 1977; Tebbetts, McConville, & Alexander, 1979). The Army and Air Force data were used to establish sizing specifications for Navy women (McConville, Tebbetts, & Churchill, 1979; Gordon, Churchill, Clauser, Bradtmiller, & McConville, 1988; Mellian, Ervin & Robinette, 1988). Although the military surveys do not reflect a broad range of the general population, they have been useful to the civilian sector as an indicator of how some average measurements have changed (i.e., increase in height and waist circumference).

International Surveys

In addition to the U.S. military surveys, a sample of 5000 adult women was measured in England in 1950, and smaller surveys have been undertaken in other countries (Cooklin, 1994; Taylor & Shoben, 1986). German surveys measured women in 1962, 1970, and again in 1983; and 8000 subjects were measured in France in 1968 (Bunn, 1983; Cooklin, 1994). In all of the surveys, common measurements were identified as important in dividing the samples into body types and size categories. Key **girth** measurements are bust, waist, and hips; the most important length measurements are waist length (from nape of neck to waist) and the length of arms, legs, and lower torso (Tamburrino, 1992a; Taylor & Shoben, 1986).

ASTM Survey of Women 55 and Older

The most recent U.S. survey completed was in 1993 under the auspices of the **American Society for Testing and Materials (ASTM)** in which 6600 U.S. women 55 years and older were measured (Goldsberry, Shim, & Reich, 1996a; Reich & Goldsberry, 1993). Body types and average measurements for each size within each body type have been extracted from these data, but a systematic set of sizing specifications has not been published. A growing number of women fit into the older age group in which physical changes in the body lead to a change from the body shape assumed in the PS 42-70 sizing specifications. Proportional changes were identified in the shoulders, back waist length, bust, waist, abdomen, and upper arm girths, even when weight did not increase (Goldsberry, 1993). The data were compared with the PS 42-70 data, and dimensions of women 55 years and older were greater in the abdominal extension, waist, sitting spread, **armscye**, bust level, back width, chest width, hip, and hip arc (Goldsberry, Shim, & Reich, 1996b).

Anthropometric Survey Using Body Scanners

The latest survey to collect anthropometric data involves the use of body scanners. The Civilian American and European Surface Anthropometry Research (CAESAR) project is primarily funded by the U.S. Air Force and NATO, although about 40 companies have also invested in the $6 million project (Ahles, 1999; Haverkampf, 1999). The project proposes that a sample of about 4000 men and women from the United

States and 6800 each from Italy and the Netherlands be studied. These European countries were chosen because Italy has the shortest population and the Netherlands has the tallest population among NATO members. The scanners are set up at large corporations where many people can be measured in one location (S. Mellian, telephone conversation, August 26, 1998). The project is scheduled to be completed by 2001. For one year after the study, only sponsoring companies and the Air Force will have access to the data, but after that apparel companies can benefit from the information.

The Textile/Clothing Technology Corporation ([TC]²) has developed its own scanner to help apparel companies improve the fit of clothing for the consumer (Haverkampf, 1999). The three-dimensional measurement data are fed directly into a computer program that matches the data with the size (in a set of size specifications) that is closest to the body dimensions. The computer program alters the matched size to the customer's measurements; the information is then relayed to an automatic pattern cutter to create a customized garment.

These scanners replace the measuring tape by collecting anthropometric data electronically with increased speed and accuracy. The availability of body scanners provides the means of updating anthropometric data more easily than in the past, and it can help make customized apparel a reality.

Table 1.1 summarizes anthropometric surveys that have influenced women's apparel sizing. Yet, in 1998, a survey by Kurt Salomon Associates found two-thirds of consumers are still dissatisfied with the fit of their clothes (Haverkampf, 1999).

Several factors contribute to the need for updated data for the U.S. population. Since the USDA survey of American women in 1940, ethnic groups have increased in the United States (Tamburrino, 1992b), lifestyles have affected physiological changes in the size and shape of the female body, and the average height and weight of the population has increased

(Abraham, 1977). However, current anthropometric data alone will not prevent poor fit in apparel if the data are used improperly in developing sizing specifications, sizing standards, and grading systems.

SIZING STANDARDS
PS 42-70 Sizing Standard
The oldest **sizing standard** for women's garments was developed from the 1940 USDA survey (O'Brien & Shelton, 1941), published in 1958. Four body types were identified: juniors, misses, half-size, and women. A few years later the specifications were revised to include junior petite, misses petite, and misses tall for a total of seven body types. The revision was published as PS 42-70 Voluntary Product Standard (U. S. Department of Commerce, 1971).

However, there is no mandatory sizing standard for domestic apparel. The PS 42-70 sizing specifications are voluntary, and few apparel manufactures actually use them per se. Apparel producers can specify in writing their acceptance of the voluntary standard as far as practicable, but they reserve the right to depart from it when expedient. Many manufacturers target a narrow consumer group with similar body characteristics. The size specifications and range of sizes used are based on what the manufacturer perceives that market to need. A unique sizing system is a means of product differentiation for manufacturers, even though it creates a dilemma for the consumer who may wear a dress size 6, 8, 10, or 12, depending upon the sizing system and size nomenclature of different manufacturers.

Existing survey data are helpful in identifying anthropometric information for population segments when developing sizing specifications, but current consumer information is essential also. The successful manufacturer first identifies a target market and then accumulates data on that consumer group before developing a sizing chart. Once the consumer group is determined, dimensions of the smallest and largest sizes within the targeted group are established. Based on the type of

garment to be produced, the manufacturer then determines the number of sizes in the size range. An efficient sizing chart has the fewest number of sizes that will provide a good fit for all persons in the specific consumer group. Although the survey data are for body measurements, the manufacturer's sizing specifications generally are for garment dimensions.

Whether a manufacturer uses a size range as wide as the PS 42-70 depends upon the type of garment being produced and the market segment targeted. A close-fitting garment requires a large range of sizes to fit the market population, but a loose-fitting garment for the same population could consist of a simple five-size range from extra small to extra large. A target market may be specific for age or figure type, which also could reduce the number of sizes in the size range. Obviously, production costs would be lower in areas of patternmaking and grading with a narrow range of sizes. There is a lack of documentation on sources of size specifications used in the industry as well as on pattern grading systems (Jones, 1989).

A significant departure from the PS 42-70 Sizing Specifications by domestic apparel producers has been **size nomenclature**. The dimensions for a size 12 in PS 42-70 may be approximately the same as a size 6, 8, or 10 in current ready-to-wear. Assigning a smaller size number to a garment that has previously carried a larger size is referred to as **vanity sizing** and is appealing to most consumers. Over time this shift in size nomenclature relative to body size has been accepted by consumers as "standard," even though the dimensional specifications depart from published standards.

ASTM D 5585-95 Sizing Standard
The ASTM D 55 Sizing Committee issued sizing standard D 5585-95 for the adult female misses figure type (Annual Book of ASTM Standards, 1997). The standard is presented in Appendix C and closely mirrors the mass-produced apparel sizing nomenclature. The standard contains sizes 2 to 20 and is based upon the PS 42-70 database and data from the military studies as well as designer and industry input. The

comparison of body dimensions for size 2 in D 5585-95 are nearest the dimensions for size 8 in PS 42-70, which demonstrates the different nomenclature used by the industry. When comparing dimensions for D 5585-95 size 2 to PS 42-70 size 8, proportional differences in some areas are apparent (see Appendixes A and C). These differences reflect the influences of military studies, designer information, and market observations (*Annual Book of ASTM Standards*, 1997). There are nine sizes in the PS 42-70 size range, whereas D 5585-95 contains ten sizes. D 5585-95 is also a voluntary standard. Apparel manufacturers may depart from the standard when tailoring their size specification to a specific target market.

ASTM D 5586-95 Sizing Standard

The ASTM has also issued Standard Tables of Body Measurements for Women Aged 55 and Older, Designation: D 5586-95 (*Annual Book of ASTM Standards*, 1997). However, the measurements are averages of the raw data, so systematic changes do not occur between sizes. Appendix B contains a systematic sizing chart along with complex and simplified grading systems that were derived from these data.

European Sizing Standard

The opening of the European Common Market in 1992 prompted the development of a sizing standard to eliminate confusion of sizing nomenclature between European countries (Mellian, 1991). Unlike the seven PS 42-70 body type classifications, the European standard classifies body types on the basis of three body lengths (short, medium, and tall) and three figure types (slim hips, normal hips, and broad hips) for each body length, resulting in a total of nine body types. Key body measurements basic to the development of the system are height, bust girth, waist girth, hip girth, and inside leg length. The labeling regulation specifies that a label on ready-to-wear carries the garment size nomenclature, a symbol to designate body type, and the bust and hip dimensions for the body type the size is to fit. Although this standard is not mandatory for all garment manufacturers in the

European Common Market, the acceptance of it by retailers and consumers may encourage the industry to adopt it.

Additional Sizing Specifications

Sets of body measurements are available in published documents, such as Fashiondex's *Apparel Design and Production Handbook* (1998), Solinger's *Apparel Manufacturing Handbook* (1988), and various pattern grading textbooks. However, these sources are not always consistent and do not necessarily disclose the source of their information. Fashiondex includes the following disclaimer: "We cannot be held responsible for sample, production, or other errors due to any information and/or measurements printed within this handbook. All measurements and information published herein are subject to change at any time, without notification by the Fashiondex, Inc."

Ultimately, the selection of body measurements to be used in the development of sizing specifications is up to the individual manufacturer, and the use of published standards is voluntary. Most apparel producers use a human **fit model** to develop a sample-size pattern. A sample-size pattern is developed for a selected garment style and fitted to the model. This master pattern is then graded into all sizes in the size range in preparation for production.

Regardless of size specifications and the grading system used, three assumptions should be made. First, the sample-size master pattern fits all critical body areas; second, the pattern is accurate with corresponding seams and notches matching; and third, a size run of the graded patterns has been completed to be sure fit and style sense are maintained across the size range.

GRADING SYSTEMS

A grading system is developed from sizing specifications, and sizing specifications are derived from anthropometric surveys. A **grade guide** dictates the system of grade distribution across the pattern (Figure 1.1). The review of available anthropometric data,

Grading System

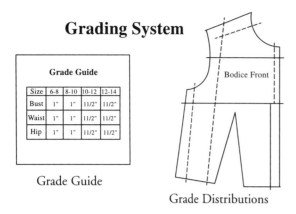

Grade Guide

Grade Distributions

■Figure 1.1 Components That Make Up a Grading System

which consists of actual body measurements, is important to understand the development of sizing specifications and how they are basic to grade guides used for pattern grading systems (Appendix A). A grade guide is determined by the mathematical differences between the dimensions of adjacent sizes.

Major Differences in Grading Systems

Grading systems differ in two major ways. The first difference is the size where the grade changes in the size range from a 1-inch to a 1 1/2-inch grade and from a 1 1/2-inch to a 2-inch grade. This numeric classification (1 inch, 1 1/2 inch, and 2 inch) indicates the dimensional change from one size to the adjacent size. In a comparison of body dimension specifications between 39 commercial apparel manufacturers and the U.S. Army specifications, the change from a 1-inch to a 1 1/2-inch grade varied from between sizes 6 and 8 to between sizes 16 and 18, with the greatest number of changes occurring between sizes 12 and 14 (Staples, 1994) The same variation was found in the sizes where the grade changed to a 2-inch grade.

The second difference in grading systems is how the total grade is distributed across the width and length of the pattern. In Chapter 2, Figure 2.4 shows the grade distribution of different systems. Using the

bodice as an example, the width grade is distributed within the neck, the shoulder, and the underarm areas. The length grade is distributed in the neck, the armscye, and the underarm to waist areas. Different systems may specify varying amounts of the total width or length grades in each of these areas, which in turn, affects how the garment fits in each of these areas. The effects of the differences in the sizes where the grade changes and how the grade is distributed within each size are most apparent in the fit of extreme sizes in a size range.

Complexity of the Body

The complex shape of the adult female body is another reason fitting problems occur. It is why so many body measurements must be taken when conducting anthropometric surveys. Taylor and Shoben (1986) reported that British survey data indicated increases in girth measurements were not equally divided between the back and front of the body. Width increase across the bust is slightly more than the increase across the back at the bust level; the width increase across the front waist is more than the increase across the back waist; the width increase across the back at the fullest part of the hips is more than the increase at the same level across the front; and the width increase across the back of the arm at the biceps is greater than across the front of the arm.

Cooklin (1994) compared survey data from the U.S., England, Germany, and France and found differences in the front and back body measurements to be similar in each data set. Table 1.2, which is an excerpt from the PS 42-70 Misses Specification Table (Table A.1 in Appendix A), includes **arc measurements** and the total girth measurements for the front bust, the front waist, and the front abdominal areas. Table 1.3 gives girth grades of the same areas; most arc grades are more than half the girth grades. The PS 42-70 back hip grade is an exception to other arc grades; it is less than half of the hip grade (Table A.2). Also, the width of the chest between the mid-armscyes is less than the width across the back between the mid-armscyes.

Both Taylor and Shoben (1986) and Cooklin (1994) discuss a **complex three-dimensional grading system** in which the suppression of darts and shape-control seams are changed in these body areas; therefore, a different set of grade rules is required for the back and for the front. As seen in Table 1.3, the front and back of the body require different width grades and a complex grading system. Taylor and Shoben along with Cooklin point out that differences in the change between the back and front of the body are small, but fitting problems will occur in extreme sizes of a wide range of sizes when using a **simplified two-dimensional grading system** in which the increase or decrease is the same for back and front. Table 1.4 is derived from the girth measurements in Table 1.2, in which the total grade is distributed equally in the bodice front and bodice back.

Taylor and Shoben point out that the closer survey data are followed, the more elaborate the grading system will be. They stress that close-fitting garments require a more complex grading system than loose-fitting garments in order to maintain satisfactory fit. The more the system is simplified, the easier it is to use, but each stage of simplification impairs the proficiency of the system.

Complex grading systems are cumbersome and time-consuming to use. Therefore, simplified systems are used in most pattern grading texts and in the apparel industry. Most manufacturers have their own unique sizing specifications, and hence each grading system may also differ; but this is not necessarily true, because the incremental differences between sizes could be similar. Pattern grading texts often present systems with no information given as to the source of the system. However, concepts of pattern grading can be grasped regardless of the grading system used.

PS 42-70 Grading System

The PS 42-70 Voluntary Product Standard lists sizes 6 to 22, a range of nine sizes (Table A.1). Table A.2 in Appendix A is the Grade Guide for the Misses Size

specification table and consists of girth, arc, width, and length measurements. A grade guide dictates the grading system by which the grades are distributed in the pattern. To use the PS 42-70 Grade Guide as is would require the development of a **complex grading system**, which can be found in Appendix A. Only a complex grading system can produce a grade distribution for the back and front body that results in the actual anthropometric measurements across a size range. Table 1.2 (an excerpt from Table A.1) contains arc measurements and total girth measurements for the bust, waist, and hips. Table 1.3 is a complex grade guide for the same measurements, and shows the difference for the back and front of the body. A simplified grade guide for the same body areas is shown in Table 1.4. It is important to know what the complex grade distribution is so that the efficiency of a simplified system developed from the same data can be evaluated. The complex grading system based on the PS 42-70 Grade Guide has been simplified by the authors of this text with the rationale illustrated in Appendix A. By comparing complex and simplified systems developed from the same data, it is apparent why garments in extreme sizes may result in fit problems and distortion of style sense when graded by a simplified system (Table A.5).

ASTM D-5585-95 Grading System

The ASTM D 5585-95 misses sizing standard is closer to size specifications used in the apparel industry than are the PS 42-70 specifications, especially in size nomenclature (Appendix C). Although the ASTM standard is rooted in the PS 42-70 database, the specifications do not contain arc measurements which are necessary for the development of a complex grading system. Arc measurements in PS 42-70 are taken across body contour and include front bust width, from side seam to side seam; front waist width, from side seam to side seam; and back hip width, from side seam to side seam. Arc measurements also identify differences between the back and front dimensions as well as show how the back and front change by different amounts between sizes.

The ASTM D 5585-95 database contains only enough information to develop a simplified grading system. This database and grade guide is used in Chapter 11.

Comparison of Authors' Simplified and ASTM D 5585 Grading Systems

As stated earlier, differences between grading systems are the size where the grade changes from a 1-inch to a 1 1/2-inch grade and from a 1 1/2-inch to a 2-inch grade and how the grade is distributed across the pattern. The only difference between the ASTM D-5585 grading system and the authors' system developed from the PS 42-70 data is in the distribution of the grade in the shoulder and neck areas of the 2-inch grade. Both systems change from a 1-inch grade to a 1 1/2-inch grade between sizes 10 and 12 and to a 2-inch grade between sizes 16 and 18. Therefore, the grading systems are alike except for the 2-inch grade in the neck and shoulder. Differences in the dimensions of the size range in the two systems are affected by the number of sizes in each system (sizes 2–20 in the ASTM versus sizes 6–22 in the PS 42-70); the number of sizes graded by a 1-inch grade (four in ASTM and two in PS 42-70); and the number of sizes graded by a 2-inch grade (two in ASTM and three in PS 42-70). The differences are not the result of the grade distributions in the grading systems. Once grading concepts are thoroughly understood, a pattern grader can use any system successfully.

The grading problems in this text are based upon the authors' grading system derived from the PS 42-70 database. Potential fit problems may result in the extreme sizes due to the modifications necessary to produce a simplified system (Table A.5). Research studies have shown that fit and garment proportion are affected when the pattern has been graded more than two sizes from the sample size (Bye & DeLong, 1994; Murphey, 1993). **With any simplified grading system, it is recommended that no more than five sizes be graded together, two on each side of the sample size.** This necessitates the use of more than one sample-size pattern for an average size range. Appropriate sample pattern sizes may vary depending upon the size range needed. Sample pattern sizes for a size range of 6 to 22 might be size 10 to grade sizes 6 to 14 and size 18 to grade sizes 14 to 22. Pattern grading exercises in this text include the complete size range (6–22) so students may experience grading across sizes where the grade changes from a 1-inch to a 1 1/2-inch grade and from a 1 1/2-inch to a 2-inch grade. This system is suitable for **rigid fabric** as opposed to **stretch fabric**. The modifications required to apply any system to **stretch garments** are explained in Chapter 9.

Taylor and Shoben (1986) have explained that when a grading system derived from anthropometric data is simplified, the proficiency of the system is impaired. Utilizing computer technology to grade close-fitting garments with a complex system in which the back and front of the garment are graded differently could provide a solution for some apparel fit problems.

PATTERN GRADING
SUMMARY

Pattern grading is the process of systematically increasing and decreasing the dimensions of a sample-size pattern into specified sizes while maintaining the style sense of the design. Specifications used to determine the amount of increase or decrease of each area of the sample-size pattern are developed from body measurements, which are derived from anthropometric studies.

The first major anthropometric study was conducted at the request of the USDA in 1940. The PS 42-70 Voluntary Product Standard, published in 1971, updated the earlier study to provide standard classifications of body types, size designation, and body measurements for use by manufacturers, retailers, and consumers. Later surveys have provided additional data, but they either do not contain extensive measurements or are limited to a specific subgroup of the population.

Grading systems are developed using the size specifications that are derived from anthropometric surveys.

The grade guide specifies the mathematical differences between the dimensions of adjacent sizes. Grading systems may be complex or simplified. Use of arc measurements such as front waist arc and back waist arc versus total waist circumference result in a complex grade guide in which the back of a garment grades differently than the front. Simplified grade guides place half the total circumference change in the front and half in the back, thereby allowing the front and back to grade by the same increment. Most ready-to-wear manufacturers use this simplified method.

The grading problems in this text are based upon the authors' grading system derived from the PS 42-70 database, and are appropriate only for patterns to be cut from rigid fabrics, unless otherwise stated. Because of modifications necessary to simplify the system, potential fit problems may result in extreme sizes when the system is used. It is recommended that no more than five sizes be graded together, two on each side of the sample size.

EXERCISES

1. Explain how custom-made clothing sizing is different from sizing used for ready-to-wear.
2. What are the three steps used to develop a grading system?
3. Why is it advantageous to collect as many body measurements as possible in an anthropometric survey?
4. It was stated that many manufacturers use a fit model to develop a sample-size pattern. What would be the advantages and disadvantages of this method?
5. How do the European sizing standards differ from the PS 42-70 sizing standards?
6. What type of body measurements are necessary to develop a complex grading system.
7. The grade between sizes is the mathematical difference between adjacent sizes. Fill in Table 1.5, a grade guide for bust, waist, and hips, using ASTM D5585 Standard Table of Body Measurements for Adult Female Misses Figure Type, Sizes 2 to 20 (Table C.1).
8. Identify where in the size range the grade changes from a 1-inch to a 1 1/2-inch grade and from a 1 1/2-inch to a 2-inch grade.
9. How much of the girth grade would go into a bodice front half pattern for 1-inch grade (_____), for 1 1/2-inch grade (_____), and for 2-inch grade (_____)?

REFERENCES

Abraham, S. (1977). *Weight by height and age of adults 18–74 in the U.S.* (Advanced Data No. 14). Rockville, MD: U.S. Department of Health, Education, and Welfare, National Center for Health Statistics.

Ahles, A. (1999, March 13). The Caesar Project Scanners may help designers create perfect fit. *The Roanoke Times*, pp. A5–6.

American Society for Testing and Materials Institute for Standards Research. (1997). *Annual book of ASTM standards* (Vol. 07.02). Philadelphia: Author.

Apparel design and production handbook. (1998). New York: Fashiondex, Inc.

Bunn, G. (1983, November). Ladieswear measurements survey. *Bobbin*, pp. 102–103.

Bye, E. K., & DeLong, M.R. (1994). A visual sensory evaluation of the results of two pattern grading methods. *Clothing and Textiles Research Journal, 12*(4), 1–7.

Churchill E., Churchill, T., McConville, J. T., & White, R. M. (1977). *Anthropometry of women of the U.S. Army* (Technical Report Natick/TR-77/024 [AD A044806]), Natick, MA: U.S. Army Natick Research and Development Command.

Cooklin, G. (1994). *Pattern grading for women's clothes.* London: Blackwell Scientific Publications.

Goldsberry, E. (1993). *Women 55 and older: How well is the domestic apparel sizing system addressing their needs?* (Research Technical Report: No. PCN 33-000006-18, ISR-06). Philadelphia: ASTM Institute for Standards Research.

Goldsberry, E., Shim, S., & Reich, N. (1996a). Women 55 years and older: Part I. Current body measurements as contrasted to the PS 42-70 data. *Clothing and Textiles Research Journal, 14*(2), 108–120.

Goldsberry, E., Shim, S., and Reich, N. (1996b). Women 55 years and older: Part II. Overall satisfaction and dissatisfaction with the fit of ready-to-wear. *Clothing and Textiles Research Journal, 14*(2), 121–132.

Gordon, C., Churchill, T., Clauser, C., Bradtmiller, B., & McConville, J. (1988). *1988 Anthropometric survey of the U.S. Army Natick R & D Center* (Technical Report Natick/TR-89/044). Natick, MA: U.S. Army Natick R&D Center.

Haverkampf, I. (1999, May 25). A size to fit all. *Style Weekly, Summer Fashion, 17*(21), 20–21.

Jones, T. R. (1989, November). Evaluating the pattern grading process. *Apparel Manufacturer*, pp. 34–37.

McConville, J., Tebbetts, I., & Churchill, T. (1979). *Analysis of body size measurements for U.S. Navy women's clothing and pattern design* (Technical Report No. 79-138). Natick, MA: Navy Clothing and Textile Research Facility.

Mellian, S. (1991, September). Uni-sizing Europe. *Apparel Industry Magazine*, pp. 82–87.

Mellian, S., Ervin, C., & Robinette, K. (1988). *Development of sizing system for Navy women's uniforms* (Technical Report No. NCTRF 182). Natick, MA: Navy Clothing and Textile Research Facility.

Murphey, I. C. (1993). *A case study of the influence of pattern grading systems on the fit and style sense of two low-neckline, fitted bodices.* Unpublished doctoral dissertation, Virginia Tech, Blacksburg, Va.

National Bureau of Standards. (1971). *Voluntary product standard: Body measurements for the sizing of women's patterns and apparel.* (NTIS No. PS 42-70) Washington DC: Government Printing Office.

O'Brien, R., & Shelton, W.C. (1941). *Women's measurement for garment and pattern construction.* (USDA Miscellaneous Publication No. 454). Washington DC: U.S. Government Printing Office.

Reich, N. & Goldsberry, E. (1993). *The development of body measurement tables for women 55 years and older and the relationships to ready-to-wear garment size.* (Research Technical Report: No. PCN 33-000006-18, ISR-06). Philadelphia, PA: ASTM Institute for Standards Research.

Solinger, J. (1988). *Apparel manufacturing handbook* (2d ed.). Columbia, SC: Bobbin Blenheim Media Corp.

Staples, N. J. (1994). *A comparison of U.S. Army and U.S. commercial misses anthropometric body dimensions specifications* (DAAK60-94-P-0145). Pendleton, SC: Clemson Apparel Research.

Tamburrino, N. (1992a, April). Apparel sizing issues: Part I. *Bobbin*, pp. 44–46.

Tamburrino, N. (1992b, May). Apparel sizing issues: Part II. *Bobbin*, pp. 52–60.

Taylor, P. J., & Shoben, M. M. (1986). *Grading for the fashion industry: The theory and practice.* London: Hutchinson.

Tebbetts, I., McConville, J., & Alexander, M. (1979). *Height/weight sizing programs for women's protective clothing* (Technical Report No. AMRL-TR-79-35). Wright-Patterson Air Force Base, Ohio: Aerospace Medical Research Laboratory.

U.S. Department of Commerce. (1958). *Body measurements for the sizing of a women's patterns and apparel* (Commercial Standard C5215-58). Washington, D.C.: U.S. Government Printing Office.

Table 1.1 Anthropometric Surveys of Adult Females

Anthropometric Survey	Date	Number in Sample
U.S. Civilian Surveys		
United States Department of Agriculture	1940	10,060
ASTM U.S. Women Age 55 and Older	1993	6,600
U.S. Military Surveys		
U.S. Army Women	1977	1,331
U.S. Air Force Women	1968	1,905
European Surveys		
England	1950	5,000
France	1968, 1970	not given
	1983	8,000
Germany	1961, 1970	not given
	1983	8,491
International Surveys		
Civilian American and European Surface Anthropometry Research (CAESAR) men and women measured	begun 1999	4,000—United States 6,800—Europe

Table 1.2 PS 42-70 Girth and Arc Body Measurements for Bust, Waist, and Hip

Size	6	8	10	12	14	16	18	20	22
Total Girth Measurements									
Bust	31 1/2	32 1/2	33 1/2	35	36 1/2	38	40	42	44
Waist	22 1/2	23 1/2	24 1/2	26	27 1/2	29	31	33	35
Hip	33 1/2	34 1/2	35 1/2	37	38 1/2	40	42	44	46
Arc Measurements									
Bust Front	17 3/4	18 1/2	19 1/4	20 1/4	21 1/4	22 1/4	23 5/8	25	26 3/8
Waist Front	11 7/8	12 1/2	13 1/8	14	14 7/8	15 3/4	17	18 1/4	19 1/2
Hip Back	16 7/8	17 1/4	17 5/8	18 1/4	18 7/8	19 1/2	20 1/4	21	21 3/4

Note: Measurements are in inches.

Table 1.3 PS 42-70 Complex Grade Guide

Size	6–8	8–10	10–12	12–14	14–16	16–18	18–20	20–22
Grades for Body Front Widths								
Bust	3/4	3/4	1	1	1	1 3/8	1 3/8	1 3/8
Waist	5/8	5/8	7/8	7/8	1 1/4	1 1/4	1 1/4	1 1/4
Hip[a]	5/8	5/8	7/8	7/8	1 1/4	1 1/4	1 1/4	1 1/4
Grades for Body Back Widths								
Bust[a]	1/4	1/4	1/2	1/2	1/2	5/8	5/8	5/8
Waist[a]	1/4	1/4	1/2	1/2	1/2	5/8	5/8	5/8
Hip	3/8	3/8	5/8	5/8	5/8	3/4	3/4	3/4
Total Girth Grades								
Bust	1	1	1 1/2	1 1/2	1 1/2	2	2	2
Waist	1	1	1 1/2	1 1/2	1 1/2	2	2	2
Hip	1	1	1 1/2	1 1/2	1 1/2	2	2	2

Note: Measurements are in inches.

[a] Measurements are the differences between PS 42-70 arc grades and total girth grades.

Table 1.4 PS 42-70 Simplified Grade Guide

Size	6–8	8–10	10–12	12–14	14–16	16–18	18–20	20–22
Grades for Body Front Widths								
Bust	1/2	1/2	3/4	3/4	3/4	1	1	1
Waist	1/2	1/2	3/4	3/4	3/4	1	1	1
Hip	1/2	1/2	3/4	3/4	3/4	1	1	1
Grades for Body Back Widths								
Bust	1/2	1/2	3/4	3/4	3/4	1	1	1
Waist	1/2	1/2	3/4	3/4	3/4	1	1	1
Hip	1/2	1/2	3/4	3/4	3/4	1	1	1
Total Girth Grades								
Bust	1	1	1 1/2	1 1/2	1 1/2	2	2	2
Waist	1	1	1 1/2	1 1/2	1 1/2	2	2	2
Hip	1	1	1 1/2	1 1/2	1 1/2	2	2	2

Note: Measurements are in inches.

■ **Table 1.5** Girth Measurement Differences Between Sizes

Size	2–4	4–6	6–8	8–10	10–12	12–14	14–16	16–18	18–20
Bust									
Waist									
Hips									

Note: Measurements are in inches.

2

Pattern Grading
Terminology

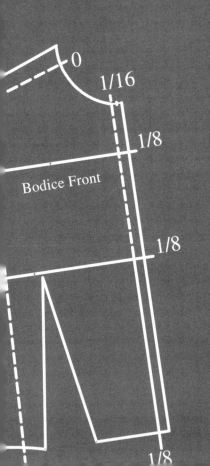

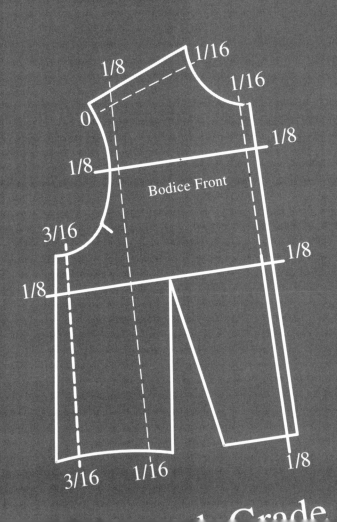

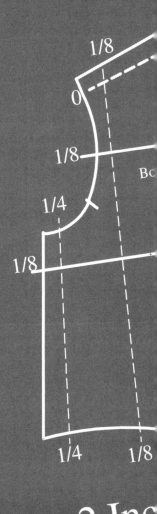

Introduction

An understanding of pattern and pattern grading terminology is essential for grasping the concepts and principles of pattern grading. Knowledge of the specific meanings of the terms allows the reader to understand their applications in the pattern grading process. If the reader does not understand the use of these terms in relation to pattern grading, the explanations provided in this text may be confusing. For example, the term *grade* has several applications and each one must be understood in relation to increasing and decreasing the dimensions of the master pattern. The terms that are defined in this chapter are also found in the Glossary. This allows easy reference when working in other chapters of the text.

PATTERN TERMINOLOGY

Four basic types of patterns are used in the design and production stages of apparel production: basic slopers, basic blocks, master patterns, and production patterns. The most simplified pattern consists of a set of **basic slopers**, which contains the minimum number of pattern pieces required for a fitted garment, with minimum ease and no seam allowances. All darts extend to their respective pivot point and lack any dart take-up. Slopers are used as the basis for flat pattern design.

Basic blocks are a set of pattern pieces for a **style** category such as a princess dress or an A-line skirt. They

are free of fashion details and usually contain only the major pattern pieces without finishing details, such as facings and pockets. Seam allowances generally are not included, but darts are shortened the appropriate distances from their pivot points. A specific company's basic blocks reflect that company's preferred fit. Sample patterns are usually developed from the basic blocks as a first step in creating the master pattern for a design. The master pattern has the added fashion details and design lines for a specific design. Dart take-up is added and all seamlines are **trued** and balanced on a master pattern, but seam allowances are optional. The master pattern usually exists in the sample size only.

The **production pattern** is the final, perfect pattern that meets all production requirements. It consists of all sizes in the size run with seam allowances and dart take-ups included. All seams are trued and balanced on all sizes.

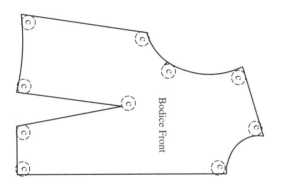

Figure 2.1 Cardinal Points

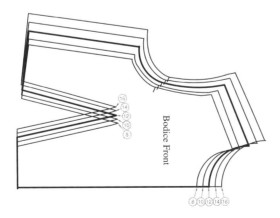

Figure 2.2 Nested Graded Pattern Block

GRADING TERMINOLOGY

The term *grade* has three definitions in the context of pattern grading. It is used as a verb and as a noun. To **grade (verb)**, in the context of this book, means to systematically decrease and increase the dimensions of the master pattern or basic blocks to create a range of sizes for production. The dimensional changes are made on the perimeter of the pattern pieces at **cardinal points** that include the intersection of seams and, in some cases, curved areas of the pattern (Figure 2.1). All sizes graded from the master pattern can be stacked into a **graded nest** so that the incremental differences are easily observed (Figure 2.2).

In a second definition, **grade (noun)** describes the *total change of the body girth*. The amount of the grade between sizes is determined from the size specifications and is equal to the difference between adjacent sizes. Refer to the grade guide for body circumference grades in Table 2.1. The waist grade between size 8 and size 10 is 1 inch in the excerpts from both the PS 42-70 and ASTM 5586 Grade Guides. This is referred to as a 1-inch grade. The waist grade between sizes 14 and 16 is 1 1/2 inches, which is a 1 1/2-inch grade (Figure 2.3). The incremental differences in larger adjacent sizes may be 2 or 3 inches, and in **alphanumeric sizes** (small, medium, large), a 4-inch grade may be used.

A third definition of **grade (noun)** is the amount of the *incremental size change at each cardinal point* on the pattern piece. The total body girth (circumference) is divided according to the location of the cardinal point to determine the grade for that specific point. For example, the total bust girth is divided by 2 to determine the front and back grades. Then the front or back grade is divided by 2 to find the increase or decrease in the front or back half-pattern since each pattern piece represents only one-half of the front or back body. (Look ahead to Figures 3.6 and 3.7.) A **grade rule** specifies the amount of increase or decrease at *each cardinal point* for *each size* in the size range relative to the sample size. A grade rule is written and applied to each cardinal point. A **grading system** is an aggregate of grade rules that specifies how the increase or decrease is distributed throughout the pattern piece. A **simplified grading system** assumes the dimensional changes occur equally in the back and front of the body.

The bust, waist, and hips are consistently increased or decreased by the same amount in a **uniform grade**. In Table 2.1 the excerpt from the PS 42-70 Grade Guide reflects a uniform grade. However, the excerpt from the ASTM D 5586 55+ Grade Guide shows the bust, waist, and hips *do not* change by the same amount between sizes. In that case a **mixed grade** is employed; grades between sizes 10–12, 12–14, and 16–18 are not the same for the bust, waist, and hips.

Grade Distribution

It is important to understand that the **total grade is distributed throughout the pattern**. Often seamstresses believe that if they just add to a side seam they have graded the pattern to the next size. This technique only increases the width of the pattern in the

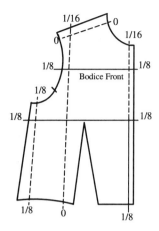

1-Inch Grade

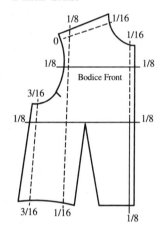

1 1/2-Inch Grade

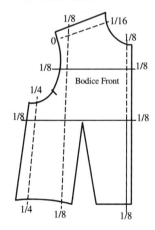

2-Inch Grade

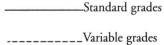

——————————Standard grades

- - - - - - - - - -Variable grades

■Figure 2.3 Grade Distributions for Total Circumference Grades

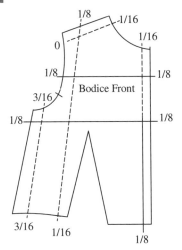

Authors' Simplified System from PS 42-70 Grade Guide

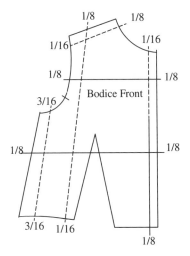

Price and Zamkoff

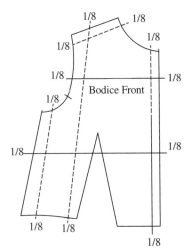

Handford

■ **Figure 2.4** Comparison of 1 1/2-inch Grading Systems

armscye, but does not affect the fit in the neck and shoulders or how the garment fits the bust contour. Although the side seams of a garment can be taken in or let out, it is difficult to adjust all the different areas of the garment where the body changes.

The key body measurements used to subdivide surveyed sample populations into classifications and size designations are (1) bust, waist, and hip girths; (2) back neck to waist; and (3) arms, legs, and lower torso lengths. Although these are considered primary measurements when applied to pattern grading, they are not sufficient to explain how the body changes between sizes and how the perimeter of the pattern should change from one size to another.

From 40 to 60 additional anthropometric measurements were taken on women measured in the large surveys discussed in Chapter 1, and many of those measurements are used to determine the system for grading the pattern. Consider the 1 1/2-inch grade distributions in which the total bust girth of a bodice is increased by 1 1/2 inches and how that grade would change a basic bodice front pattern piece. First of all, the bodice front pattern represents only one-fourth of the bust girth, so that half-pattern piece would be increased 3/8 inches from a size 12 to a size 14 when using a 1 1/2-inch grade (Figure 2.3). The 3/8 inches must be distributed so that there is some increase in the neck width, some in the shoulder length, and some in the underarm width. It is these additional measurements that must be used to define the **grade distribution** across the pattern in a grading system. A grading system specifies both the distribution of the grade within the pattern block and the total grade (1-inch, 1 1/2-inch, or 2-inches) used between specific sizes. Garments will fit the wearer differently when different grading systems are used to grade a master pattern. Figure 2.4 presents a comparison between the authors' grading system, developed from the PS 42-70 Grade Guide, and systems used by Price and Zamkoff (1996) and Handford (1980). The differences are most apparent in the extreme sizes because the changes are cumulative across the size range.

Cross (Width) Grades

Figure 2.3 indicates where the body increases or decreases occur between sizes and how those changes affect the grade at the cardinal points of a pattern piece. Consider the 1 1/2-inch grade distribution illustrated in Figure 2.3 and the cross width and cross length grades in Figure 2.5. The distribution of the **width grade**, beginning at the center front, includes the **neck grade** of 1/16 inch, a **cross shoulder grade** of 3/16 inch (which includes the 1/16 inch of the neck grade plus an additional 1/8 inch increase in the shoulder width), and the total **cross body grade** increase of 3/8 inch (which includes the neck grade of 1/16 inch, the shoulder grade of 1/8 inch, and the 3/16 inch that is added to the underarm width). These **cross grades** are **variable grades** because the incremental changes vary between the 1-inch, the 1 1/2-inch, and the 2-inch grades (Figures 2.3 and 2.5). The cross grades are assumed to be the same for the front and back pattern pieces in simplified grading systems.

Length Grades

Incremental changes in length between sizes remain constant regardless whether a 1-inch, a 1 1/2-inch, or a 2-inch grade is used (Figure 2.5). Therefore, the **length grade** is a **standard grade** with few exceptions. The adult body changes less in length than in width between sizes. When a pattern is graded into a wide range of sizes, the length grade may be omitted in some lower body length areas (hem length) in the largest sizes. The total length grades of the bodice back and front generally are assumed to be the same.

Grading Methods

Patterns may be graded by physically moving the pattern to increase and decrease it through a process of **manual grading**. In **machine grading** this is accomplished mechanically. Or the pattern could be processed for **computer grading**. These methods are discussed in Chapter 4. Computer grading is the most efficient and accurate of the three methods, when accurate information is entered into the computer. A prerequisite for any method is a thorough understanding of grading concepts.

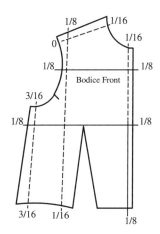

1 1/2-Inch Grade

|1| Cross waist/bust grade
|2| Cross shoulder grade
|3| Neck grade
|4| Armhole width grade
|5| Armhole length grade
|6| Side seam length grade
|7| Center front length grade
|8| Center front to bust point grade
|9| Neck to bust grade

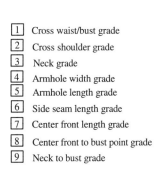

Cross Grades

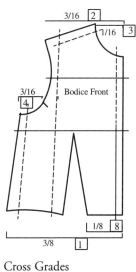

Length Grades

■Figure 2.5 Cross Width Grades and Length Grades

PATTERN GRADING
SUMMARY

Pattern grading (systematically increasing or decreasing the dimensions of a pattern) takes place at cardinal points on the pattern. All seam intersections, as well as some curved areas of patterns, are designated as cardinal points. The amount of increase or decrease at each cardinal point is determined from size specifications. The simplified pattern grading system is based on the assumption that all changes occur equally around the body. Therefore, the change at each cardinal point is the same on both the front and back of a garment.

The bust, waist, and hip are the three primary body girth measurements applied to pattern grading. Generally, the amount of total body girth change is the same for the bust, the waist, and the hip. This difference designates the amount of grade for the garment and is referred to as a uniform grade. If the change in all three body areas is 1 inch, then the pat-

tern has a 1-inch grade. A mixed grade occurs if the change in one of the three body areas, such as the waist, is different than in the others. In a mixed grade, each area is designated as having its own grade (i.e., bust: a 2-inch grade; waist: a 1 1/2-inch grade; hip: a 2-inch grade.) Because the change in girth measurements varies between sizes (usually 1 inch, 1 1/2 inch, or 2 inches), these areas are designated as variable grades. Dimensions for length grades do not tend to vary between sizes, therefore, they are usually designated as standard grades.

Although the primary body measurements indicate the total increase or decrease of the **pattern dimensions**, the grading system used determines how the total change is distributed within the pattern piece. The grading may be accomplished through manual, machine, or computer grading techniques. These methods are discussed in detail in later chapters.

EXERCISES

1. Define the following terms:
   Grade (noun, two definitions)
   Grade (verb)
   Cardinal points
   Graded nest
   Mixed grade
   Standard grade
   Production pattern
2. How does a master pattern differ from a basic block?
3. Calculate the amount of the grade for a half pattern from the full-pattern grade.

	Full-Pattern Grade	Half-Pattern Grade
Bust circumference	1 1/2″	
Front chest width	1/4″	
Center front length	1/4″	

4. Why is it important to know how a grade is distributed in a pattern?
5. The grade distribution is usually divided into width grades and length grades.
   a. What are the three width distribution grades in the upper bodice?
   b. Are they variable or standard grades?
6. Use Figure 2.6 to identify cardinal points on the bodice front. Write them on the half-pattern.
7. Draw vertical lines through the upper pattern block areas in Figure 2.7 where width grades are distributed in the pattern.
8. Label Figure 2.8 with the following cross and length grades:
   a. Cross shoulder grade
   b. Cross waist grade
   c. Armscye length grade
   d. Center front length grade
9. Compare the grade distribution in Figure 2.3 with those found in other text books. How are they the same or different?

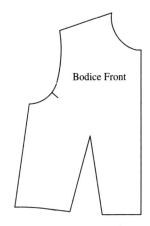

■ Figure 2.6 Cardinal Points

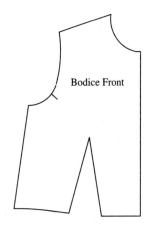

■ Figure 2.7 Grade Distributions

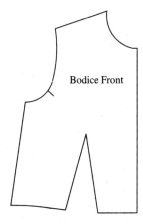

■ Figure 2.8 Cross Grades and Length Grades

REFERENCES

Handford, J. (1980). *Professional pattern grading for women's, men's and children's apparel.* Redondo Beach, CA: Plycon Press.

Price, J., & Zamkoff, B. (1996). *Grading techniques for modern design* (2nd ed.). New York: Fairchild Publications.

■**Table 2.1** Comparison of PS 42-70 Misses and ASTM D 5586 Misses 55+ Sizes for Bust, Waist, and Hips

Excerpt From PS 42–70 Grade Guide (Appendix Table A.2)							
Size	**6–8**	**8–10**	**10–12**	**12–14**	**14–16**	**16–18**	**18–20**
Bust	1	1	1 1/2	1 1/2	1 1/2	2	2
Waist	1	1	1 1/2	1 1/2	1 1/2	2	2
Hips	1	1	1 1/2	1 1/2	1 1/2	2	2
Excerpt From ASTM D 5586 55+ Grade Guide (Appendix B.6)							
Size	**6–8**	**8–10**	**10–12**	**12–14**	**14–16**	**16–18**	**18–20**
Bust	1	1	1 1/2	1 1/2	1 1/2	2	2
Waist	1	1	1 1/2	1 1/2	1 1/2	2	2
Hips	1	1	1	1	1 1/2	1 1/2	2

Note: Measurements are in inches.

NOTES

3

Grading on the Cartesian Graph

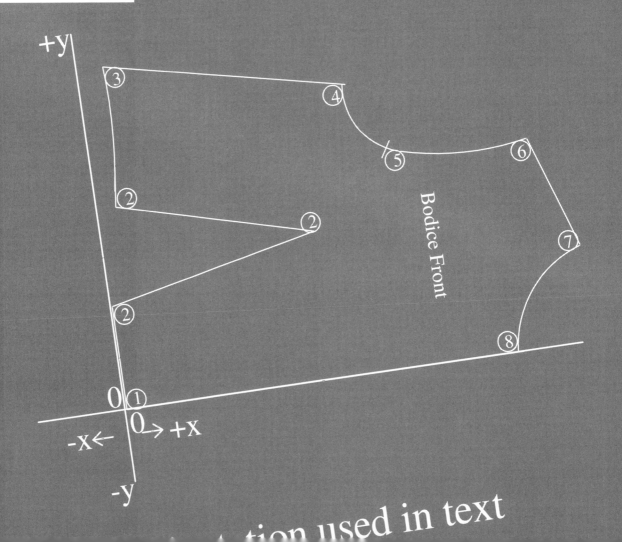

+y

③

④

⑤

⑥

②

②

Bodice Front

⑦

②

⑧

0 ①

−x← 0 → +x

−y

...tion used in text

Introduction

While manual and machine grading methods change pattern dimensions in increments, computer grading is rooted in the **Cartesian graph** concept. Regardless of the method used for pattern grading, manual or computer, pattern movement within a Cartesian graph can be applied. Students who do not have access to a computer can gain the basic grading knowledge to apply later when they are introduced to computerized grading.

The general procedure for grading patterns using the Cartesian graph is to first determine the **pattern orientation**. This establishes the **zero, zero (0,0) point of reference**, which is imperative because the x,y coordinates of a grade rule are based on the pattern orientation. The next step is to label the cardinal points of the pattern and then develop the grade rules for those points. Grading a pattern on the computer utilizes the same initial procedure. The additional steps required for computer grading are discussed in Chapter 4.

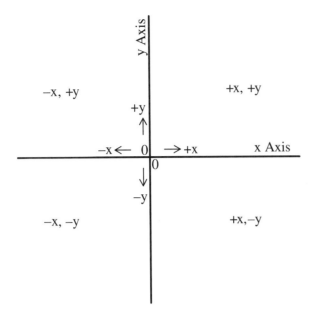

Figure 3.1 Cartesian Graph

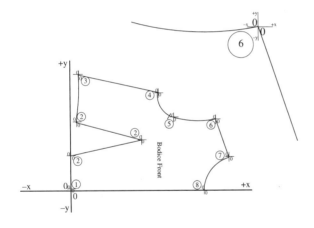

Figure 3.2 All cardinal points are theoretically 0,0

THE CARTESIAN GRAPH

The Cartesian graph contains a horizontal *x* axis and a vertical *y* axis; these axes intersect to form four right angles. The 0,0 point on the graph is the point where the **x,y axes** intersect, and all **x,y points** on the graph have a value that is relative to the 0,0 point (Figure 3.1). This 0,0 point becomes the point of reference for the pattern as it is graded. The graph is divided into **quadrants** by the intersecting axes and each *x* and *y*

value at any point on the graph is a plus (+) or a minus (−), depending upon the quadrant in which it is located. The quadrant above the *x* axis and right of the *y* axis contains +*x*,+*y* points; the quadrant above the *x* axis and left of the *y* axis contains −*x*,+*y* points; the quadrant below the *x* axis and right of the *y* axis contains +*x*,−*y* points; and the quadrant below the *x* axis and left of the *y* axis contains −*x*,−*y* points (Figure 3.1). The order of the values of any point on the graph is *x*,*y*. The value of *x* **always** precedes the value of *y*.

NUMBERING CARDINAL POINTS

Cardinal points are placed at key locations that control the change in the perimeter of a pattern piece when it is graded. Most seam intersections and some curved areas have designated cardinal points. There is a convention for numbering cardinal points that is followed for either manual or computerized grading. The cardinal point of the pattern that is placed at the 0,0 point of the Cartesian graph is assigned point number 1. After this 0,0 point of reference has been established, all succeeding cardinal points are numbered in a clockwise order (Figure 3.2).

As each cardinal point is graded, the pattern block is moved away from the 0,0 point the specified amount along the *x* and *y* axes of the Cartesian graph. If the pattern is graded to a smaller size, cardinal point number 1 (Figure 3.2) is moved into either or both the −*x*, −*y* quadrant(s). Even though the cardinal point being graded remains in the +*x*,+*y* quadrant (example, cardinal point 6), the graded cardinal point is a minus grade. Thus, **all points on the pattern are moved by the specified amount from their own 0,0 point**. This concept will be important when developing grade rules for each cardinal point on the pattern for a range of sizes.

PATTERN ORIENTATION

Before grade rules can be written for the cardinal points of a pattern piece, the orientation of the pattern piece must be determined in relation to the 0,0 point of reference. The pattern can be graded correctly regardless of its orientation, but corresponding cardinal points are numbered and assigned *x,y* values based on their orientation (Figure 3.3). The pattern placement in relation to the 0,0 point should be carefully considered so that the most efficient bank of grade rules can be developed. Although each cardinal point is initially 0,0 before any point is graded, the grade rule used to determine the amount of growth (movement) at any point is based on the 0,0 point of the pattern orientation (i.e., the center front/waist intersection on the bodice front in this text). This 0,0 point is the point of reference for the entire pattern piece, and each graded cardinal point reflects the sum of all grade distributions between that cardinal point and the 0,0 point.

Problems in this text are oriented with the waist center front and the waist center back located at the 0,0 point and with the body of the bodice pattern in the +*x*,+*y* quadrant and the body of the skirt or the pant pattern in the −*x*, +*y* quadrant. This orientation allows all size changes to radiate from the center waist of the body. It enables the grader to use the same width rules for the bodice, skirt, and pant, and it thereby improves the efficiency of the grading process and the accuracy of the graded patterns. A grade rule may be assigned repeatedly to cardinal points on other pattern pieces if there is consistency in the orientation of the pattern pieces relative to the 0,0 point of reference.

At the initial placement of the master pattern on the graph, every cardinal point theoretically is also a 0,0 point for the purpose of pattern grading (Figure 3.2). The enlargement of cardinal point 6 illustrates the *x,y* axes that are at each cardinal point.

DEVELOPING GRADE RULES

A set of grade rules that includes all sizes in the size range is developed for each pattern piece in the master pattern; each rule is calculated by applying an appropriate formula. As discussed in Chapter 1, a grade guide is derived from size specifications, and the grade between adjacent sizes is the difference between the

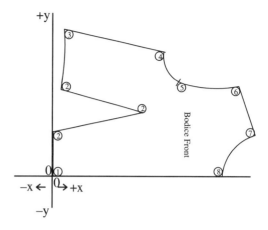

Orientation used in text

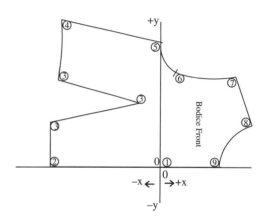

Alternate orientation

■**Figure 3.3** Different 0,0 Point Orientations

dimensions of those two sizes. For example, the bust girth for the PS 42-70 misses size 12 is 35 inches, and size 14 is 36 1/2 inches (Table A.1); therefore, the grade between sizes 12 and 14 is 1 1/2 inches. This girth grade indicates the total increase in the circumference of the garment (Figure 3.4).

Grade rules are developed for the **bodice half-pattern**, which represents only one-fourth of the total increase in circumference. Therefore, when a grade rule is written to increase or decrease a horizontal girth grade, the total increment is divided by 4.

Width measurements on a pattern are divided by 2 because they represent left and right sides of the body.

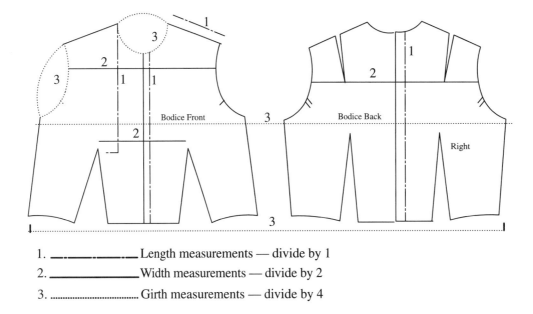

1. _____ Length measurements — divide by 1
2. _____ Width measurements — divide by 2
3. .... Girth measurements — divide by 4

Figure 3.4 Length, Width, and Girth Grades

Length measurements are used without division because the pattern piece represents the total body length for a specific area. The following information is useful in identifying the appropriate formula:

• Circumference measurements are divided by 4: body areas are waist, bust, hips, and neck.
• Width measurements are divided by 2: body areas are bodice back width and chest width. The armscye girth is also divided by 2.
• Length measurements are divided by 1: body areas are shoulder length, center back and center front lengths, sleeve and skirt or pant lengths.
• Neck and armscye half-pattern grades must be calculated from other measurements to determine length and width distributions.

Cumulative Grades

Each grade rule represents the sum of all grade distributions between the specific grade point and the 0,0 point of reference along each axis, and the sum of all sizes graded from the master pattern. The **cumulative grades** along the x axis are the sum of length grades and the cumulative grades along the y axis are the sum of width grades.

Pattern Block-Grade Distributions

The total **width and length grades** are distributed within the pattern piece. Figure 3.5 shows the center front/waistline of the bodice front located at the 0,0 point of reference and the bodice in the $+x, +y$ quadrant of the Cartesian graph. Each grade rule must reflect all changes in the pattern between the 0,0 point and the cardinal point for which the rule is written. The grade rules illustrated in Figure 3.5 are written as 32nds of an inch using only the numerator. Appendix D contains a conversion table for fractions to 32nds of an inch and to decimals. The unit of measurement is discussed under computer grading in Chapter 4.

Grade Rule 2 has been assigned to three cardinal points on the pattern because the width change of 1/8 inch between the center front and each of the points is constant. Since the change is along the y axis, and there is no change in dart length, the grade rule is 0,4/32 inch (0,4). Grade rule for cardinal point 3 is additive; the width change between 0,0 and point 3 is 1/8 inch between the center front and the dart plus 1/4 inch (1/16" plus 3/16") between the dart and the side seam for a total of 3/8 inch. The grade rule for point 3 is 0,12/32 inch (0,12). All of the changes have been along the *y* axis. It is helpful to note that width changes are indicated by horizontal lines and length changes are indicated by vertical lines on the pattern. **Length changes are *never* added to width changes.** Length changes occur along the *x* axis and width changes are along the *y* axis because of pattern orientation.

Grading a Size Range

All sizes in a size range are graded from the master pattern, which in this case is size 12. Logically, the dimensional difference between the master size 12 and size 16 is greater than the difference between size 12 and 14. Therefore, to determine the grade for size 16, the incremental grade from size12 to 14 and the incremental grade from size 14 to 16 must be added together. Table 3.1 is an excerpt from Table A.2 for the waist girth grade between sizes; it shows the grade across a size range.

Table 3.2 shows grades from the master size 12 to each of the other sizes. The + indicates that the increment must be added to all increments between the specified size and size 12. The increments change when the grade changes from a 1 1/2-inch to a 1-inch grade and from a 1 1/2-inch to a 2-inch grade (refer to Figure 2.3). Total additive circumference and cross bust/waist grades from size 12 to each size are illustrated in Table 3.3.

Note in Table 3.3 that when grading to smaller sizes in a range, the total grade is a negative number. For example, if the grade is from size12 to size10, it would be −1 1/2 inches instead of +1 1/2 inches. Table 3.1 shows the total waist circumference grade for a size range. Generally, the pattern piece represents only one-fourth of the waist circumference, so calculations for cross bust/waist grades are in Table 3.3.

Grade Rule Table

The development of a set of grade rules must be completed for each pattern piece in the garment style and for all sizes in the size range before grading the master block or master pattern manually or by computer. A **grade rule table** is used to record the relative grade

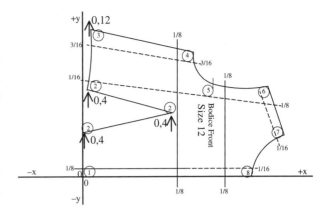

■Figure 3.5 Center Front/Waistline at 0,0 Point

rules for each cardinal point for all pattern sizes in the size range.

COMPUTERIZED GRADING

Pattern grading on the computer is accurate and efficient. This is the method used almost exclusively by the industry. A pattern grader must have as thorough an understanding of pattern grading principles when grading on the computer as when grading by hand. Moreover, any errors are compounded faster in computer grading. A thorough understanding of this chapter and Chapter 2 is imperative to comprehend pattern grading concepts. See Chapter 4 for additional information on computerized grading.

Before the pattern can be graded on the computer, the pattern piece is entered into the computer by **digitizing**, or entering, the cardinal points of the perimeter of the pattern on the Cartesian graph. The process is begun by establishing the 0,0 point of reference. Grade rules that have been written for all sizes in the size range for each cardinal point are entered into the computer. The digitized pattern pieces can be viewed on the computer screen, and the grade rule assigned to each cardinal point determines the movement of the cardinal point during the grading process.

The procedure for writing grade rules for computerized grading is the same as for manual grading. Only the format of the rules is different. Most changes within a pattern piece are fractions of an inch, but entering fractions into the computer is cumbersome. Therefore, only the numerator of the fraction is entered. *Because only the* **numerator** *is used, all fractions must have the same* **denominator**, as explained next.

Unit of Measurement

Many computer systems are based on 32nds or 64ths of an inch, while some use decimals. Some offer the option of selecting the unit of measurement. Working with such small increments makes it difficult to maintain accuracy when grading manually but not when grading by computer. In this text 32nds of an inch is used for consistency. Therefore, all fractions must be converted to 32nds before writing a grade rule. Table D.1 in Appendix D shows the conversion of decimals to fractions and fractions to 32nds of an inch. A conversion chart of fractions to 32nds of an inch is also included for use with the grading exercises in this text.

Grading Increment Values

The positive sign (+) is generally not used with numbers in pattern grading. All increments of fractions, whole numbers and decimals, are assumed to be positive unless a negative sign (−) precedes them. The inch (″) mark is not used when entering numbers into the computer, except for whole inches. For example, 1 inch can be entered as 32 or as 1″. If a number greater than an inch is needed, for example, 1 3/8 inches, 32 (1″) and 12 (3/8″) are added to equal 44, which is the number entered. Memorizing the numerators for the most commonly used fractions is helpful for speed and accuracy in entering increment values.

Relative Grading and Incremental Grading

Grade rule tables may be written using either **relative** or **incremental grades** for both manual and computer grading. In the relative grading method, grade rules reflect the changes in the pattern dimensions from the master size to each of the graded sizes; that is, all changes are "relative" to the master size. In the incremental grading method, the grade rules reflect the change from the adjacent size; that is, they give the increments of change for only one size. These increments remain constant for all areas that reflect a standard grade but change for variable grades. The variable grades are constant for 1-inch grades, for 1 1/2-inch grades, and so on, with changes occurring only when the total girth grade changes. At first glance, it would seem that incremental grading is much simpler than relative grading. However, cardinal points may have a variable grade in one direction (such as the y) and a standard grade in the other direction (such as x). Incremental grading can be very complex and sometimes confusing. Relative grading is used in this text.

Production Patterns

The **production patterns** used in the industry are different from the familiar home-sewing patterns. Generally, when the graded production patterns are laid on the fabric to be cut, the fabric is a single ply instead of being folded as home-sewing patterns usually recommend. In home-sewing patterns, symmetrical pieces such as bodices, skirts, and collars are represented by a pattern for half of the garment part. In some cases the pattern is placed on the fold. Because there is no fold in the production lay of the fabric, a full-pattern piece that represents both sides of the garment part or a pattern piece for the left side and one for the right side of the garment must be used (Figure 3.6). If grade rules were written for the full-pattern piece, almost twice the number would be required, resulting in inefficiency and added production costs. Therefore, symmetric pattern blocks used for production are graded as half-patterns. In computerized grading, the mirror image command converts the half-pattern with a fold line to a full representation of both sides of the garment (production pattern). Pattern pieces without a fold line use an opposite or flip command to grade the side that is the opposite of the one the grade rules are written for, that is, left back and right back.

In developing grade rules that can be used for both the bodice back and front half-pattern pieces, the back and front patterns must be oriented alike in relation to the 0,0 point on the Cartesian graph. Visualize using the right bodice front of a full body pattern and the left bodice back, as worn on the body (Figure 3.6). When the patterns are positioned with the intersection of the waist and center front or center back at the 0,0 point and the body of the pattern in the $+x,+y$ quadrant, they are oriented alike on the graph (Figure 3.7).

The centers of both pieces lie along the $+x$ axis and the waistlines lie along the $+y$ axis. Because the front and back pieces increase the same amount between sizes in a simplified grading system, the corresponding cardinal points on the two pieces will be assigned the same grade rule. If the left side of both pattern pieces were used, and oriented so that the intersection of the waistline and the center of the patterns were at the 0,0 point, one piece would be above the x axis and the other would be below the x axis. Although the cardinal points would be increased the same amount, a different set of grade rules would be needed for the two pieces, because at the location where one piece would increase in the plus direction along the y axis, the other would increase in the minus direction. Inconsistent orientation of pattern pieces requires more grade rules, which increases the cost of the grading process and the chance of errors.

VARIATIONS IN PATTERN ORIENTATION

Each company or pattern grader may have a specific method for grading a pattern. Although this text explains the basic principles of manual and computer grading on the Cartesian graph, there are variations to these principles.

Before beginning the process of writing a set of grade rules, the pattern orientation on the Cartesian graph must be established. All cardinal points on the pattern are assigned a grade rule that indicates the change in the pattern between that cardinal point and the 0,0 point of reference on the Cartesian graph for each of the sizes in the size range. Figure 3.8 illustrates differ-

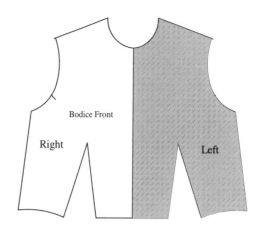

Full Front

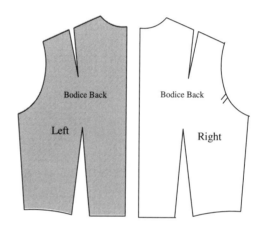

Left and Right Back

Figure 3.6 Production Patterns

ent pattern orientations. Any orientation can be used, but the grade rules for specific cardinal points differ for each orientation since all grade rules are written in relation to the point of reference on the pattern piece, which is the 0,0 point of the x,y axes.

Consider the cardinal point at the center front/neckline intersection. On the bodice in Figure 3.8 (Front/Waist line), the change between the 0,0 point and this cardinal point along the x axis is a total of 1/4 inch, so grading from a size 12 to a size 14, the grade rule would be 8,0. Because there is no change between the cardinal point at the neck and the 0,0 on the y axis, y

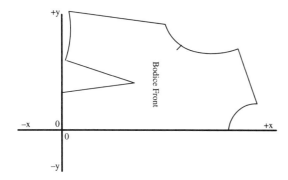

Right Front

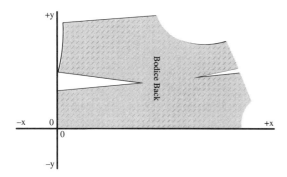

Left Back

Figure 3.7 Pattern Orientation for Grading Half-Patterns

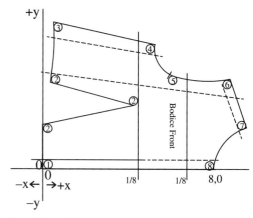

Front/Waistline

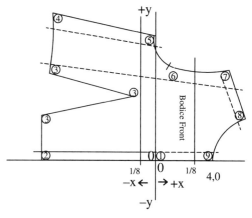

Underarm/Side Seam

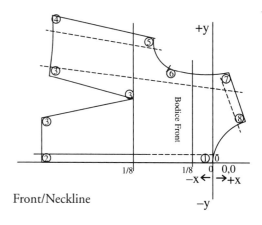

Front/Neckline

Figure 3.8 Effect of Orientation on Grade Rules

is 0. In Figure 3.8 (Underarm/Side Seam) the 0,0 point is at the underarm level, and the change along the *x* axis is 1/8-inch difference between the reference point and the neck. The grade rule with this orientation is 4,0. In Figure 3.8 (Front/Neckline), the 0,0 point is at the center front/neckline so the grade rule is 0,0. The numbering of the cardinal points changes with the change in pattern orientation **with the 0,0 point of reference always being 1**. Figure 3.8 shows only one *x,y* value illustrating the grade from size 12 to 14. However, when grading across a size range, an *x,y* value is assigned at each cardinal point for all sizes in the size range.

The orientation used in Figure 3.8 (Front/Waistline) represents the most efficient use of grade rules. **Caution should be exercised if using an orientation with the 0,0 point at the center front/neckline** in

Figure 3.8 (Front/Neckline). When grading on some computers, the neckline will become distorted; instead of the neckline forming a right angle at the center front, a peak or dip will be formed.

PATTERN GRADING
SUMMARY

Understanding the concept of the Cartesian graph is essential to applying pattern grading principles to computer grading. The concept is also easily applied to manual or machine grading. Each cardinal point on a pattern piece is graded relative to the orientation of the pattern at the 0,0 point on the Cartesian graph. Each cardinal point also maintains its own x,y axes. Starting with the 0,0 point of reference for the pattern piece, movement for each of the individual cardinal points is identical to the cumulative movements of all preceding pieces.

Manual and machine grading involve physically connecting lines between graded cardinal points, thereby allowing the pattern grader to make judgments when completing the pattern. The graded cardinal points are joined mathematically in computerized grading. This places additional constraints on pattern orientation. However, if all grading is approached as if it were being implemented on the computer, the guidelines and principles used remain consistent regardless of the method used.

The most efficient pattern orientation is with the center waist of each pattern piece located at the 0,0 point of reference on the Cartesian graph. This orientation makes the center waist the point of reference with all pattern growth radiating from the center point of the body. The pattern orientation used in this text places the center of each full-pattern piece along the x axis, with the bodice on the $+x$ axis and the skirt and pants on the $-x$ axis. The body of the garment is in the $+y$ quadrants (see Figure 3.7). Exceptions will be noted as they occur.

A grade rule table is developed using size specifications to determine the amount of growth from size to size. The total difference in body dimensions for each body area must be divided according to the portion of the body the pattern is designed to cover. Individual grade rules reflect the pattern movement for each cardinal point.

Grade rule tables must use a consistent format. Some computer systems use decimals as the unit of measurement, while others use fractions. Some provide the option of choosing which to use. This text uses primarily fractions, with the exception of specific problems. Only the numerator is used with computer systems; therefore, all fractions must have the same denominator. This text uses 32nds of an inch to maintain consistency.

The master pattern is used as the base size in grade rule tables. Generally, the perimeter of a smaller-size bodice moves into the $-x$ and $-y$ quadrants from each 0,0 point, while the larger sizes move into the $+x$ and $+y$ quadrants. In relative grading, all dimensions are relative to the master size and movement for each size reflects the dimensional change from the master size to the size being graded. Incremental grading reflects only the dimensional change from the adjacent size.

Grade rule tables provide a systematic record of growth for each pattern piece. Since individual rules reflect the growth of a specific body area, they may be used repeatedly on other garment styles that cover the same body area. Although the grade guide does not have to be in the form of a grade rule table for manual grading, grade rule tables organize grade rules and are valuable tools for pattern grading. They make the transition to computer grading much easier and more logical.

An understanding of this chapter is imperative to grasping computer grading concepts, which are applied to manual and machine grading. Repeated readings with a focused concentration on the material will save time and errors later on.

EXERCISES

1. On the Cartesian graph in Figure 3.9 label the following: x axis; y axis; 0,0 point; and the plus (+) and minus (−) quadrants.

2. Using a ruler with 1/8-inch increments, plot the following points on the graph: (1/8,1/8), (−1/2,3/4), (−3/8, −1), (1/2, −1/4)

3. In computerized grading, why is a common denominator used for a grade rule table?

4. In the grade rule table, all coordinates are additive from the master-size pattern. Add the following fractions and state the answer in 32nds of an inch.
   1. 1/4 + 3/8 = x/32
   2. 3/8 + 1/2 = x/32
   3. 1/16 + 1/8 = x/32
   4. 3/16 + 1/4 + 1/8 = x/32
   5. 3/32 + 5/8 + 1/16 = x/32

5. Grade rules developed from specifications require that girth and width measurements be divided to determine the grade for a half-pattern. Divide the following equations.
   1. 1/16 ÷ 2 = x/32
   2. 1/8 ÷ 4 = x/32
   3. 3/8 ÷ 2 = x/32
   4. 3/8 ÷ 4 = x/32
   5. 5/8 ÷ 4 = x/32

6. What is the difference between relative and incremental grading?

7. Why is it important to establish the pattern orientation before grade rules are developed?

8. Using a multisized commercial pattern, identify the 0,0 point of reference from which the pattern was graded.

9. Use the grade distributions shown in Figure 3.10 to write the grade rule for cardinal point A on each of the pattern orientations.

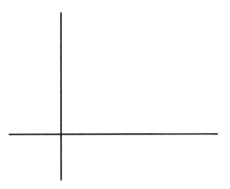

Figure 3.9 Cartesian Graph

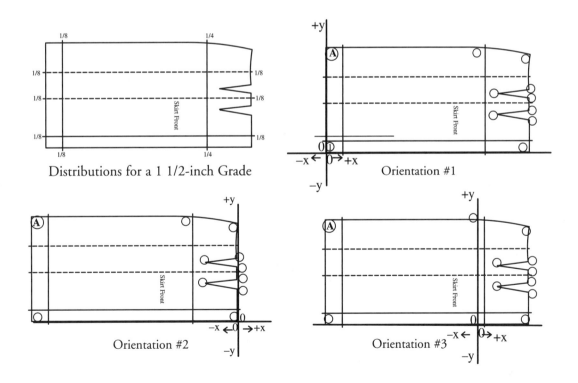

Distributions for a 1 1/2-inch Grade

Orientation #1

Orientation #2

Orientation #3

Figure 3.10 Orientations for Skirt Pattern

█Table 3.1 Misses Grade Guide for Total Waist Girth—PS 42-70

Size	6–8	8–10	10–12	12–14	14–16	16–18	18–20	20–22
Waist	1	1	1 1/2	1 1/2	1 1/2	2	2	2

Note: Measurements are in inches.

█Table 3.2 Grades from Size 12 to Other Sizes

Size	6	8	10	12	14	16	18	20	22
			1 1/2	**0**	1 1/2				
		1+	1 1/2	**0**	1 1/2+	1 1/2			
	1+	1+	1 1/2	**0**	1 1/2+	1 1/2+	2		
				0	1 1/2+	1 1/2+	2+	2	
				0	1 1/2+	1 1/2+	2+	2+	2

Note: Measurements are in inches.

█Table 3.3 Total Circumference Grades Relative to Master Size 12

Circumference Grade		Cross Bust/Waist Grades (Circ. divided by 4)
Size 12 to 10	−1 1/2	−3/8
Size 12 to 8	(1 1/2 + 1) = −2 1/2	−5/8
Size 12 to 6	(1 1/2 + 1+ 1) = −3 1/2	−7/8
Size 12		
Size 12 to 14	1 1/2	3/8
Size 12 to 16	(1 1/2 + 1 1/2) = 3	3/4
Size 12 to 18	(1 1/2 + 1 1/2 + 2) = 5	1 1/4
Size 12 to 20	(1 1/2 + 1 1/2 + 2 + 2) = 7	1 3/4
Size 12 to 22	(1 1/2 + 1 1/2 + 2 + 2 + 2) = 9	2 1/4

Note: Measurements are in inches.

NOTES

4

Manual, Machine, and Computer Grading

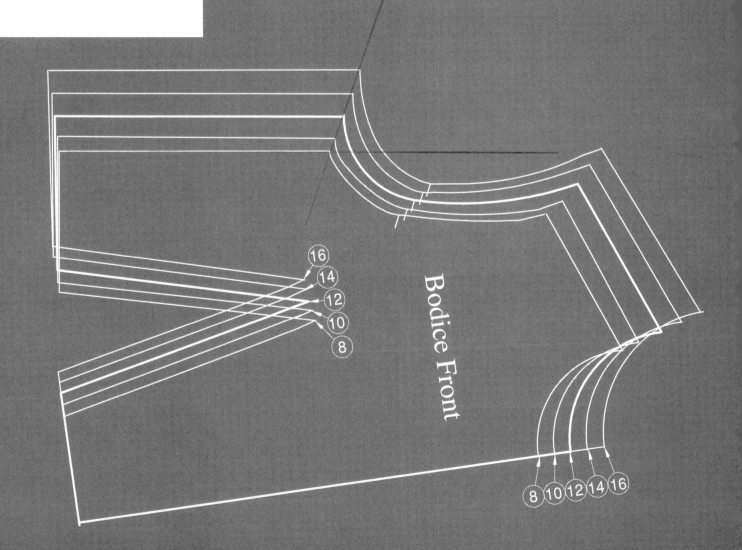

Introduction

The basic concepts and principles of pattern grading are applicable to manual, machine, and computer grading. Writing grade rules relative to the placement of the pattern block on the Cartesian graph is the first step in all three methods of grading in this text. In manual and machine grading the grader physically moves the pattern block, marks the graded sizes at each cardinal point, and blends seam lines between cardinal points. In computer grading each pattern block is digitized into the computer, grade rules are input and applied to the computer image of the pattern block, and the computer then generates the blending of the seamlines.

Success in grading by any of the methods can be achieved only if a well-developed, accurate master pattern is used. Seam lengths, notch placement, and any other markings should match on seams that will be joined in the construction process. All seam lines should be smooth, whether straight or curved. The same elements should be checked on the graded patterns for each size in the size range in all three grading methods.

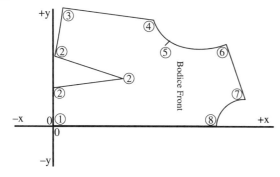

a. Trace master size on pattern paper

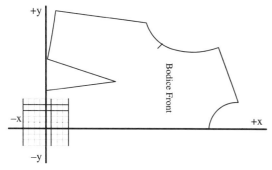

b. Grid placed at 0,0 point

■**Figure 4.1** Preparation for Manual Grading

MANUAL GRADING

Pattern grading concepts are best understood by a hands-on approach to increasing and decreasing the pattern block. Even if the grader has access to a grading machine or a computer, the introduction to pattern grading should consist of manually moving, marking, and blending several pattern blocks.

Block Movement Method for Manual Grading

The Cartesian graph concept of pattern grading was explained in Chapter 3. Grade rules for each pattern piece of a style are determined by where the block is placed on the graph and by the distribution of the pattern grade between each cardinal point relative to the 0,0 point of reference. Therefore, it is necessary to draw the x,y axes on a piece of paper that is large enough to accommodate the largest size to be graded. The master pattern block is then traced with the ori-

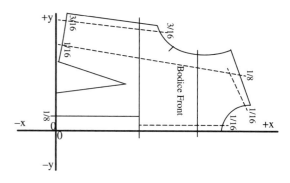

a. 1 1/2–Inch Grade Distribution

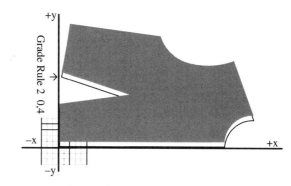

b. Movement for Grade Rule 2

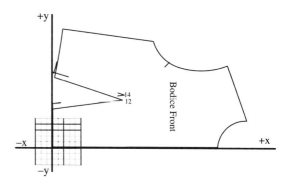

c. Marking on traced master pattern

■**Figure 4.2** Movement to Grade Pattern from Size 12 to Size 14

entation appropriate in relation to the 0,0 point on the graph. Figure 4.1a illustrates a bodice front block traced with the center front/waistline of the axes at the 0,0 point and the pattern in the $+x, +y$ quadrant. Table 4.1 contains grade rules for grading a size 12 block up to a size 14 and down to a size 10. The numerator of a fraction is used with a common denominator of 32 for all numbers in the grade rule table.

Moving the Pattern Block

To facilitate accurate movement of the block as each cardinal point is graded, a 4 × 4 inch square of graph paper with 1/8 inch divisions can be inserted at the 0,0 point to serve as a measurement guide (Figure 4.1b). The block is moved the specified distance away from 0,0 along the *x* and *y* axes either by hand or machine. If the movement is less than 1/8 inch, the grader must determine the appropriate movement within the 1/8 inch square. The example in Figure 4.2b for grading size 12 to size 14 is a movement of 1/8 inch along the *y* axis to mark the three dart points at cardinal point 2; Figure 4.2c illustrates the marked points for size 14. Grade Rule 2 is 0,4 (1/8 inch = 4/32 inch).

Each movement of the block reflects the grade distribution explained in Chapter 2 (see Figure 2.3). Figure 4.3a illustrates the movement of 1/8 inch on the *x* axis and 3/8 inch on the *y* axis for Grade Rule 4 (cardinal point 4) at the side seam/armhole intersection with a value of 4,12. In Figure 4.3b, the markings for Grade Rules 2, 3, and 4 are indicated. Figure 4.3c and d illustrate Grade Rule 6. **As the pattern block is moved, the center front must remain parallel to the *x* axis.** Otherwise, the graded points will be incorrect.

When grading to a smaller size from the master pattern, the master pattern block is shifted in the opposite direction into the −*x*,−*y* quadrants. Figure 4.4a illustrates the movement of the block for marking Grade Rule 2. The block is moved along the *y* axis, across the *x* axis, into the −*y* region. Grade Rule 2 is 0,−4 for size 10. Figure 4.4b shows the marked **grade points**.

Marking Cardinal Points

When the block has been moved the correct distance, lightly mark the new grade points by drawing a line about 1/2 inch long from the intersection of the seams in each direction (Figure 4.3). Keep the marks as light as possible, because during the process of blending seamlines you may need to erase some of these marks. Continue clockwise around the pattern piece and

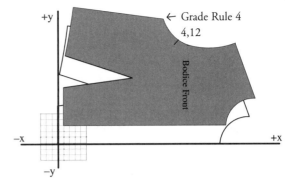

a. Movement for Grade Rule 4

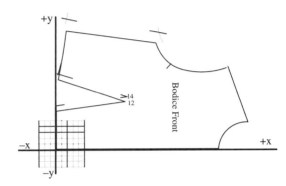

b. Marking on traced master pattern

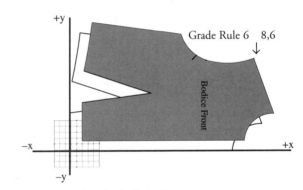

c. Movement for Grade Rule 6

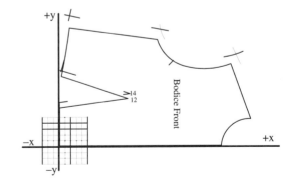

d. Marking on Traced Master Pattern

■**Figure 4.3** Grading Process from Size 12 to 14 With a 1 1/2–Inch Grade

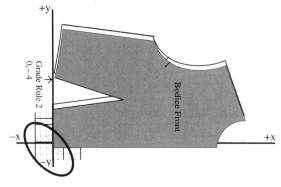

a. Movement for Grade Rule 2

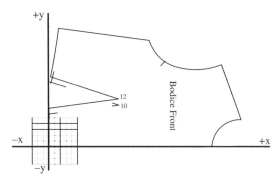

b. Marking on traced master pattern

Figure 4.4 Block movement to grade pattern Size 12 to 14

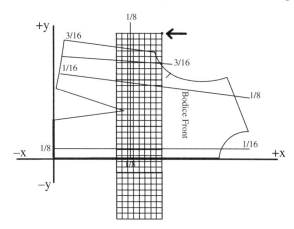

a. Ruler enlarged to illustrate method

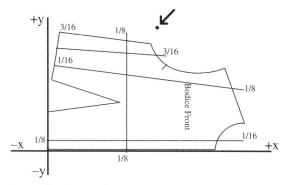

b. Dot indicating grade point

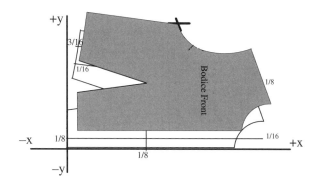

c. Movement of block to mark grade point

Figure 4.5 Marking By Measurement

mark the new grade point location at each cardinal point. Do not mark entire seamlines, or in the case of the first graded point, dart lines. After all cardinal points have been graded, the seamlines must be blended. (Blending is illustrated and discussed later in this chapter.) **Complete the blending for each graded size before marking grade points for subsequent sizes. It is easier to maintain the character of curved seams when the blending of one size is completed before grading the next size.** Assign the graded size to at least one of the cardinal points.

Measurement Method for Manual Grading

A pattern may be graded easily by the **measurement method** at each cardinal point instead of manually moving the pattern block. Begin by drawing the *x,y* axes on the pattern paper. Trace the master pattern as instructed for marking the new grades by moving the pattern. However, because each point on the master pattern is theoretically 0,0, the grade rule for each cardinal point indicates exactly how the new grade point changes from 0,0.

For example, Grade Rule 4 is 4,12, so the new grade point would be moved by 1/8 inch in the *x* direction and 3/8 inch in the *y* direction. A transparent ruler can be used to quickly mark that point. Place the ruler so that 1/8 inch extends above the cardinal point on the master pattern and mark a point 3/8 inch beyond and 1/8 inch above the cardinal point (Figure 4.5a). **It is imperative that the ruler is perpendicular to the *x* axis before the point is marked or the point will be incorrect.** Figure 4.5b shows the marked point as a dot (.) for Grade Rule 4. Use of the ruler in this manner simulates computerized grading.

After marking each point, lay the master pattern on the paper with the **grainline parallel to the *x* axis** and the cardinal point placed at the newly marked point. Trace about 1/2 inch of the seamlines at the graded point (Figure 4.5c). Rather than tracing around the corner of the cardinal point, it is best to trace the end of each seamline; remove the block and use a ruler to extend each line just beyond the intersection until crosshairs are formed at the point where the seams intersect.

Blending in Manual Grading

When all graded cardinal points for one size have been marked, trace in the perimeter of the pattern by blending marked lines (Figure 4.6). Blending requires visual evaluation in both manual and machine grading. It is extremely important that all seamlines retain the shape of the master pattern; the curved seams require the greatest attention. During the grading procedure each grade point was lightly marked along the pattern edge for about 1/2 inch from the intersection of seams at the cardinal points. Starting at these points, allow the curves of the master pattern to function as a curved ruler for blending the curves in the new size. Lay the master pattern on the graded size with the intersections of the master pattern curved seamlines aligned with the ends of the half-inch lines at the graded points. Curves and seamlines maintain the greatest accuracy if the seamlines for each size are blended before any additional sizes are graded. Blending should always be completed for adjacent sizes before continuing to grade additional sizes.

a. Master pattern

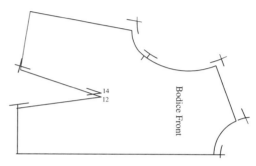

b. Marked grade points

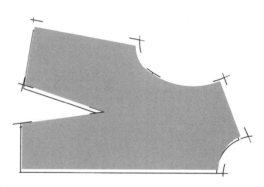

c. Blended dart legs

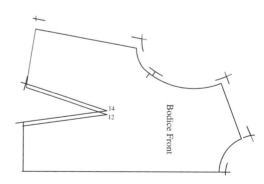

d. Graded size marked on traced pattern

Figure 4.6 Blending Seamlines Between Marked Grade Points

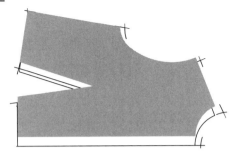

a. Blend waistline between dart and side seam

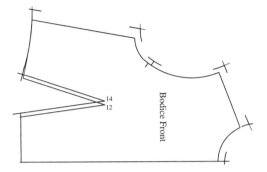

b. Blended waistline

Figure 4.7 Blending Waistline

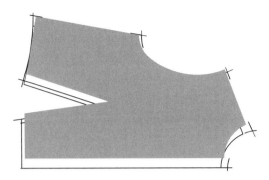

a. Blend side seam

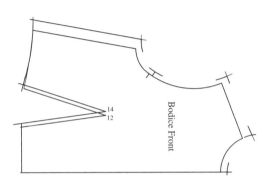

b. Blended side seam

Figure 4.8 Blending Side Seam

Figure 4.6 illustrates the blending of the dart legs. The waistline curve is blended in Figure 4.7, and the side seam, in Figure 4.8. Lightly mark the armhole curve at several places and then lift the pattern to see if the new curve looks like the master pattern curve. If the shape of the master pattern has been maintained, complete the entire seamline with a permanent line (Figure 4.9). Figure 4.10 illustrates the blending of the shoulder seam, and Figure 4.11 the blending of the neckline. Erase any marks that do not coincide with the final seamlines. The blending of the seamlines completes the grading of the master pattern to an adjacent size. Continue to grade new sizes according to assigned exercises. A graded nest for sizes 8 through 16 is shown in Figure 4.12. When multiple sizes are graded, the seamlines of one size may sometimes cross over the seamlines of the adjacent size so that a portion of the new seamline is within the boundary of the original size and a portion is outside the original size seamline (see the necklines in Figure 4.12). This varies depending upon the curved shape and the original point of reference.

Check Corresponding Seam Lengths and Notches

When all pattern pieces of a style have been graded, check all corresponding seams in each size to be sure they are the same length. Check notch placement on corresponding seams to assure they match. Graded patterns should maintain the integrity of the original design. The shapes of the graded pattern pieces should reflect the shapes of the original master pattern.

MACHINE GRADING

The procedures for writing grade rules for machine grading are the same as for manual grading. Draw a Cartesian graph on a large piece of paper, trace the pattern block oriented appropriately relative to the 0,0 point on the graph, and determine the grade rules accordingly.

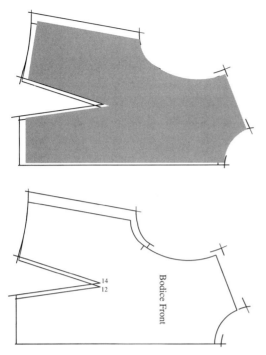

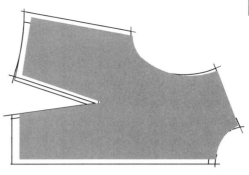

a. Blend shoulder seam

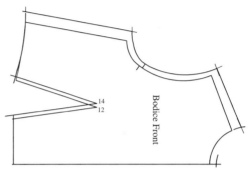

b. Blended shoulder seam

a. Blend underarm seam from side seam to notch

Figure 4.10 Blending Shoulder Seam

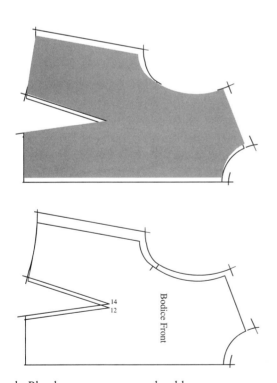

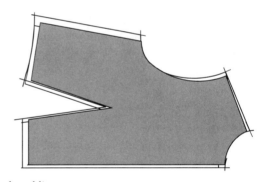

a. Blend neckline

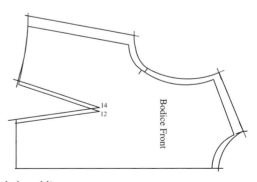

b. Blend upper armscye to shoulder

b. Blended neckline

Figure 4.9 Blending Armscye

Figure 4.11 Blending Neckline

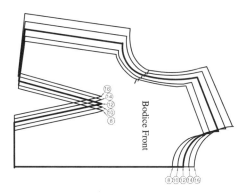

Figure 4.12 Nested Graded Pattern Block Sizes 8 Through 16

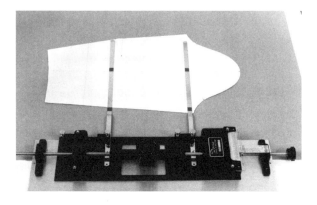

Figure 4.13 Pattern Block Mounted in Grading Machine

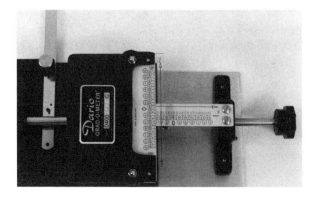

Figure 4.14 Ruled Bars on Grading Machine

Mounting Pattern Block in Grading Machine

Machine grading entails clamping the pattern block into a grading machine (Figure 4.13). Instructions for the specific machine should be followed for this procedure. The block should be clamped into the machine so that it precisely coincides with the traced block on the Cartesian graph when the knobs are set at 0.

Moving the Pattern Block

Grading machines have two small knobs that move the pattern block. As a knob is turned, a pointer on the knob moves along a ruled area marked in 1/16-inch increments (Figure 4.14). If a movement of less than 1/16 inch is required, the pointer can be stopped between the increment markings. One knob moves the pattern along the x axis, and the other one moves the pattern along the y axis. Turning the knobs in the clockwise direction moves the pattern toward the positive quadrants. Turning the knob in the counterclockwise direction moves the pattern into the negative quadrants. With both knobs set to 0, the pattern block in the machine must be adjusted so that it coincides with the traced pattern block on the graph. Then as each cardinal point is graded, the knobs are turned to move the pattern block the designated amount for the graded size.

Marking, Blending, and Checking Graded Size

Follow the marking and blending instructions for manually moving the pattern block. When the grading process is completed, all graded pattern blocks should be checked for accuracy.

COMPUTER GRADING

Computer grading requires the use of the same concepts that apply to manual grading. As in manual grading, the first step is to write the grade rules. Once the grade rules for each pattern piece and all sizes in a style have been established, the pattern pieces are digitized into the computer. As in manual grading the grade rules for each individual cardinal point determine the new (graded) location of that point. The lines between the points are connected using the same relationship between points as in the original master pattern.

Pattern Preparation

Pattern preparation for digitizing includes identifying specific information about each piece. Although individual computer systems may vary, most will need the following information: style name, piece name, master size, grade reference line, and grain line.

The style name, piece name, master size, and grain line are identified on all pattern pieces regardless of the method used for grading (Figure 4.15). The grade reference line is unique to computer grading. **The grade reference line is always *parallel* to the *x* axis of the Cartesian graph for the pattern piece.** Its orientation is used as the reference for the position of all other points and lines on the pattern during the grading process. Depending upon the computer system, the exact placement of the grade reference line within the pattern piece may be a matter of choice, but for continuity, exercises in this text always place the grade reference line along the center front or center back line of bodices and skirts and along the center line of sleeves. The grade reference line extends to within about 1/2 inch of the top and bottom of the pattern piece to ensure that it maintains its parallel relationship to the center line. The grade rule number for each cardinal point should also be written on the pattern piece so the grade rules may be entered into the computer with the pattern rather than added later (Figure 4.15).

Digitizing

Digitizing is the process of entering the pattern piece along with its identifying information into the computer. The exact process will be somewhat different for each computer system. Therefore, only general steps are identified in this text. The digitizer surface resembles a drawing board, but it contains a computerized grid beneath the surface (Figure 4.16).

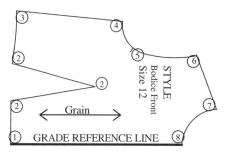

Figure 4.15 Pattern Prepared for Digitizing

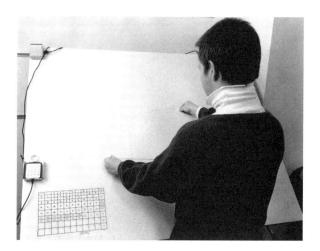

Figure 4.16 Digitizing Board

Pattern Input and Pattern Information

The location of all pattern information is transferred to the computer by use of a mouse-type instrument that contains a view scope with crosshairs and a multifunction keypad (Figure 4.17). The crosshairs indicate the location of each point and the multifunction keys are used to provide information about the point.

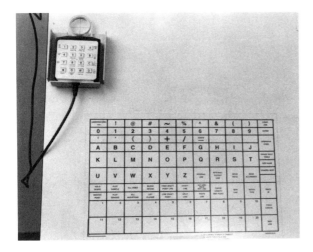

Figure 4.17 Mouse Pad on Digitizing Board

Once the pattern is prepared, it is placed on the digitizer so that the surface is flat, with the grade reference line on the horizontal and the pattern oriented with the top to the right and the bottom to the left. The first step in digitizing is to enter pattern identification information, which includes the style name, piece name, and size. Most grading systems have the option of entering the grade rules with the pattern piece or adding them later. If they are entered with the pattern, the name of the grade rule table containing the grade rules is also required.

Actual pattern input usually starts with locating the grade reference line. **The crosshairs of the view scope should be placed exactly on the ends of the grade reference line as the orientation of this line is key to the accuracy of all grading operations.** Other information that falls within the perimeter of the pattern piece is then digitized. This includes information such as the grain line, annotation points (the location of written information on the pattern), and drill holes (indicating darts, pockets, etc.) or other construction information.

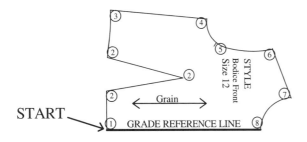

Figure 4.18 Orientation and Starting Point for Digitizing Pattern

The perimeter of the pattern is usually entered in a clockwise direction. The first point should be the bottom left seamline intersection of the piece (Figure 4.18). As each point of the pattern is digitized, information about the point, including the grade rule number, is entered using the mouse keypad. Moving the mouse crosshairs along the line and entering information via the keypad identifies the perimeter lines of the pattern. It is important to identify enough curve points along a curved line for the computer to be able to translate the points into a smooth curve, rather than a line composed of a series of straight lines. Refer to the specific computer manual for the number and type of points required to enter the pattern piece into the computer. Each pattern piece in a style is entered in the same style file and uses the same grade rule table for grading. Most computer systems provide a method of entering oversize pieces for garments with pattern pieces larger than the digitizer surface. Check individual computer manuals for the procedures.

Lines and points on each pattern piece may be modified after the pattern is digitized to indicate mirror lines (fold lines on home-sewing patterns), notch points, drill holes, and annotation points. Refer to individual computer grading system manuals for specific information on these and other pattern identification markings.

Entering Grade Rules into the Computer

The grade rules for each pattern piece are written based on the size specifications for the style. After the rules have been written, they are entered into a grade rule table for computer grading. Each grade rule table has a specific name. There may be numerous grade rule tables in a computer, but all pieces in a style must use only one grade rule table. The grade rules are numbered in the table and may be used repeatedly for various styles. New rules may be added to a grade rule table after it is created. Refer to the individual computer manual for the specific methods of entering grade rules. Most computer systems require the user to specify the unit of measurement and whether the method of grading is relative or incremental. Relative grading bases all changes (increases or decreases) in the perimeter of the pattern on the master size, whereas incremental grading bases changes on the adjacent size. Exercises in this text use 32nds of an inch as the unit of measurement and the relative method of grading unless otherwise specified.

Assignment of Grade Rules

Each cardinal point on a pattern piece requires a grade rule to specify the amount of change that takes place between the master size and the graded size. If the grade rule was not assigned to the cardinal point prior to digitizing, it must be assigned before the piece can be successfully graded. Grade rules may be modified (changed) and new rules may be added to the grade rule table after the initial grade rule table is created. Modifying rules requires caution, as changing the values in a rule changes the grade on all styles and pieces that have that specific rule assigned to them.

Nested Graded Pattern

Most computer systems allow the user to view a graded pattern piece both as an individual size and as a graded nest. A graded nest shows all the sizes in the size range nested together (Figure 4.12). The pattern grader can often identify any areas of a pattern that are not being graded correctly by viewing a graded nest. The changes between sizes within each grade (1 inch, 1 1/2 inches, and 2 inches) will appear uniform on a nest. Checking the grade of each pattern piece in this manner is a good habit for the pattern grader to develop.

Plot Graded Patterns

The last step in computerized pattern grading is to plot all pieces in a style and to examine the lines and curves. Some complex patterns may require additional grade rules or alternate reference axes (see Chapter 8) to control the movement of various areas of the pattern. It is sometimes difficult to determine exactly how many grade rules may be needed until a pattern is plotted. All seamlines and notches on the plotted pattern should be checked to be sure they match corresponding seams and notches.

PATTERN GRADING
SUMMARY

Manual, machine, and computer grading may all be approached in the same manner. In manual grading, the pattern grader physically moves the pattern the designated distances along the x and y axes. In machine grading, the pattern is clamped into arms on the grading machine and designated movements along the x and y axes are controlled by turning the knobs on the grading machine. These knobs move the arms of the grading machine, thus moving the pattern piece. With computer grading, the designated movement along the x and y axes is accomplished by entering grade rules in a grade rule table. The pattern piece is digitized into the computer system and the computer redraws the new size pattern as specified by the grade rules. Therefore, having a written record of the movement along the x and y axes for each graded size is the first step in all three methods of grading. The grade rules that are written in subsequent chapters represent these movements.

Manual and machine grading require the pattern grader to mark the intersections of all seams (cardinal points) on the new size either by tracing about a half inch of each intersecting seamline or by marking the location of the new intersection with a ruler. The master pattern is used as a guide to blend the seamlines between the marked intersections.

In all methods it is imperative that the center line of the pattern is kept parallel to the x axis. The computer replicates the manual methods by using a grade reference line to keep the pattern parallel to the x axis and by using grade rules to designate the movement of cardinal points for each graded pattern size. The computer then replicates the shapes of the original lines and curves that connect the cardinal points.

All three methods require the pattern grader to examine the graded pattern to see that it maintains the same style sense as the original master pattern. It is also necessary to check corresponding seamlines to be sure the principles of patternmaking are maintained and that seams are trued with one another.

EXERCISES

1. For manual grading, it is recommended that the basic pattern blocks be cut from tag board or other stiff paper. Prepare the bodice front pattern block for manual grading.

2. After moving and marking a pattern during grading, what is the final step? What problems could occur if the last step is not done?

3. What pattern information is needed for computerized grading? How are grade rules assigned to cardinal points if computerized grading is used?

Table 4.1 Grade Rule Table: Bodice Front

Pattern Piece: Bodice front with waist dart
Unit: Inches   **Denominator:** 1/32
Size Range: Misses 10–14
Master size: Misses 12
Grade Rules: 1–8

Notes: The left bodice back pattern is used

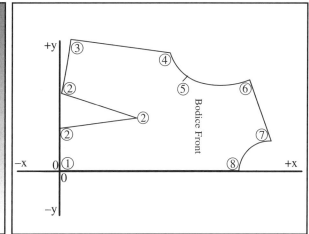

Size	Rule 1		Rule 2		Rule 3		Rule 4		Rule 5		Rule 6	
	X	Y	X	Y	X	Y	X	Y	X	Y	X	Y
10	0	0	0	–4	0	–12	–4	–6	–4	–6	–8	–6
12	0	0	0	0	0	0	0	0	0	0	0	0
14	0	0	0	4	0	12	4	12	0	0	8	6

Size	Rule 7		Rule 8	
	X	Y	X	Y
10	–10	–20	–8	0
12	0	0	0	0
14	10	2	8	0

5

Grading the Basic

Pattern Blocks

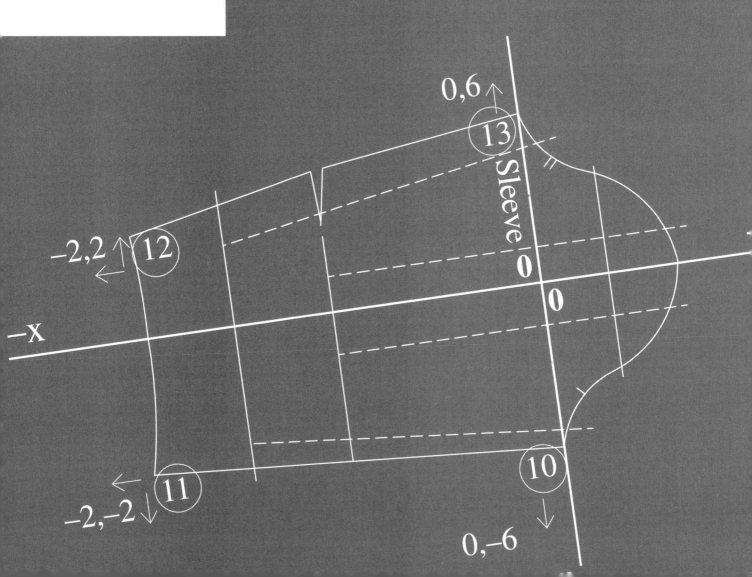

Introduction

This chapter contains grading instructions for the basic blocks: the bodice front and back, sleeve, skirt front and back (Figure 5.1). Explanations for grading pant front and back are also included. Most garment designs are developed from the basic pattern block, so when the distribution of the grade (how the body changes) is understood for the basic pattern block, the knowledge can be applied to grading master patterns with design variations. Figure 5.2 illustrates the grade distribution for the bodice front in misses sizes. An enlargement of an inch, showing fractions and the breakdown to 32nds of an inch, is provided with each basic block to aid in conversion of fractions for the writing of grade rules. All basic blocks are graded without seam allowances or dart take-up for greater accuracy. To convert basic blocks or master patterns to production patterns, add seam allowances and dart take-up to all pattern pieces following the principles of flat pattern making.

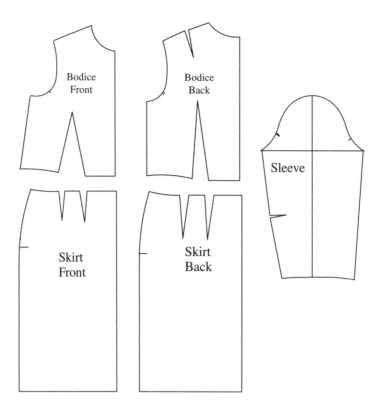

■**Figure 5.1** Basic Blocks

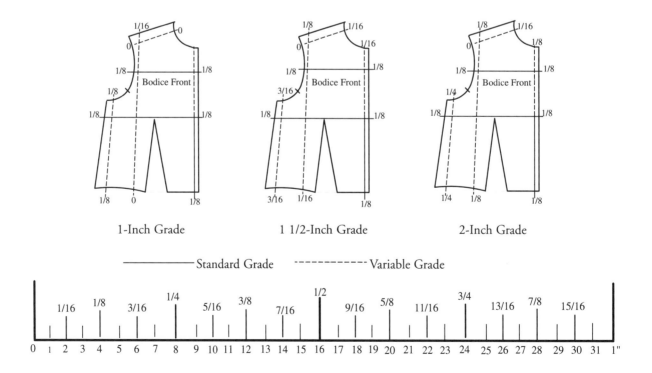

■**Figure 5.2** Grade Distributions for Bodice Front

GRADING PROCEDURES

The development of a grade rule table is necessary for both computer and manual grading. Understanding the development of the *x,y* coordinate is extremely advantageous for students who may not have access to computer grading in the classroom. In pattern grading the positive sign (+) is generally not written with the numbers. All increments of fractions, whole numbers, and decimals are assumed to be positive unless a negative sign proceeds them.

As each grading problem is introduced in this chapter, the orientation of the block on the Cartesian graph is shown. If necessary, review the discussion of pattern orientation in Chapter 3. The bodice front is graded first; a grade rule for each cardinal point on the block is assigned. Each cardinal point has a *x,y* value for each size, and the set of *x,y* values becomes the grade rule. **All grade rule values are determined in relation to the 0,0 point on the graph.** As individual grade rules are written for each piece, a bank of grade rules is created and used on subsequent grading problems (Table 5.1). The bodice front requires a total of eight rules. The bodice back is graded next; it is positioned on the Cartesian graph in the same manner as the bodice front. This allows grade rules developed for the front to be applied to the back. Cardinal points are identified on each grading problem; a circle around a number indicates an established grade rule, and a rectangle indicates that a new rule is needed for that cardinal point (Figure 5.3).

Each cardinal point on the block is assigned the appropriate grade rule number, and each rule consists of *x,y* movements for the range of sizes. Refer to Figure 5.2 and note how the increments change across the size range between the 1-inch, 1 1/2-inch and 2-inch grades. Pattern movement for each graded cardinal point is indicated by a small arrow (look ahead to Figure 5.5 for the first example). Note that arrows pointing up (↑) indicate +*y* movement; arrows pointing down (↓) indicate −*y* movement; arrows pointing to the right (→) indicate +*x* movement; and arrows to the left (←) indicate −*x* movement.

Patterns Graded in This Chapter

A basic fitted bodice with long sleeves, a fitted skirt, and a fitted pant are graded in this chapter. Terminology is important for understanding the pattern grading exercises. Width generally refers to changes across the body; length generally refers to up and down movement on the body. Exceptions are the shoulder length, which refers to the change in length from the neck to armscye, and the neckline length, which relates to the change in neckline circumference. A master pattern for each of the following basic block pieces should be made from tag board to facilitate grading the pattern manually:

- Bodice front with one waistline dart
- Bodice back with shoulder dart and waistline dart

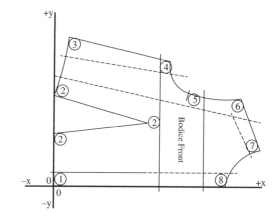

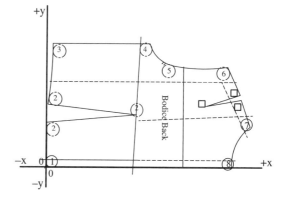

Figure 5.3 Block Orientation/Cardinal Points

- Skirt front with two waistline darts
- Skirt back with two waistline darts
- Set-in long sleeve with elbow dart
- Pant front with two waistline darts
- Pant back with two waistline darts

BODICE FRONT

What you should know to grade the bodice front:

1. Pattern orientation and 0,0 point for placement on Cartesian graph (Figure 5.3).
2. Cardinal points and grade rules of the pattern to be graded (Figure 5.3).
3. Master size and size range of pattern. Misses size 12 is the master pattern used for this example.
4. Unit of measurement and common denominator. Inches are the unit of measurement and the common denominator used is 32.
5. Distribution of the grade within the pattern and the difference between standard and variable grades (Figure 5.2).
6. Sizes at which the girth changes from a 1-inch to a 1 1/2-inch and a 2-inch grade.
7. Completion of the x,y values within a grade rule table.
8. Method for moving a pattern block for grading and blending of lines (Chapter 4).

What you should know to develop a grade rule table:

1. Each cardinal point in a grade rule has a set of x,y values for each size.
2. All grade rules are additive from the master size. For Table 5.1 the misses size 12 is the master size.
3. The common denominator for this grade rule table is 32.
4. Location within the pattern where standard and variable grades occur. (Figure 5.2)
5. Incremental changes of standard grades remain the same regardless of the 1-inch, the 1 1/2-inch, or the 2-inch grade.

6. Variable grade increments change between the 1 1/2-inch and the 1-inch grades and between the 1 1/2-inch and the 2-inch grades.
7. Width grades (indicated by vertical lines) are never added to length grades (indicated by horizontal lines).
8. Each cardinal point has its own 0,0 point from which each grade rule's coordinates are referenced (Figure 5.3).
9. Generally, when grading from the master bodice patterns to larger sizes, the grade rules are $+x,+y$; when grading to smaller sizes, the grade rules are $-x,-y$.

Grading Size 12 Up to Size 14
Grade Rule 1: Cardinal Point 0,0

The bodice front is placed on the Cartesian graph so the waistline/center front intersection is at the 0,0 point and the block lies in the $+x,+y$ quadrant. This 0,0 point is assigned Grade Rule 1; it is the reference point from which all other grade rules for the bodice front are developed. Before the grading process is begun, all cardinal points on the block are 0,0 (Figure 5.4).

Grade Rule 2: Dart

The second cardinal point on the bodice front refers to the three points of the waistline dart. Since the size of the dart is determined by the angle of the dart legs, it is important that the legs remain the same distance apart if the dart length does not change. Therefore, these three points are given the same grade rule (Figure 5.5).

As seen in the beginning bodice diagram (Figure 5.4), the change in distance from the center front to the dart is 1/8 inch. With this pattern orientation, the movement for this grade rule is only in the y direction. Grading from size 12 to size 14, the x,y coordinates for Grade Rule 2 are 0,4.

Grade Rule 3: Waistline/Side Seam

It is important in grading to keep the waistline level and the center front perpendicular and parallel to the *x,y* axes. The cardinal point at the waistline/side seam reflects an additive grade. The bodice diagram shows the body width changes in three areas between the center front and the side seam. A change of 1/8 inch occurs between the center front and the first dart leg. A change of 1/16 inch occurs closest to the dart, and an additional 3/16-inch change occurs closer to the side seam. The distance from the reference point, which is held constant, is a total of 3/8 inch in the *y* direction (1/16 inch plus 3/16 inch plus the 1/8 inch from the previous Grade Rule 2.) The movement for Grade Rule 3 is 0,12 (Figure 5.6).

Grade Rule 4: Side Seam/Armhole

It is important to remember in a uniform grade that the amount of change in circumference of the body at the waist is the same as across the bust. Notice that the three lines that were used to develop the *y* movement for Grade Rule 3 are the same for Grade Rule 4 (Figure 5.7). The *y* movement for this rule is the same as in Grade Rule 3, or 12/32 inch.

The *x* movement for Grade Rule 4 is different from Grade Rule 3. Grade Rule 4 incorporates growth in the length of the side seam. The bodice diagram shows a line from the center front to the side seam (above the waistline dart point) and indicates a change of 1/8 inch. Since the waistline of the bodice has not moved in the *x* direction, this movement of 1/8 inch is shown in Grade Rule 4. This movement indicates the growth of the side seam length in the positive +*x* direction. The *x,y* movement for Grade Rule 4 from the size 12 to size 14 is 4,12 (Figure 5.7).

Grade Rule 5: Armhole Notch

The notch in the armhole of the bodice is usually placed at the break point of the arm. This is the location where the armhole begins to deepen and curve under the arm. A grade rule is normally placed at this location to help maintain the curved shape of the armhole (Figure 5.8).

The *x* movement for Grade Rule 5 is the same as for Grade Rule 4. The 1/8-inch increase in length is the

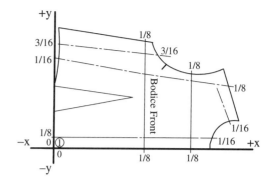

■**Figure 5.4** Bodice Front Orientation (Grade Rule 1)

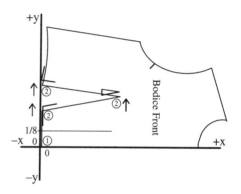

■**Figure 5.5** Grade Rule 2, Size 12 to Size 14

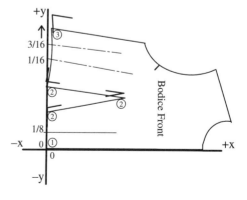

■**Figure 5.6** Grade Rule 3, Size 12 to Size 14

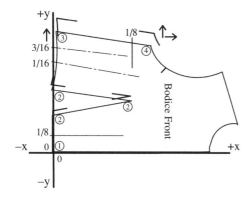

Figure 5.7 Grade Rule 4, Size 12 to Size 14

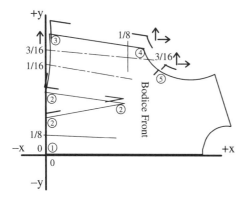

Figure 5.8 Grade Rule 5, Size 12 to Size 14

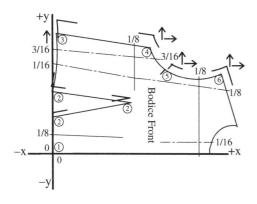

Figure 5.9 Grade Rule 6, Size 12 to Size 14

same increase used for the side seam. The *y* movement is different because it does not include the 3/16 inch used in the armhole width. Note that the width measurement nearest the center front changes at the bust line from 1/8 inch at the waist to 1/16 inch at the neck. The 1/8-inch growth through the shoulder is maintained above the bust line (Figure 5.2). The addition of the 1/16 inch and 1/8 inch equals a total girth growth of 3/16 inch. The *x,y* movement for Grade Rule 5 is 4,6 (Figure 5.8).

Grade Rule 6: Armhole/Shoulder

The change in body width is not the same above and below the bust. This is due to the difference in muscle and fat tissue in these body areas. Half of the cross bust grade goes into the armhole width and the remainder is distributed in the shoulder length (1/8 inch) and neck width (1/16 inch) (Figure 5.2). The *x* movement for this point incorporates the length in the side seam plus the armhole length. The *x* movement is 1/4 inch or 8/32 inch.

The *y* movement for Grade Rule 6 is the summation of the 1/16 inch closest to the center front at the neckline and the 1/8 inch which bisects the shoulder line. The *x,y* movement for Grade Rule 6 from size 12 to size 14 is 8,6 (Figure 5.9).

Grade Rule 7: Shoulder/Neckline

The *x* movement for Grade Rule 7 is not the same as for Grade Rule 6. In order to increase the neckline measurement, 1/16 inch is added to the neckline curve. Note that this measurement does not extend into the armhole. Therefore, the *x* movement for Grade Rule 7 is 1/16 inch plus the 1/4 inch movement seen in Grade Rule 6. The total *x* movement is 5/16 inch, or 10/32 inch (Figure 5.10).

The *y* movement is changed to indicate the difference in the shoulder length grade and the neckline length grade. From the center front reference point to Grade Rule 7 the *y* movement is only 1/16 inch. In Grade Rule 7 the *x,y* coordinates are 10,2.

Grade Rule 8: Neckline/ Center Front

From the Reference point (Grade Rule 1) to Grade Rule 8 the movement is in the x direction only (length). The neckline/center front increases in length 1/8 inch in side seam length and an additional 1/8 inch in the armhole depth. For size 12 to size 14, the x,y coordinates for Grade Rule 8 are 8,0 (Figure 5.11).

Blend and Check Seamlines

Before grading to another size, blend all seamlines between cardinal points. Corresponding seams and notches should also be checked for accuracy. Label the size on the graded pattern.

Grading Size 12 Down to Size 10
Grade Rule 1: Cardinal Point 0,0

When the master pattern is graded into smaller sizes, the block is moved from the 0,0 point into the $-x$ and $-y$ quadrants. Even though the cardinal points on the master pattern block physically lie in the $+x,+y$ quadrant of the overall graph, each cardinal point has moved into the $-x,-y$ quadrant from its own Cartesian graph (Figure 3.2) and the grade points carry minus numbers.

Keep in mind that all grade rules are determined in relation to the 0,0 point and all cardinal points are 0,0 for master size 12. Grade Rule 1 is located at the 0,0 point (Figure 5.12).

Grade Rule 2: Dart

The dart legs are graded according to the change between the center front and the dart leg. To mark the grade points for size 10, the master size 12 pattern block is moved into the $-y$ quadrant in order to decrease the distance from center front to the dart legs. Grade Rule 2 for grading down to size 10 is 0,-4 (Figure 5.13), instead of 0,$+4$ as it was when grading up from size 12 to 14.

Grade Rule 3: Waistline/Side Seam

Figure 5.14 illustrates the movement of the block in the $-y$ direction on the Cartesian graph. Because a 1 1/2-inch grade is used between size 12 and 14 and

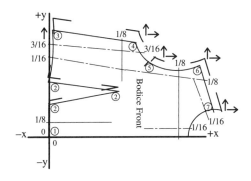

Figure 5.10 Grade Rule 7, Size 12 to Size 14

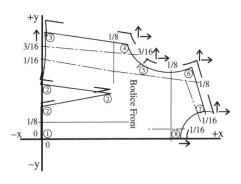

Figure 5.11 Grade Rule 8, Size 12 to Size 14

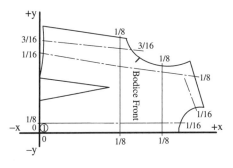

Figure 5.12 Bodice Front Orientation (Grade Rule 1)

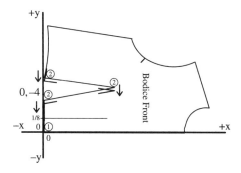

Figure 5.13 Grade Rule 2, Size 12 to Size 10

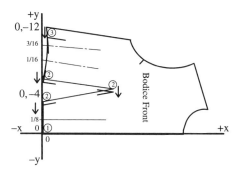

Figure 5.14 Grade Rule 3, Size 12 to Size 10

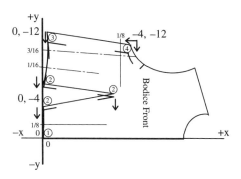

Figure 5.15 Grade Rule 4, Size 12 to Size 10

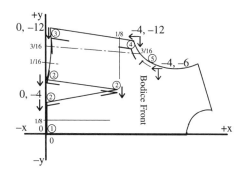

Figure 5.16 Grade Rule 5, Size 12 to Size 10

between size 12 and 10, the amount of grade is the same; only the direction is different. Therefore, Grade Rule 3 is $0, -12$ for size 10 instead of $0, 12$ for size 14.

Grade Rule 4: Side Seam/Armhole

Grade Rule 4 reflects length and width decreases as the block is moved into the $-x, -y$ quadrant. Figure 5.15 indicates that Grade Rule 4 is $-4, -12$.

Grade Rule 5: Armhole Notch

The width change of 3/16 inch along the y axis is half the width change for Grade Rule 4, which is 3/8 inch; whereas the 1/8-inch length on the x axis is the same for both cardinal points. Grade Rule 5 is $-4, -6$ (Figure 5.16).

Grade Rule 6: Armhole/ Shoulder Seam

Length along the x axis at Grade Rule 6 is decreased another 1/8 inch in the armhole depth for a total change of 1/4 inch. Since there is no change in width, Grade Rule 6 for y remains 3/16 inch. Grade Rule 6 is $-8, -6$ (Figure 5.17).

Grade Rule 7: Shoulder Seam/Neckline

There is an additional change of 1/16 inch in the neck length that was not reflected at the armhole/shoulder seam. The total length change at the shoulder seam/neckline intersection is 5/16 inch, and consists of 1/4 inch in center front length plus 1/16 inch in neck (Figure 5.18).

The width change of 1/6 inch in the neck determines the y value for Grade Rule 7. Grade Rule 7 is $-10, -2$.

Grade Rule 8: Neckline/ Center Front

In Figure 5.19 a grade change occurs only along the x axis. This cardinal point is decreased by 1/4 inch in the length of the center front. Since there is no change in y, Grade Rule 8 is $-8, 0$.

Blend and Check Seamlines

After grading each size, blend and check seamlines. Label each new size.

BODICE BACK WITH SHOULDER DART

What you should know to grade the bodice back with shoulder dart:

1. Purpose of using the left bodice back pattern for grading (see Chapter 3).
2. Cardinal points and grade rules of the pattern to be graded (Figure 5.3).
3. Unit of measurement and common denominator used is 32.
4. Pattern orientation and 0,0 point for placement on Cartesian graph (Figure 5.3).
5. Distribution of the grade within the 1-inch, 1 1/2-inch, and 2-inch grades and the difference between standard and variable grades (Figure 5.20).
6. Sizes at which the girth changes from a 1-inch to a 1 1/2-inch grade and from a 1 1/2-inch to a 2-inch grade (Table 5.2).
7. A 1 1/2-inch grade is used when grading up from size 12 to size 14 and when grading down from size 12 to size 10. The increments for all grade rules are the same when grading up and down except for the direction of movement.
8. Development of a grade rule table (Table 5.2).
9. Method for moving a pattern block and blending of lines for manual grading (Chapter 4).

Grading Size 12 Up to Size 14

Pattern orientation allows the grade rules for the bodice back to follow those of the bodice front (Figure 5.21). Grade Rules 1 through 8 are the same. Because the bodice back has a shoulder dart, the 1/8 inch shoulder width grade (Grade Rule 6 reflects this change) is divided and 1/16 inch is placed on each side of the dart. Thus an additional rule, Grade Rule 9, has been added to the bodice back.

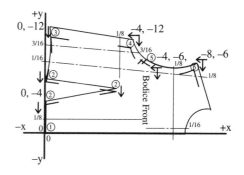

Figure 5.17 Grade Rule 6, Size 12 to Size 10

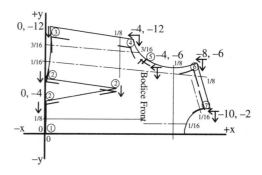

Figure 5.18 Grade Rule 7, Size 12 to Size 10

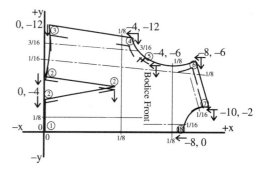

Figure 5.19 Grade Rule 8, Size 12 to Size 10

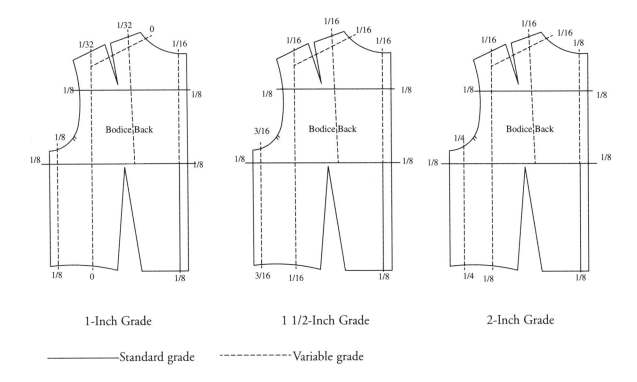

1-Inch Grade   1 1/2-Inch Grade   2-Inch Grade

————————Standard grade   - - - - - - - - - Variable grade

Figure 5.20 Grade Distributions for Bodice Back

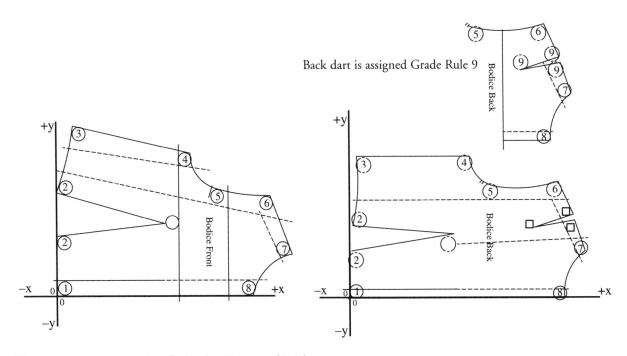

Back dart is assigned Grade Rule 9

Figure 5.21 Orientation for Bodice Front and Back

Grade Rule 9: Back Shoulder Dart

The three points of the dart at the shoulder are moved the same amount. The 1/8-inch shoulder grade is divided and 1/16 inch is placed on each side of the dart. The *x,y* movement for Grade Rule 9 is 10,4 (Figure 5.22).

SLEEVE

What you should know to grade the sleeve:

1. Grade distribution for bodice front and back (Figures 5.2 and 5.20).
2. The shape and location of sleeve parts.
3. Cardinal points and grade rules of the pattern to be graded (Table 5.3).
4. Pattern orientation and 0,0 point for placement on Cartesian graph.
5. Distribution of the grade within the 1-inch, the 1 1/2-inch, and the 2-inch grades and the

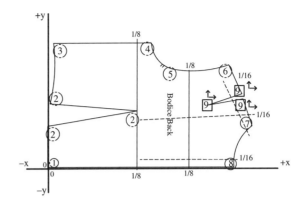

Figure 5.22 New Grade Rule for Cardinal Point 9

difference between standard and variable grades (Figure 5.23).

6. In the 2-inch grade the total sleeve cap line seam grade is 7/8 inch while the armscye total girth grade is 3/4 inch. See sleeve discussion in Appendix A for explanation.
7. Development of Grade Rule Table 5.3.

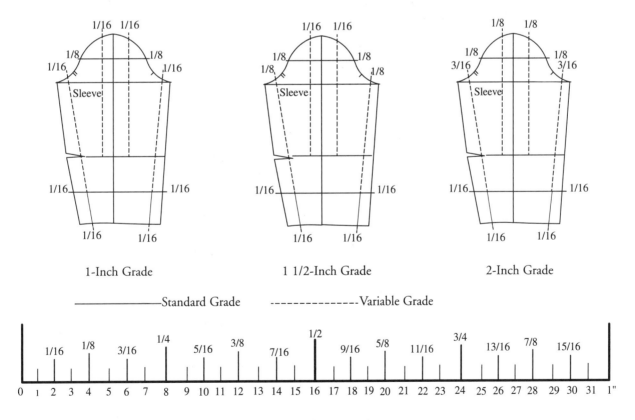

Figure 5.23 Grade Distributions for Sleeve

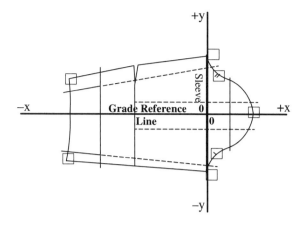

New grade rules to be assigned to sleeve

■Figure 5.24 Orientation for Grading Sleeve

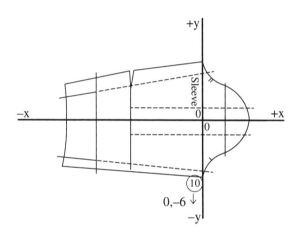

■Figure 5.25 Grade Rule 10, Size 12 to Size 14

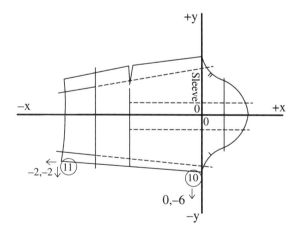

■Figure 5.26 Grade Rule 11, Size 12 to Size 14

Grading Size 12 Up to Size 14

The reference orientation for the sleeve can vary in accordance with the wishes of the grader or manufacturer. For this text, the 0,0 reference point is placed at the intersection of the bicep line and the center of the cap (Figure 5.24). It should be noted that the y axis follows the bicep line and the x axis follows the center line of the sleeve cap. This orientation of the sleeve allows the biceps line to remain at the 0 y location for all sizes and the center of the sleeve cap to be at the 0 x location for all sizes. Grade rules are assigned in a clockwise direction.

Grade Rule 10: Front Bicep (Sleeve Cap/Underarm Seam Intersection)

Grade Rule 10 is located on the y axis, which is the bicep line. The movement for this position represents one-half of the total growth in the bicep circumference. The movement to grade the bicep from size 12 to size 14 is 1/16 inch across the cap curve plus the 1/8 inch distributions in underarm width. This 3/16-inch increase is the same amount seen in the bodice front armhole grade width. The x movement for Grade Rule 10 is 0, and the y movement is 3/16 inch. The coordinates for Grade Rule 10 are 0,−6 (Figure 5.25).

Grade Rule 11: Front Wrist

Continuing in a clockwise direction, Grade Rule 11 is located at the intersection of the wrist and underarm seams. The x movement represents the growth in length from the bicep. In Figure 5.23 it is seen that there is a standard growth of 1/16 inch from elbow to wrist. This 1/16-inch growth is to the left of the 0,0 point and therefore is a negative x movement of −2.

The y movement for the front wrist is smaller than Grade Rule 10. The 1/16-inch growth in the cap is not reflected in the wrist, and the 1/8-inch growth near the underarm seam is reduced to 1/16 inch at the wrist.

Grade Rule 11 is a variable grade, and for the size 12 to 14 the coordinates are −2, −2 (Figure 5.26).

Grade Rule 12: Back Wrist

The back wrist and underarm intersection point has the same movement or growth as the front wrist. Note that the grade distributions are the same for the front and back of the sleeve. A new grade rule is needed because the movement from the reference, or 0,0 point, is in a different quadrant of the Cartesian graph. The coordinates for Grade Rule 12 are −2,2 (Figure 5.27).

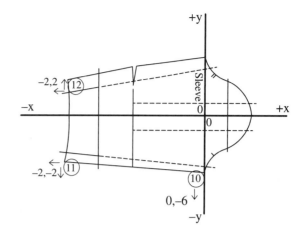

Figure 5.27 Grade Rule 12, Size 12 to Size 14

Grade Rule 13: Back Bicep (Underarm/Sleeve Cap Intersection)

Grade Rule 13 reflects the growth in the back bicep area of the sleeve. This growth is the same for both the front and back of the sleeve. Note that the distributions for Grade Rule 13 are the same as for Grade Rule 10. However, Grade Rule 13 is located in a different quadrant therefore, the *x,y* coordinates for this point have a different sign even though the movements are the same. The coordinates for Grade Rule 13 are 0,6 (Figure 5.28).

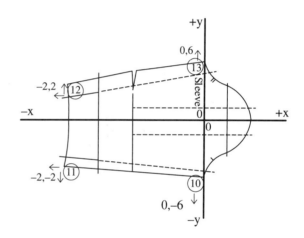

Figure 5.28 Grade Rule 13, Size 12 to Size 14

Grade Rule 14: Back Break Point

The cap of the sleeve is usually notched at the break points to denote the front (one notch) and back (two notches) of the piece. These notches guide the stitcher when the garment is being assembled and also identifies the position at which the sleeve seam begins to curve under the arm. A grade rule is needed for these points so the grade can be evenly distributed between the shoulder and bicep.

In the *x* direction there are no grade distributions between the 0,0 point and Grade Rule 14. In the *y* direction, there is one grade distribution which bisects the sleeve cap through the bicep. Note that this is a variable grade from a 1 1/2- to a 2-inch grade. The distribution which is parallel to the underarm seam is not included in Grade Rule 14.

The *x,y* coordinates for Grade Rule 14 for size 12 to 14 are 0, 2 (Figure 5.29).

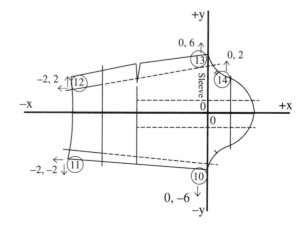

Figure 5.29 Grade Rule 14, Size 12 to Size 14

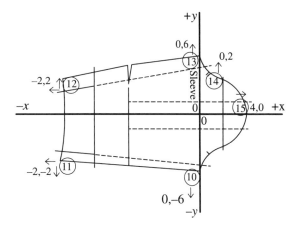

Figure 5.30 Grade Rule 15, Size 12 to Size 14

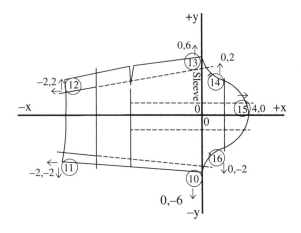

Figure 5.31 Grade Rule 16, Size 12 to Size 14

Grade Rule 15: Sleeve Cap/Shoulder point

Since the shoulder point is in the center of the sleeve, there is no growth or movement in the y direction. Grade Rule 15 is used to show the length grade in the cap of the sleeve. Note that there is a standard 1/8-inch increase in the cap of the sleeve between Grade Rule 15 location and the bicep. The movement for Grade Rule 15 is 4,0 (Figure 5.30).

Grade Rule 16: Front Break Point

Grade Rule 16 has the same growth as Grade Rule 14. As stated before, it is necessary to write new grade rules for points in which the sign changes for either the x or y movements.

The x,y coordinates for Grade Rule 16 are 0,−2 (Figure 5.31).

Computerized Pattern Grading for Sleeves

Grading a sleeve by means of a computerized grading system simplifies the grading procedure. Many computer grading systems allow the pattern grader to designate a cardinal point as an opposite grade rule. These systems allow the pattern grader to specify that the axis *perpendicular* to the grade reference line is the opposite value of a previous rule. This eliminates the need for writing new rules that differ only in the direction of movement. For example, notice that the only difference between Grade Rule 11 for the front wrist and Grade Rule 12 for the back wrist is the positive or negative sign of the y value. Therefore, instead of writing a new rule for cardinal point 12, Grade Rule 11 can be used with the opposite designation. The same concept would apply to cardinal points 10 and 13 for the front and back biceps as well as to cardinal points 14 and 16 for the back and front break points. Individual computer manuals define the procedure. This text uses the principle of writing rules for each cardinal point to facilitate understanding the principles of pattern grading. Experienced pattern graders who use computer systems can take advantage of the time-saving feature of designating rules as opposite grades.

SKIRT FRONT

What you should know to grade the skirt front:

1. Cardinal points and grade rules for the basic bodice front (Table 5.1).
2. Cardinal points and grade rules of the pattern to be graded (Table 5.4).
3. Distribution of the grade within the 1-inch, the 1 1/2-inch and the 2-inch grades and the difference between standard and variable grades (Figure 5.32).
4. Pattern orientation and 0,0 point for placement on Cartesian graph (Figure 5.33).

5. Sizes at which the girth changes from a 1-inch to a 1 1/2-inch grade and from a 1 1/2-inch to a 2-inch grade (Table 5.4).

Grading Size 12 Up to Size 14

The skirt front and back are oriented so that the waistline area of the skirt can follow the same grade rules as the bodice area even though the skirt lies in the $-x, +y$ quadrant of the Cartesian graph. As the size is increased, the grade rules will be $-x, +y$; whereas, grade rules for decreased sizes will be $+x, -y$. Using this pattern orientation, in which the center front and waistline intersection does not move, allows existing grade rules to be used for a dress or jacket that combines a bodice and skirt pattern.

All of the grade rules for a skirt front are explained. It should be noted that some of the grade rules devel-

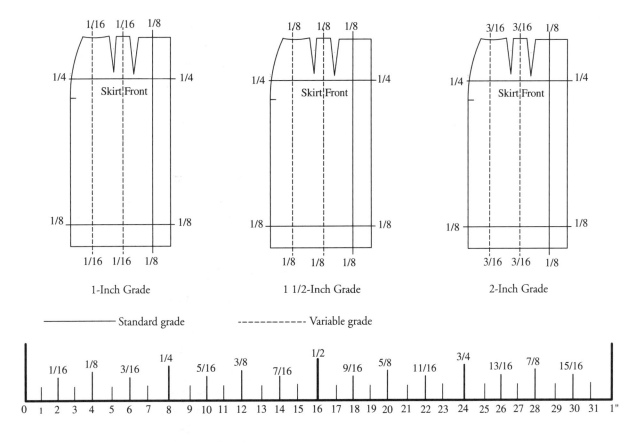

Figure 5.32 Grade Distributions for Skirt

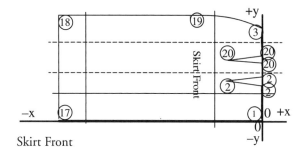

Skirt Front

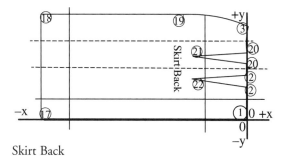

Skirt Back

◼ **Figure 5.33** Skirt Front and Back Orientation/Cardinal Points

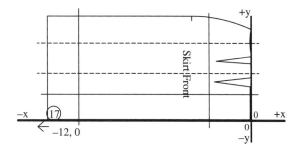

◼ **Figure 5.34** Grade Rule 17, Size 12 to Size 14

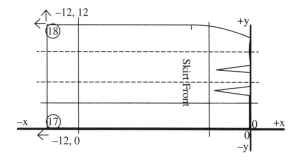

◼ **Figure 5.35** Grade Rule 18, Size 12 to Size 14

oped for the bodice front are used and the previously assigned grade rule numbers will be used. New grade rules are noted on the Grade Rule Table 5.4.

Grade Rule 1: Cardinal Point 0,0

In the skirt front pattern, the 0,0 cardinal point is at the center front/waistline intersection. This position is used in order that the bodice and skirt patterns may be combined to form a torso or dress pattern. The grade rules used for the bodice and skirt can then be used for the dress pattern as well (Figure 5.33).

As before, the x,y movement for Grade Rule 1 is 0,0.

Grade Rule 17: Center Front/Hemline

The center front moves a total of 3/8 inch in the $-x$ direction (1/4 inch between the waistline and hipline and 1/8 inch below the hip), but does not move at all in the y direction. Grade Rule 17 for size 12 to 14 is $-12,0$ (Figure 5.34).

Grade Rule 18: Hemline/Side Seam

Grade Rule 18 will have the same x value as Grade Rule 17; however, the y value changes to reflect the grade distribution in the width of the skirt. The width increases 3/8 inch (1/8 inch + 1/8 inch + 1/8 inch). Therefore, the grade rule for size 12 to 14 is $-12,12$ (Figure 5.35).

Grade Rule 19: Hip Level

Grade Rule 19 has the same y value as Grade Rule 18; the pattern block is still the same distance from 0,0 as it was when the hemline/side seam was marked. However, only the length change of 1/4 inch is between the hipline and the waistline, so x becomes -8; Grade Rule 19 is $-8,12$ (Figure 5.36).

Grade Rule 3: Side Seam/Waistline

Grade Rule 3 for the waistline/side seam of the bodice can be applied to the skirt at this location. Because it is necessary to maintain the same increase in waist and hip circumference, y is the same as Grade Rule 19. The side seam/waistline intersection has now been moved back along the x axis to 0,0, so x is 0. Grade

Rule 3 is applied to the side seam waistline cardinal point and is 0,12 (Figure 5.37).

Grade Rule 20: Second Dart from Center Front

The skirt has two waistline darts. The grade rule written for the bodice dart will be used for the first skirt dart, but an additional rule must be written for the second dart. The waistline position is not changed from the previous rule in relation to the x axis. Even though the width cross grade is variable, the grade distribution between the center front and the first dart is a standard 1/8 inch for a 1-inch, a 1 1/2-inch, and a 2-inch grade. Therefore, the remainder of the cross grade is divided, with half going between the darts and the remainder between the second dart and the side seam. The grade rule at the second dart is 0, 8 (Figure 5.38). The length of the skirt front darts does not change across the size range. Therefore, the dart end point is assigned the same rule as the dart legs.

Grade Rule 2: First Waistline Dart

The front skirt pattern has a waistline that is fitted at the same area of the body as the bodice front, and many times the bodice and skirt are sewn together. When the bodice and skirt are sewn together, the darts closest to the center front should match. Therefore, grade rule 2 (0,4) written for the waistline dart can be used at the first waistline dart on the skirt (Figure 5.39).

SKIRT BACK

What you should know to grade the skirt back:

1. Reason for using the skirt left back pattern for grading.
2. Pattern shape differences between the skirt front and back patterns.
3. Cardinal points and grade rules of the pattern to be graded.
4. Pattern orientation and 0,0 point for placement on Cartesian graph.

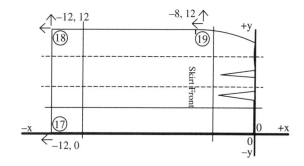

Figure 5.36 Grade Rule 19, Size 12 to Size 14

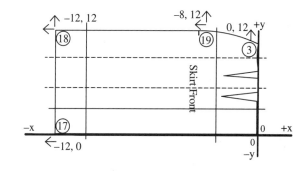

Figure 5.37 Grade Rule 3, Size 12 to Size 14

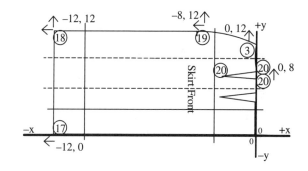

Figure 5.38 Grade Rule 20, Size 12 to Size 14

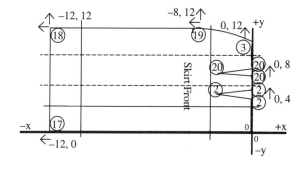

Figure 5.39 Grade Rule 2, Size 12 to Size 14

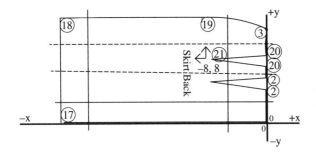

Figure 5.40 Grade Rule 21, Size 12 to Size 14

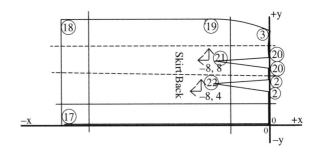

Figure 5.41 Grade Rule 22, Size 12 to Size 14

5. Distribution of the grade within the 1-inch, the 1 1/2-inch, and the 2-inch grades and the difference between standard and variable grades (Figure 5.32).
6. Development of the grade rule table (Table 5.5).
7. Sizes at which the girth changes from a 1-inch to a 1 1/2-inch grade and from a 1 1/2-inch to a 2-inch grade (Table 5.5).

Grading Size 12 Up to Size 14

As stated before, the skirt front and back are graded similarly. The skirt back darts are longer than the skirt front darts and, therefore, need to include a length grade of 1/8 inch. Note the differences between the location of the dart end points on the skirt front and back. The darts in the skirt back extend farther down than the darts in the front, and the dart legs need to be extended accordingly. The lengthwise grade distribution crosses the ends of the back darts. Changing the length of a dart without changing the distance between the dart legs theoretically changes the fullness of the dart; this fullness is accounted for in the overall grade of the waist and the hip. The change in dart length keeps the dart in the correct location for the corresponding body length. Therefore, the dart endpoints require a different grade rule than the top of the dart legs at the waistline. All other grade rules developed for the skirt front may be used on the skirt back.

Grade Rule 21: End of Second Dart on Skirt Back

Since the lower torso length grade lengthens the back skirt darts, rules are needed for each dart end. For the second dart, y remains the same as Grade Rule 20, but the end point has moved 1/4 inch on the x axis to reflect the grade between the waistline and hip line. The grader may choose to lengthen the dart by only 1/8 inch because the end of the dart stops short of the hip line. Grade Rule 21 is −8,8 (Figure 5.40).

Grade Rule 22: End of First Dart on Skirt Back

The Grade Rule 22 assigned to the end of the dart closest to center front is −8,4 (Figure 5.41). The movement along x is the same as Grade Rule 21 and the movement along y is the same as Grade Rule 2.

PANT FRONT AND BACK

What you should know to grade the pant front and back:

1. Cardinal points and grade rules for the skirt front and back (Tables 5.4 and 5.5).
2. Pattern orientation and 0,0 point for placement on Cartesian graph.
3. Distribution of the grade within the 1-inch, 1 1/2-inch, and 2-inch grade and the difference between standard and variable grade (Figures 5.42 and 5.43).

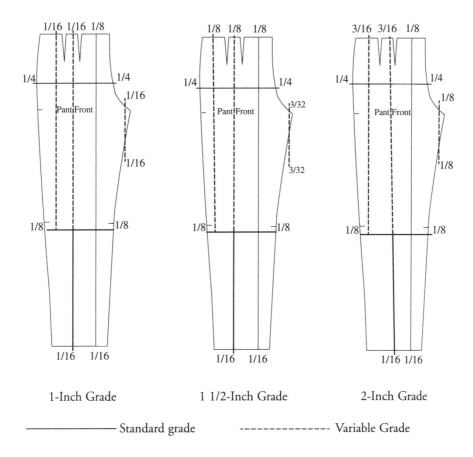

1-Inch Grade   1 1/2-Inch Grade   2-Inch Grade

———————— Standard grade   - - - - - - - - - - - Variable Grade

Figure 5.42 Grade Distributions for Pant Front

4. Location of new cardinal points (Table 5.6 and 5.7).
5. Sizes at which the girth changes from a 1-inch to a 1 1/2-inch grade and from a 1 1/2-inch to a 2-inch grades.

Four new rules, in addition to the grade rules written for the bodice and skirt, are needed to grade pants. The pant block is oriented on the Cartesian graph in the $-x, +y$ quadrant, in the same manner as the skirt. Therefore, some of the rules used to grade the skirt can be assigned to the pant. Cardinal points that require new grade rules are the crotch curve, crotch/inseam, the ankle/inseam, and the ankle/side seam intersections (Figure 5.44). Grade Rules 17 and 18 assigned to the skirt can be assigned or eliminated when grading the pants; the knee width grade is greater than the leg opening, but when the seam line

is blended between the hip/crotch level and the leg opening, that difference will be accounted for.

Grading Size 12 Up to Size 14

A 1 1/2-inch grade is applied when grading up from size 12 to size 14 and when grading down from size 12 to a size 10. The example is graded from a size 12 to size 14. To grade down from a size 12 to size 10, the grade rule increments remain the same, but the signs are opposite, because the garment size is being decreased instead of increased. For example, Grade Rule 24 for the front crotch/inseam intersection is $-8, -2$ when grading size 12 to size 14 and 8,2 when grading size 12 to size 10.

Grade Rule 23: Crotch Curve

A grade rule is added to the crotch curve. This cardinal point is at the hip level and is used to maintain the

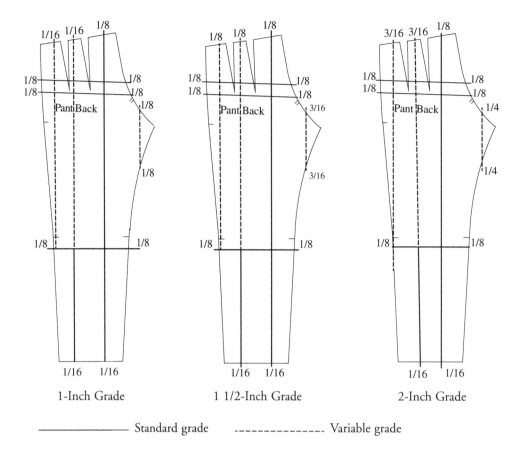

_____ Standard grade   - - - - - - - - - - - - - - - Variable grade

■**Figure 5.43** Grade Distributions for Pant Back

curve of the crotch seam as it is graded in length. This point is located along the center line of the crotch and reflects only the length grade. Movement is along the x axis from size 12 to size 14, so Grade Rule 23 is $-8,0$ (Figure 5.45).

Grade Rule 24: Front Crotch/ Inseam Intersection

The front crotch/inseam intersection is graded in length the same as the skirt hip level grade, -8. To grade from size 12 to size 14, the movement is into the $-y$ quadrant 3/32 inch (one-fourth of the hip grade). Grade Rule 24, which is $-8,-3$, is assigned to this intersection (Figure 5.46).

Grade Rule 25: Ankle/ Inseam Intersection

The 0,0 point is at the waistline/crotch intersection, so all length increases are in the $-x$ direction and are additive. The increase in length between the waistline

and hipline is 1/4 inch when grading from size 12 to size 14; an additional 1/8-inch length increase is found between the crotch/inseam intersection and the leg opening for a total 3/8-inch increase in length. There is no increase in width from the 0,0 point along y. Grade Rule 25 is assigned to this cardinal point and is $-12,0$ (Figure 5.47).

Grade Rule 26: Ankle/Side Seam Intersection

The length increase at the leg opening/side seam intersection is the same as Grade Rule 25, which is -12. However, the total increase in the leg opening width of 1/8 inch from size 12 to size 14 is reflected in Grade Rule 26. Grade Rule 26 is $-12, 4$ (Figure 5.47).

Grade Rule 27: Back Crotch/ Inseam Intersection

Grade Rule 24 was assigned to the front crotch/inseam intersection, but because the crotch width grade

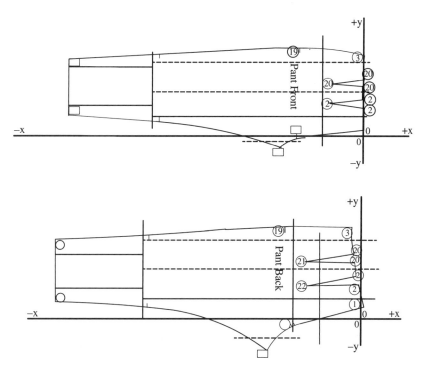

□New grade rules are needed for crotch/inseam and ends of leg

Figure 5.44 Pant Front and Back Orientation

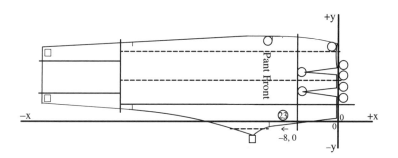

Figure 5.45 Grade Rule 23, Size 12 to Size 14

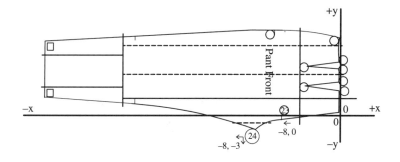

Figure 5.46 Grade Rule 24, Size 12 to Size 14

for back and front is not the same, a new grade rule is assigned to the back crotch/inseam intersection. The front crotch grade is the hip grade (3/8 inch) plus one-fourth (3/32 inch) of the hip grade; the back crotch grade is the hip grade (3/8 inch) plus one-half (3/16 inch) of the hip grade. Grade Rule 27 is $-8, -6$ (Figure 5.48).

Completing the Pant Grade

Complete the process of grading the pant by applying the grade rules previously developed for the skirt hip, waist, and dart (front and back, respectively). Blend and true the lines between the graded points to complete the graded pattern. Check seamlines and notches for accuracy. Label the new pattern size.

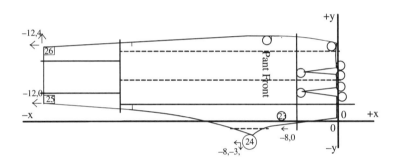

Figure 5.47 Grade Rules 25 and 26, Size 12 to Size 14

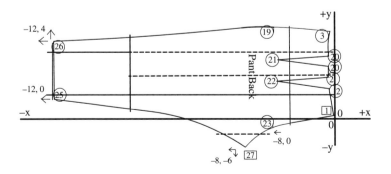

Figure 5.48 Grade Rule 27, Size 12 to Size 14

PATTERN GRADING
Summary

Most garment designs are developed from basic pattern blocks, so when grade distributions (how the body changes between sizes) are understood for the basic pattern block, the knowledge can be applied to grading other patterns. Information required to grade a pattern includes: cardinal points and their corresponding grade rules; the master size and size range of the pattern; the unit of measurement and the common denominator; the distribution of the grade; the differences between standard and variable grades; and the sizes at which the girth changes between a 1-inch grade, a 1 1/2-inch grade, and a 2-inch grade.

The development of a grade rule table is the first step for both manual and computer grading. This requires an understanding of the Cartesian graph. All grade rule values are determined in relation to the 0,0 point of reference and the orientation of the pattern location at the $0x,0y$ point of the graph. The grading procedure for the basic pattern blocks explained in this chapter develops the beginning grade rule tables for these pattern pieces. The pattern blocks are then graded according to the method explained in Chapter 4. The grade rules that are developed for each pattern block may be applied to similar pattern blocks. Therefore, consistent pattern orientation on the Cartesian graph is necessary.

EXERCISES

1. Why is the pattern orientation used in this chapter recommended?

2. Why is the left back bodice used for grading? When would the left back not be appropriate? How would the grade rules differ for the right bodice back as compared to the left bodice back?

3. How would the grade rules differ if a pattern has seam allowances added before grading?

4. Why are bodice front darts graded using the same rule for each dart leg and the dart point?

5. Once grade rules have been written for the basic pattern blocks, the rules can be applied to other designs. Write grade rules for the shift dress front (Table 5.8). The grade distributions for the dress are shown in Figure 5.49.

6. Skipping sizes while grading is not recommended. Try grading directly from the size 12 to the size 20. Compare the final pattern with a size 20 that was graded through all the sizes.

7. It was recommended that no more than two sizes of a pattern be graded from the master pattern. To illustrate how a pattern can be distorted, compare the size 20 pattern from Question 6 graded by other graders in your class.

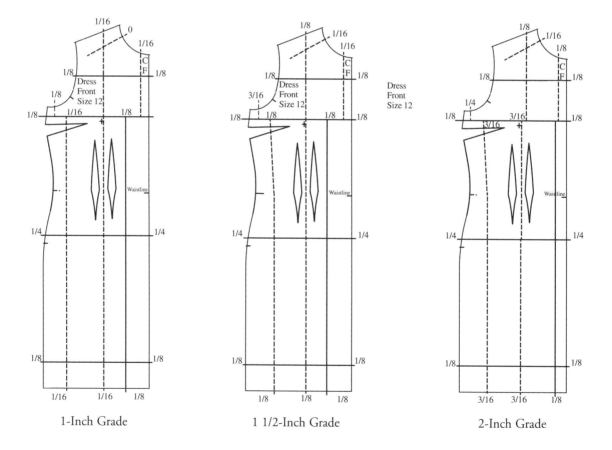

1-Inch Grade　　　　1 1/2-Inch Grade　　　　2-Inch Grade

Figure 5.49 Dress Front Grade Distributions

■Table 5.1 Grade Rule Table: Bodice Front

Pattern Piece: Bodice front with waist dart

Unit: Inches   **Denominator:** 1/32

Size Range: Misses 6–22

Master Size: Misses 12

Grade Rules: 1–8

Notes:
1-inch grade between sizes 6–8 and 8–10
1 1/2-inch grade between sizes 10–12, 12–14 and 14–16
2-inch grade between sizes 16–18, 18–20 and 20–22

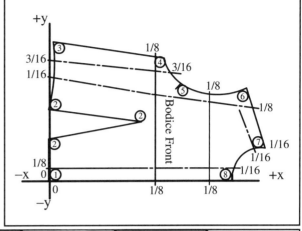

Size	Rule 1		Rule 2		Rule 3		Rule 4		Rule 5		Rule 6	
	X	Y	X	Y	X	Y	X	Y	X	Y	X	Y
6	0	0					−12	−28			−24	−14
8	0	0					−8	−20			−16	−10
10	0	0	0	−4	0	−12	−4	−12			−8	−6
12	0	0	0	0	0	0	0	0	0	0	0	0
14	0	0	0	4	0	12	4	12			−8	−6
16	0	0					8	24			16	12
18	0	0					12	40			24	20
20	0	0					16	56			32	28
22	0	0					20	72			40	36

Size	Rule 7		Rule 8	
	X	Y	X	Y
6	−26	−6		
8	−18	−4		
10	−10	−2	−8	0
12	0	0	0	0
14	10	2	8	0
16	20	4		
18	30	8		
20	40	12		
22	50	16		

■Table 5.2 Grade Rule Table: Bodice Back with Shoulder Dart

Pattern Piece: Bodice back with shoulder dart

Unit: Inches   **Denominator:** 1/32

Size Range: Misses 6–22

Master Size: Misses 12

Grade Rules: 1–9

Notes: The left bodice back pattern is used

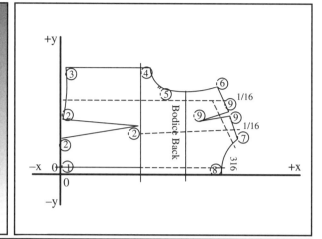

Size	Rule 1		Rule 2		Rule 3		Rule 4		Rule 5		Rule 6	
	X	Y	X	Y	X	Y	X	Y	X	Y	X	Y
6												
8												
10												
12	0	0	0	0	0	0	0	0	0	0	0	0
14												
16												
18												
20												
22												

Size	Rule 7		Rule 8		Rule 9	
	X	Y	X	Y	X	Y
6					−26	−10
8					−18	−7
10					−10	−4
12	0	0	0	0	0	0
14					10	4
16					20	8
18					30	14
20					40	20
22					50	26

Table 5.3 Grade Rule Table: Sleeve with Elbow Dart

Pattern Piece: Sleeve with Elbow Dart

Unit: Inches   **Denominator:** 1/32

Size Range: Misses 6–22

Master Size: Misses 12

Grade Rules: 10–16

Notes: Orientation of the *x,y* axes is located such that the *y* axis is the bicep line of the sleeve

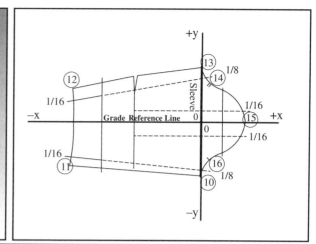

Size	Rule 10		Rule 11		Rule 12		Rule 13		Rule 14		Rule 15	
	X	Y	X	Y	X	Y	X	Y	X	Y	X	Y
6												
8												
10												
12	0	0	0	0	0	0	0	0	0	0	0	0
14												
16												
18												
20												
22												

Size	Rule 16	
	X	Y
6		
8		
10		
12	0	0
14		
16		
18		
20		
22		

Table 5.4 Grade Rule Table: Skirt Front

Pattern Piece: Skirt front

Unit: Inches   **Denominator:** 1/32

Size Range: Misses 6–22

Master size: Misses 12

Grade Rules: 1, 2, 3, 17, 18, 19, 20

Notes: Grade rules are listed in the clockwise order seen on the skirt pattern. Previously developed grade rules have been included and should be filled in by the reader.

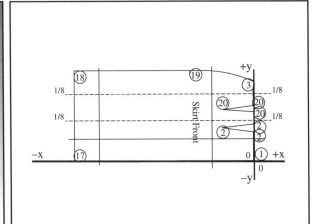

Size	Rule 1		Rule 17		Rule 18		Rule 19		Rule 3		Rule 20	
	X	Y	X	Y	X	Y	X	Y	X	Y	X	Y
6												
8												
10												
12	0	0	0	0	0	0	0	0	0	0	0	0
14												
16												
18												
20												
22												

Size	Rule 2	
	X	Y
6		
8		
10		
12	0	0
14		
16		
18		
20		
22		

Table 5.5 Grade Rule Table: Skirt Back

Pattern Piece: Skirt Back
Unit: Inches   **Denominator:** 1/32
Size Range: Misses 6–22
Master Size: Misses 12
Grade Rules: 1, 2, 3, 17, 18, 19, 20, 21, 22

Notes: The left back skirt pattern is used

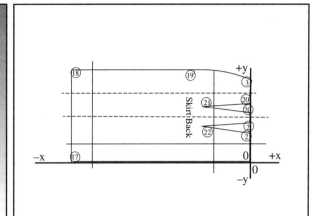

Size	Rule 1		Rule 17		Rule 18		Rule 19		Rule 3		Rule 20	
	X	Y	X	Y	X	Y	X	Y	X	Y	X	Y
6												
8												
10												
12	0	0	0	0	0	0	0	0	0	0	0	0
14												
16												
18												
20												
22												

Size	Rule 21		Rule 2		Rule 22	
	X	Y	X	Y	X	Y
6						
8						
10						
12	0	0	0	0	0	0
14						
16						
18						
20						
22						

Table 5.6 Grade Rule Table: Pant Front

Pattern Piece: Pant front
Unit: Inches   **Denominator:** 1/32
Size Range: Misses 6–22
Master size: Misses 12
Grade Rules: 1, 2, 3, 19, 20, 23, 24, 25, 26

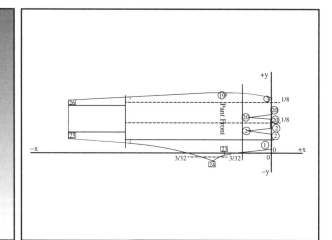

Size	Rule 1		Rule 23		Rule 24		Rule 25		Rule 26		Rule 19	
	X	Y	X	Y	X	Y	X	Y	X	Y	X	Y
6												
8												
10												
12	0	0	0	0	0	0	0	0	0	0	0	0
14												
16												
18												
20												
22												

Size	Rule 3		Rule 20		Rule 2	
	X	Y	X	Y	X	Y
6						
8						
10						
12	0	0	0	0	0	0
14						
16						
18						
20						
22						

Table 5.7 Grade Rule Table: Pant Back

Pattern Piece: Pant back
Unit: Inches   **Denominator:** 1/32
Size Range: Misses 6–22
Master size: Misses 12
Grade Rules: 1, 2, 3, 19, 20, 21, 22, 23, 25, 26, 27

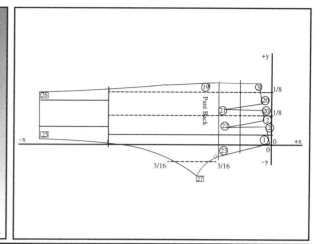

Size	Rule 1		Rule 23		Rule 27		Rule 25		Rule 26		Rule 19	
	X	Y	X	Y	X	Y	X	Y	X	Y	X	Y
6												
8												
10												
12	0	0	0	0	0	0	0	0	0	0	0	0
14												
16												
18												
20												
22												

Size	Rule 3		Rule 20		Rule 21		Rule 2		Rule 22	
	X	Y	X	Y	X	Y	X	Y	X	Y
6										
8										
10										
12	0	0	0	0	0	0	0	0	0	0
14										
16										
18										
20										
22										

Table 5.8 Grade Rule Table: Shift Dress Front

Pattern Piece: Dress Front
Unit: Inches   **Denominator:** 1/32
Size Range: Misses 6–22
Master size: Misses 12
Grade Rules:

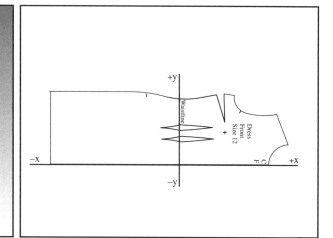

Size	Rule		Rule		Rule		Rule		Rule		Rule	
	X	Y	X	Y	X	Y	X	Y	X	Y	X	Y
6												
8												
10												
12	0	0	0	0	0	0	0	0	0	0	0	0
14												
16												
18												
20												
22												

Size	Rule		Rule		Rule		Rule		Rule		Rule	
	X	Y	X	Y	X	Y	X	Y	X	Y	X	Y
6												
8												
10												
12	0	0	0	0	0	0	0	0	0	0	0	0
14												
16												
18												
20												
22												

NOTES

6

Sleeve/Bodice

Combinations

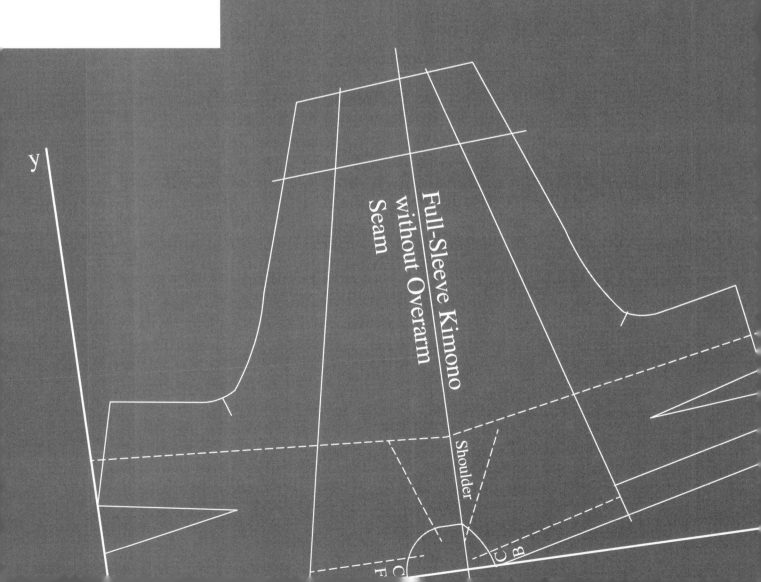

y

Full-Sleeve Kimono
without Overarm
Seam

Shoulder

C   B

C
F

Introduction

The bodice and sleeve patterns may be com-

bined to produce new styles referred to as a sleeve/bodice combinations. Although these styles are actually developed by combining two basic patterns, new grade rules are required when the pattern orientation is different from the basic blocks. For this chapter, new grade rules will be developed for all the cardinal points. Some manufacturers may develop a new grade rule table for each new style, even though many of the new grade rules will be the same or duplicates of previously developed grade rules. Duplicate rules can be transferred to the new table. Other manufactures may use the same grade rule table with the previously developed rules and just add new ones as necessary. Developing a new grade rule table helps the student understand the relationships of the grade rules.

A thorough understanding of how width and length grades are distributed within a basic block will make any new garment style easy to grade. A grader should be able to identify the grade rules developed for the basic pattern blocks in Chapter 5.

An understanding of the procedures used to develop a grade rule table and the methods used for manually grading a pattern are prerequisites for the information that follows. This chapter gives a brief explanation of the pattern to be graded, along with the distribution of the grade in the 1-inch, the 1 1/2-inch, and the 2-inch grades, and provides a grade rule table showing the location of the appropriate cardinal points. Pattern orientation is shown on the grade rule table for each example.

Grading of three basic sleeve/bodice patterns is explained in this chapter; they are the kimono with overarm seam, the kimono with underarm gusset, and the raglan sleeve.

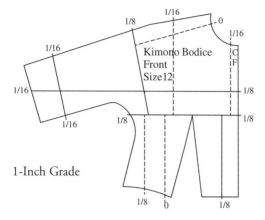

1-Inch Grade

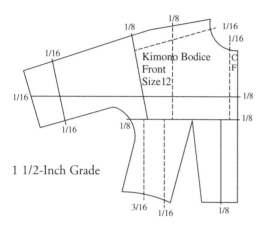

1 1/2-Inch Grade

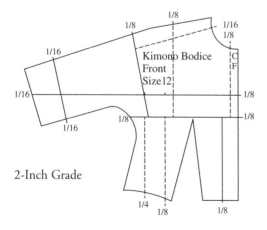

2-Inch Grade

——————— Standard grade

------------ Variable grade

Figure 6.1 Grade Distributions for Kimono Sleeve

KIMONO SLEEVE WITH OVERARM SEAM

The kimono sleeve pattern is developed from the basic bodice and sleeve. Therefore, it is understandable that the grading of this pattern involves many of the same grade rules used for the basic bodice and sleeve blocks.

In Figure 6.1, compare the grade distribution of the kimono sleeve pattern with those of the basic bodice pattern block (Figure 5.2) and the sleeve pattern block (Figure 5.23). Note that the divisions showing the distributions for a 1-inch, a 1 1/2-inch, and a 2-inch grade are the same. New grade rules may be written for all the cardinal points or a manufacturer may use previously established grade rules. **However, in this text new grade rules will be written for all new grading problems in each chapter, and the first digit of these rule numbers will refer to the chapter number.** For this chapter, all grade rules start with a 6 (the chapter number) followed by a decimal point and the grade rule number. Grade rule numbers for each new grade rule table will continue in sequence from the previous grade rule table. If a computer system automatically drops the 0 after a decimal (changing 6.10 to 6.1), then a hyphen may be used instead of a decimal (i.e., 6-1, 6-2, etc.).

What you should know to grade the kimono sleeve with overarm seam:

1. Basic grade rules and distribution of the grade for the basic bodices and sleeve (Chapter 5).
2. Orientation and location of cardinal points on the kimono sleeve (Figure 6.2).
3. New grade rules are written for all the cardinal points for the kimono sleeve. Each grade rule begins with a 6, as a reference to the chapter number. New grade rules are numbered consecutively around the pattern piece in the clockwise direction.
4. New grade rules are required when there is a movement change on the *x,y* axes or a change in grade distribution within a pattern.

5. The underarm/sleeve intersection on the kimono sleeve must be identified and graded. This point is not a defined intersection, so the grader must approximate the location and grade the curve.

6. Method for moving a pattern for grading and blending of lines (Chapter 4).

Pattern Orientation and Grade Rules

The kimono sleeve pattern is oriented like the bodice front (Figure 6.2). The orientation of point 0,0 is the waistline/center front intersection labeled Grade Rule 6.1. This is the same as Grade Rule 1 used in the bodice front in Chapter 5. Grade Rules 6.2, 6.3, 6.4 are the same as Grade Rules 2, 3, 4 for the bodice front (Chapter 5). Additional Grade Rules 6.7, 6.8, 6.9 are the same as Grade Rules 6, 7, 8 for the bodice front.

New grade rules have been established for the sleeve area because the pattern orientation is different from the basic sleeve. Two additional grade rules are needed. One is needed for the underarm seam at the wrist. This reflects the length change of the sleeve. The second rule for the overarm seam at the wrist reflects the same length change as well as the width change needed in the sleeve circumference.

The movement for the grade at each of the pattern's cardinal points is cumulative because it includes all grade distributions between it and the 0,0 point of reference. This concept is applied as new grade rules for the sleeve portion of the kimono are determined. The amount of growth in the sleeve is the same as for the basic set-in sleeve, but the movement of the bodice is incorporated into the sleeve's grade rules because the sleeve is attached to the bodice. Coordinates are given for specific sizes in Table 6.1 to aid the grader in establishing the correct x,y coordinates.

KIMONO SLEEVE WITH UNDERARM GUSSET

The grade distributions of the kimono sleeve with underarm gusset are the same as for the kimono sleeve.

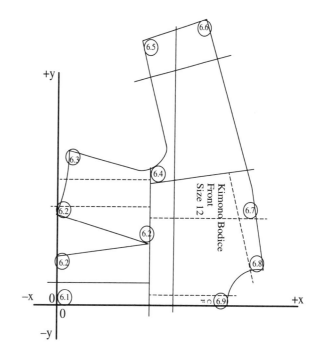

Figure 6.2 Orientation for Kimono Sleeve

The gusset and its placement in the sleeve require grading; new cardinal points are necessary to designate their movement. The angle of the sleeve from the bodice can vary and careful consideration is necessary to determine if new grade rules are to be used for the sleeve or if the previously developed kimono sleeve grade rules may be applied. (Additional x,y axes may also be necessary, and further discussion of this type of grading is explained in Chapter 8.)

This kimono sleeve with underarm gusset is developed by lowering the angle of the sleeve to approximately 45 degrees of the bodice. The overlap of the underarm area between the bodice and sleeve becomes the location of the gusset. The gusset is a separate piece and is graded with new cardinal points and grade rules. The grade distribution in the gusset is a standard grade. The ends of the gusset are graded, but the width of the gusset remains constant from size to size.

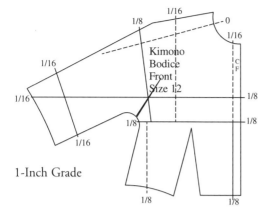

1-Inch Grade

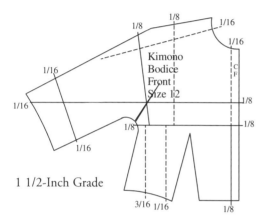

1 1/2-Inch Grade

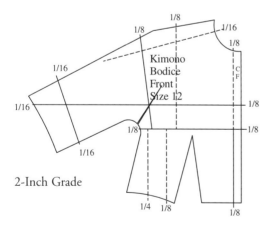

2-Inch Grade

——————— Standard grade

- - - - - - - - - Variable grade

Figure 6.3 Grade Distributions for Kimono Sleeve with Gusset

What you should know to grade the kimono sleeve with underarm gusset:

1. Grade distribution for the kimono sleeve with underarm gusset (Figure 6.3).
2. Basic grade rules and grade distributions for the kimono sleeve (Table 6.1 and Figure 6.2).
3. Location of cardinal points for the kimono sleeve with underarm gusset (Table 6.2 and Figure 6.4).
4. The development and location of a gusset pattern in the underarm.
5. Orientation and cardinal points for the gusset pattern piece (Figure 6.4).
6. Method for moving a pattern for grading and blending lines (Chapter 4).
7. Completion of a grade rule table by adding grade rules not previously specified for sleeve/bodice combinations.

RAGLAN SLEEVE

The raglan sleeve is a sleeve/bodice combination in which a portion of bodice shoulder area becomes the top portion of the sleeve. The two basic pattern pieces for the front and back are a raglan bodice and a raglan sleeve. Note that the sleeve consists of two pieces, a front and back (Figure 6.5). The raglan bodice pattern uses the same orientation and grade rules as the basic bodice (see Chapter 5). This pattern should be very easy for the beginning grader to understand and grade. The raglan sleeve pattern requires new grade rules because its orientation and grades are a combination of rules used for the sleeve and the bodice (Figure 6.6). Understanding how a raglan sleeve pattern is developed and the grade distribution for the basic bodice and sleeve make the rules for the raglan pattern more understandable.

In each chapter the grade rules continue in sequence from the previous grade rule table. Grade rules that were developed previously in this chapter will be noted on the grade rule table but not recorded again in Table 6.3. Grade rules that were written for the

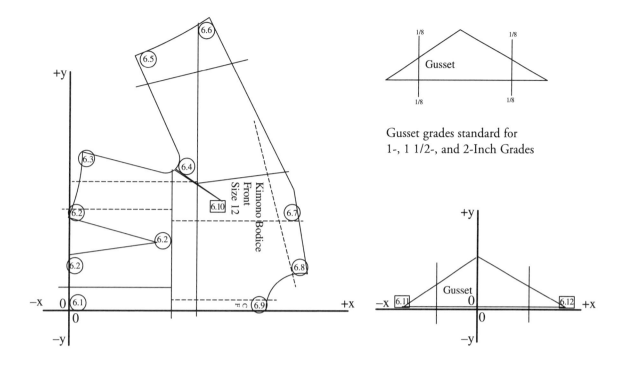

Figure 6.4 Orientation for Kimono Sleeve With Gusset

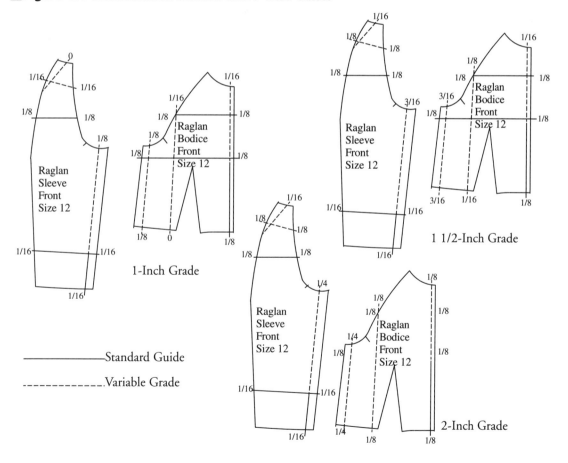

Figure 6.5 Grade Distributions for Raglan Sleeve/Bodice

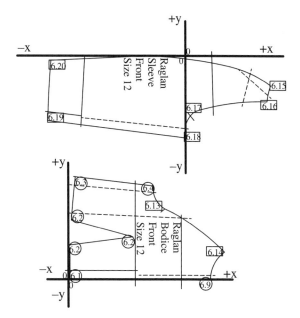

Sleeve/Bodice Front

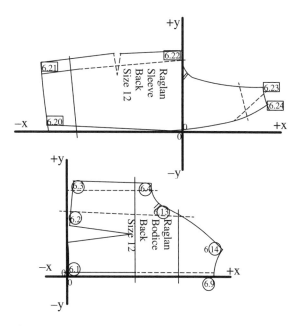

Sleeve/Bodice Back

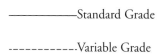

——————Standard Grade

------------Variable Grade

Figure 6.6 Orientation for Raglan Sleeve/Bodice Front and Back

basic bodice front in Chapter 5 should be reviewed. Grade Rules 6.13, 6.17, 6.18, and 6.19 are the same as previously written grade rules for the basic bodice and sleeve. It is important to note the pattern orientation for the raglan sleeve pattern. The orientation used will enable the grader to reference similar grade rules developed for the basic sleeve (Table 5.3).

New *x,y* coordinates are needed for Grade Rule 6.14. This point is located midway between the center front/neck and the shoulder/neckline intersection. This point was not identified in the basic bodice and does not have the same *x,y* coordinates as Grade Rule 7 or Grade Rule 6.8. **Check grade rule numbers after adjusting pattern shape.**

The raglan sleeve pattern has part of the bodice attached to the sleeve. Grade Rules 6.15 and 6.16 on the front raglan sleeve and Grade Rules 6.23 and 6.24 on the back raglan sleeve have a grade distribution that includes grades from the bodice and the sleeve. These are new grade rules that must be determined.

What you should know to grade the raglan sleeve:

1. Grade distribution for the raglan sleeve front and back (Figure 6.5).
2. Basic grade rules and grade distributions for the kimono sleeve (Table 6.1).
3. Basic grade rules and grade distributions for the basic bodice and basic sleeve (Table 5.1 and 5.3).
4. Location of cardinal points for the raglan bodice and sleeve (Table 6.3 and Figure 6.6).
5. Orientation of the raglan bodice and sleeve patterns (Figure 6.6).
6. Method for moving a pattern for grading and blending of lines (Chapter 4).

PATTERN GRADING
SUMMARY

Bodice/sleeve combination styles, which combine the bodice and sleeve patterns, use the same grade distributions as the basic bodice and sleeve. However, new grade rules are required because the orientation of portions of the pattern are different from the basic blocks. Understanding the procedures used to develop a grade rule table enables the pattern grader to apply knowledge of grading basic patterns to new styles. New grade rule tables are developed for each style to aid in understanding the grading process and the relationship of grade rules to one another. In this and subsequent chapters, the grade rules all start with the chapter number followed by a decimal and the grade rule number. This makes referencing the grade rules easier for the beginner.

Grading kimono sleeve and raglan sleeve styles requires studying the grade distributions for the basic pattern blocks and transferring the information to the new pattern combination. Pattern grading explanations in this chapter guide the pattern grader through this process. Completing the grade rule tables provided in the text reinforces the information presented.

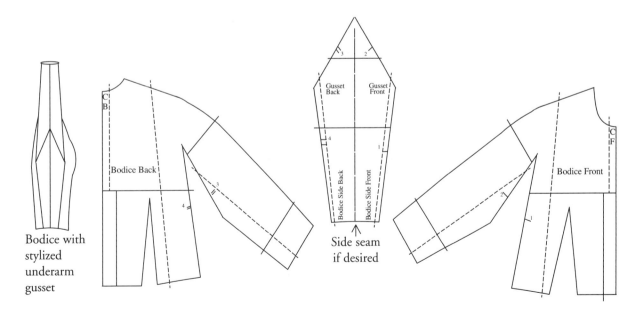

Figure 6.7 Grade Distributions for Kimono Sleeve with Stylized Gusset

EXERCISES

1. Use Figure 6.1 (grade distributions) and Figure 6.2 (orientation) to write grade rules in Table 6.1 for the kimono sleeve for grading from size 12 down to size 10 and up to size 14.

2. Complete the grade rule table developed in Exercise 1 for all other sizes.

3. There are many design variations for the kimono sleeve. How might the underarm curve or the angle of the sleeve affect the grading?

4. Develop the grade rules for the kimono sleeve with a stylized gusset. The grade distribution is given in Figure 6.7 and pattern orientation in Figure 6.8. A blank grade rule table can be found in Appendix D.

5. Develop the grade rules for the full-sleeve kimono. The pattern orientation and grade distribution lines are illustrated in Figure 6.9. Be aware that all of the center front and center back length grades are placed above the underarm seam because of the lowered armhole.

6. Find examples of other sleeve/bodice combinations.

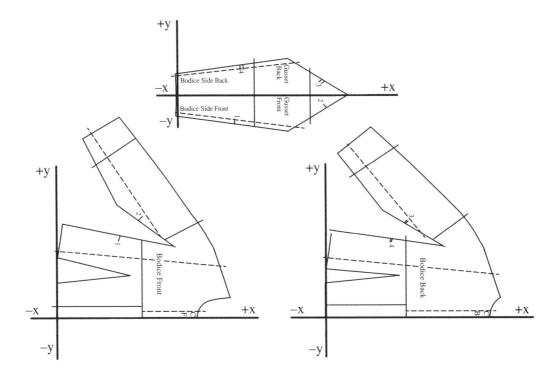

Figure 6.8 Orientation for Kimono Sleeve with Stylized Gusset

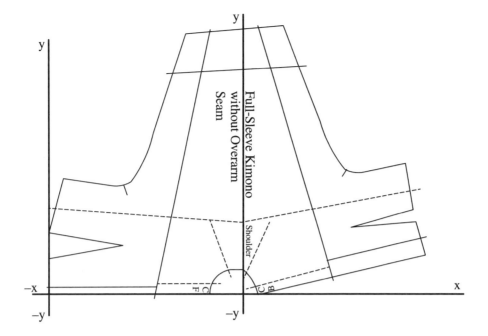

Figure 6.9 Orientation for Full-Sleeve Kimono

Table 6.1 Grade Rule Table: Kimono Sleeve with Overarm Seam

Pattern Piece: Kimono Sleeve
Unit: Inches   **Denominator:** 1/32
Size Range: Misses 6–22
Master size: Misses 12
Grade Rules: 6.1 through 6.9

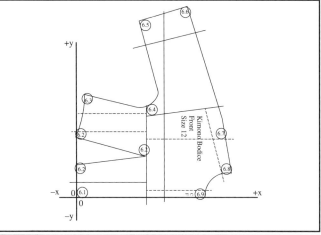

Size	Rule 6.1		Rule 6.2		Rule 6.3		Rule 6.4		Rule 6.5		Rule 6.6	
	X	Y	X	Y	X	Y	X	Y	X	Y	X	Y
6												
8	0	0	0	–8	0	–20	–8	–20	–8	–22	–12	–22
10	0	0	0	–4	0	–12	–4	–12	–4	–12	–6	–12
12	0	0	0	0	0	0	0	0	0	0	0	0
14												
16												
18												
20												
22												

Size	Rule 6.7		Rule 6.8		Rule 6.9	
	X	Y	X	Y	X	Y
6						
8	–18	–10	–18	–4	–16	0
10	–10	–6	–10	–2	–8	0
12	0	0	0	0	0	0
14						
16						
18						
20						
22						

Table 6.2 Grade Rule Table: Kimono Sleeve with Underarm Gusset

Pattern Piece: Kimono Sleeve with Gusset
Unit: Inches   **Denominator:** 1/32
Size Range: Misses 6–22
Master size: Misses 12
Grade Rules: 6.10 through 6.12

Notes: Grade Rules 6.1 to 6.9 are found on
Table 6.1: Kimono sleeve

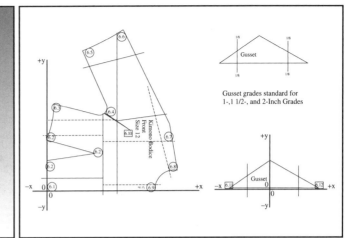

Size	Rule 6.10		Rule 6.11		Rule 6.12		Rule		Rule		Rule	
	X	Y	X	Y	X	Y	X	Y	X	Y	X	Y
6												
8												
10												
12	0	0	0	0	0	0	0	0	0	0	0	0
14												
16												
18												
20												
22												

Size	Rule		Rule		Rule		Rule		Rule		Rule	
	X	Y	X	Y	X	Y	X	Y	X	Y	X	Y
6												
8												
10												
12	0	0	0	0	0	0	0	0	0	0	0	0
14												
16												
18												
20												
22												

Table 6.3 Grade Rule Table: Raglan Bodice and Sleeve

Pattern Piece: Raglan Bodice and Sleeve
Unit: Inches   **Denominator:** 1/32
Size Range: Misses 6–22
Master size: Misses 12
Grade Rules:

Notes: Grade Rules 6.1 to 6.4 are found on
Table 6.1: Kimono sleeve

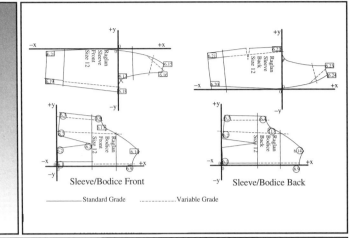

Standard Grade   Variable Grade

Sleeve/Bodice Front   Sleeve/Bodice Back

Size	Rule 6.13		Rule 6.14		Rule 6.15		Rule 6.16		Rule 6.17		Rule 6.18	
	X	Y	X	Y	X	Y	X	Y	X	Y	X	Y
6												
8												
10												
12	0	0	0	0	0	0	0	0	0	0	0	0
14												
16												
18												
20												
22												

Size	Rule 6.19		Rule 6.20		Rule 6.21		Rule 6.22		Rule 6.23		Rule 6.24	
	X	Y	X	Y	X	Y	X	Y	X	Y	X	Y
6												
8												
10												
12	0	0	0	0	0	0	0	0	0	0	0	0
14												
16												
18												
20												
22												

NOTES

7

Design

Variations

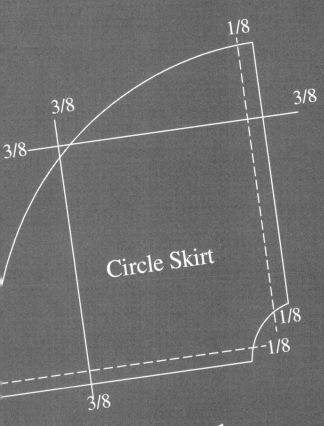

1/8

3/8

3/8

3/8

1/8

1/8

1/8

Circle Skirt

3/8

1 Inch Grade

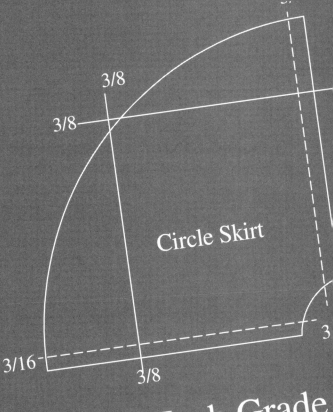

3/8

3/8

Circle Skirt

3/16

3/8

3

1 1/2 Inch Grade

Variable grade

Introduction

By this point the reader should be familiar with the grade rules necessary to grade basic garment designs. This chapter features designs that are variations of basic styles or designs that combine two or more grade distributions. The basic cardinal points are identified and the new grade rules are provided for each design. As in Chapter 6, the grade rule numbering is independent of previous chapters. The grade rules are identified by the chapter number plus rule number and continue in consecutive order. See information in Chapter 6 for computer systems that automatically drop zeros after decimals.

The designs presented in this chapter are the princess bodice, full-roll collar, circle skirt, jumpsuit, and surplice bodice. Other designs are discussed relative to element proportions and how the proportions are affected by the pattern grading process. A grade distribution for the 1-inch, the 1 1/2-inch, and the 2-inch grades and a grade rule table are given to show pattern orientation and location of cardinal points. This chapter provides guidelines for developing grade rules and information about factors that influence the grading of the design.

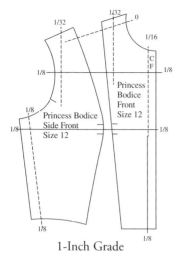

1-Inch Grade

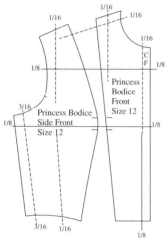

1 1/2-Inch Grade

2-Inch Grade

———— Standard grade ---------- Variable grade

Figure 7.1 Grade Distributions for Princess Bodice

PRINCESS BODICE

The princess bodice is developed from the basic bodice pieces. It is easier to understand the movements used for grading the princess bodice if the two pattern pieces are viewed as a bodice with shoulder and waistline darts, not as two independent pieces. For a manufacturer, it is advantageous to keep the two pattern pieces together for grading purposes because the two pattern pieces can use grade rules that were developed for a basic bodice block. If changes are made to the design, new grade rules may not be necessary. (Grade rules in this chapter may not carry the same number on similar cardinal points as in previous chapters because the numbering begins anew in each chapter.)

As seen in the bodice back with shoulder dart, the shoulder length growth is divided on each side of the shoulder dart. The same principle is used when grading a princess bodice; the shoulder growth is divided on each side of the princess line within the bodice (Figure 7.1). The x,y coordinates necessary for the princess bodice are the same as in the basic bodice back with shoulder dart.

In order to maintain the shape of the garment, the bust point or curve must be identified and moved to show the difference in the bodice length between the shoulder area and the lower sections of the bodice. A new grade is needed for the bust area to control the growth that occurs in the bodice.

What you should know to grade the princess bodice:

1. Basic grade rules and distributions of the grade for the basic bodice back (Chapter 5). An additional grade rule is needed for the bust point (Table 7.1).
2. Location of cardinal points for the princess bodice (Table 7.1).
3. New grade rules are written for all the cardinal points for the princess bodice because numbering begins anew in each chapter. Each

grade rule is preceded by 7, as a reference to the chapter number.

4. Princess bodice center front and side front are graded together and have a common 0,0 point of reference.

5. Grade distributions for princess bodice (Figure 7.1).

6. Orientation for princess bodice (Figure 7.2).

FULL-ROLL COLLAR

The full-roll collar is very easy to grade. The grade division is the combination of the front and back neckline grades (Figure 7.3). Because the neckline seam on the full-roll collar is essentially a straight line, the amount of change for larger and smaller sizes is an additive grade of the neckline divisions. Both the partial-roll and the flat collar have necklines that curve and require two *x,y* axes for grading. This procedure is explained in Chapter 8. Since the grade distributions in the full-roll collar are the same as the distributions in the bodice front and back necklines, the neckline distributions are added and the collar is graded in one direction. This same method of adding or subtracting grade distributions can be applied to other designs, such as a straight waistband or cuffs.

Convertible collars and band collars are graded like the full-roll collar. The collar and the stand of a two-piece band collar both use the same grade distributions and procedure.

What you should know to grade the full-roll collar:

1. Basic grade rules and distributions of the grade for the basic front and back bodice necklines (Chapter 5) and the application to collars (Figure 7.3).

2. Location of cardinal points for the full-roll collar (Table 7.2).

3. Pattern orientation of the collar and the 0,0 reference point (Figure 7.4).

4. New grade rules are written for all the cardinal points for the full-roll collar. Each grade

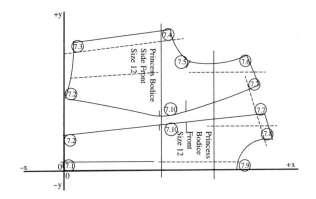

Figure 7.2 Orientation for Princess Bodice

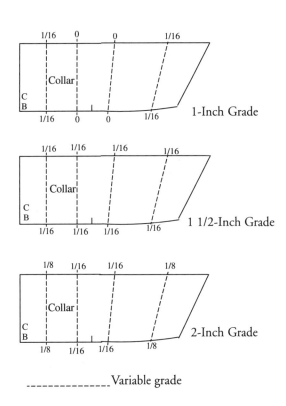

Figure 7.3 Grade Distributions for Roll, Band, and Convertible Collars

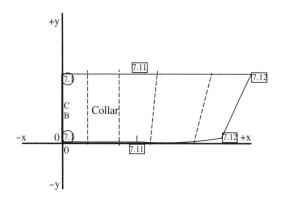

Figure 7.4 Orientation for Roll, Band, and
Convertible Collars

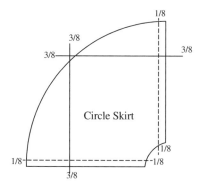

1-Inch Grade

rule is preceded by a 7, as a reference to the
chapter number.

5. The grade rules are additive from the 0,0
   point.

CIRCLE SKIRT: MANUAL GRADING

A true circle skirt pattern in which the side seams and
center front of half the skirt are perpendicular to each
other utilizes a unique method of grading. The
method described in this section is appropriate for all
manual or machine grading, but is appropriate for
computer grading *only if the skirt has four seams*, center front, center back, and each side seam. Computer
grading of a skirt with a fold at the center front and/or
center back must use a different approach which will
be explained in the next section. Computer grading of
a skirt with a center fold using this first orientation
will cause it to grade into itself at the center. Other
flared skirt designs may require the use of two reference axes, and the procedure for grading these skirts is
discussed in Chapter 8.

In this example, the circle skirt pattern is for one-
fourth of the total garment, and the grade distribution
shown is one-fourth of the circumference grade
(Figure 7.5). This pattern could also represent one half
of a skirt design, in which case the grade rules would

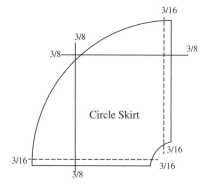

1 1/2-Inch Grade

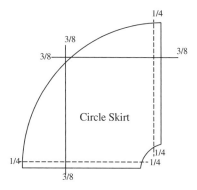

2-Inch Grade

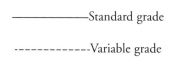

Figure 7.5 Grade Distributions for Circle Skirt

be different. The grader should be aware of the pattern shape and style when assigning grade rules.

The circle skirt is unique in that the *x,y* axes are placed in the center of the waist curve and the center and side seams are moved in *x,y* directions. The 0,0 point is located in the curve of the waistline in order for the curve to be maintained as the seams are moved (Figure 7.6). The grader will want to review the information presented in Chapter 4 related to the blending of curved lines. Because this pattern is composed of curves representing one-quarter of a circle, each of the cardinal points must move so the curve can maintain a circle-like appearance and not become an ellipse. The graded hemline curve should remain parallel to the master block.

Four grade rules will be used for the circle skirt. The two waistline cardinal points reflect the waist circumference grade. The cardinal points at the hemline reflect the circumference grade and the length grade. Each point has different *x,y* coordinates mainly due to their location within the Cartesian graph.

What you should know to grade the circle skirt manually:

1. How a circle skirt pattern is developed.
2. Grade rules and distribution of the grade for the basic skirt.
3. Grade distributions for the circle skirt (Figure 7.5).
4. Location of cardinal points for the circle skirt (Table 7.3).
5. New grade rules are required when there is a sign change or a movement change within a grade rule.
6. Orientation of the circle skirt (Figure 7.6).

CIRCLE SKIRT: COMPUTER GRADING

The circle skirt is a style that requires an orientation for computer grading that is different from the orientation described for manual grading. Although the computer grading procedure can be applied success-

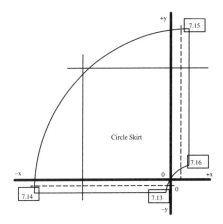

■ **Figure 7.6** Orientation for Circle Skirt

fully to manual grading, the process is more complex than the one described for manual grading. Therefore, both methods are presented. The grade distribution for the circle skirt remains the same for either method (Figure 7.5). However, the skirt must be oriented with the center front/back line along the −*x* axis and the side seam along the +*y* axis for computer grading (Figure 7.7).

In order to maintain the shape of the curves, the waist and hem must grade so they are parallel to one another along the entire curve (Figure 7.8). If the center line/waist intersection were to remain constant at 0,0 as it does in other skirts that have been graded, the curves would become elliptical as they grade. Therefore, the center line/waist intersection must grade the same amount as the side seam/waist intersection. Determining the grade rules for this type of grade involves working with the radius of the circles necessary to give the specified waist circumference rather than the differences in waist circumference.

Table 7.4 gives the radius for the waist circumferences specified in PS 42-70. Seam allowances have not been included. Note that the exact waist measurement has been used and that no **fitting ease** has been allowed because of the bias nature of the waistline seam. Some fabrics may even require a reduced circumference for the same reason. The *difference in the waist radius* from the sample size to the graded size will be the *x* value

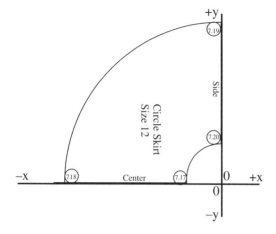

Figure 7.7 Orientation for Circle Skirt (Computer Grading)

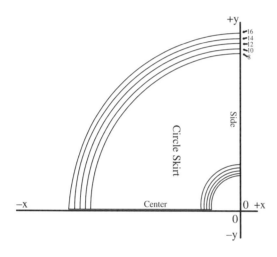

Figure 7.8 Graded Nest for Circle Skirt

lating the radius needed to produce the specified circumference. The waist radius can be determined by using the following mathematical formula:

$$\text{radius (r)} = \text{circumference (c)} \div 2\pi$$

Divide the waist specification (circumference) by 2π (6.2832) to determine the radius required to create a circle (waist seamline) equal to the waist size specification. Use the conversion chart, Table D.1 in Appendix D, to convert the decimals to fractions for the grade rule table. Even though the waist is a horizontal circumference measurement, it is not divided by four when grading a half-front or half-back circle pattern. This is because *the grade rule is based on differences in the radius for each size*, and the radius is comparable to a length grade on the body (Table 7.5).

The waist grade must be added to the length grade to determine the grade rules for the hemline of the circle skirt. Refer to the grade distribution, shown in Figure 7.5, for the length grade. Like the waist, the *x* increment for the center line/hem and the *y* increment for the side seam/hem intersection will be the same number but with opposite signs. The *y* for the center line/hem and the *x* for the side seam/hem will both be 0. Complete Grade Rule Table 7.6 for all sizes using the grade guide provided in Table 7.5.

The same method of grading circles can be used for any circular pattern, such as a cascade ruffle that must fit the circumference of the adjacent pattern piece. Pattern pieces that are circular but not a full circle also can be graded using this method. The radius will need to be adjusted to represent the portion of the circle used for the pattern. *Patternmaking for Fashion Design* by Armstrong (1995) contains a radius chart and complete instructions for developing circular patterns.

Some computerized grading systems incorporate options for alternative methods of grading that can be used for garments that have seamlines or edges that remain parallel to one another when graded. Refer to individual computer grading manuals for information on the procedure.

for the center front/center back. The same difference will be the *y* value for the side seam; however, the sign will be opposite because of the orientation on the Cartesian graph. The *y* value for the center front/center back and the *x* value for the side seam will both remain 0 on all sizes. The hem length is an additive grade and must include the growth in length as well as the change in waist radius for each size.

Size specifications other than the one illustrated may have different waist dimensions. This requires calcu-

What you should know to grade the circle skirt on the computer:

1. How a circle skirt pattern is developed.
2. Distributions of the grade for the circle skirt (Figure 7.5).
3. Pattern orientation of the circle skirt and the 0,0 reference point (Figure 7.6).
4. Location of cardinal points for the circle skirt (Table 7.6).
5. New grade rules are required when there is a sign change or a movement change within a grade rule.
6. The radius of the circle that is equal to the waist specification.

JUMPSUIT

The jumpsuit design is a good example of the application of basic grade rules from more than one basic block. Once a grader has become familiar with how a grade is distributed in basic garment designs, the application of grade rules for different design variations becomes simple. The grade distributions in the jumpsuit front, Figure 7.9, should be compared to the grade distribution of the basic pant and basic bodice fronts. The jumpsuit pattern is developed by combining a bodice pattern to a pants pattern. A grade rule table for a jumpsuit is the combination of the grade rule tables for the bodice and pants. The use of these two grade rule tables is possible because of the orien-

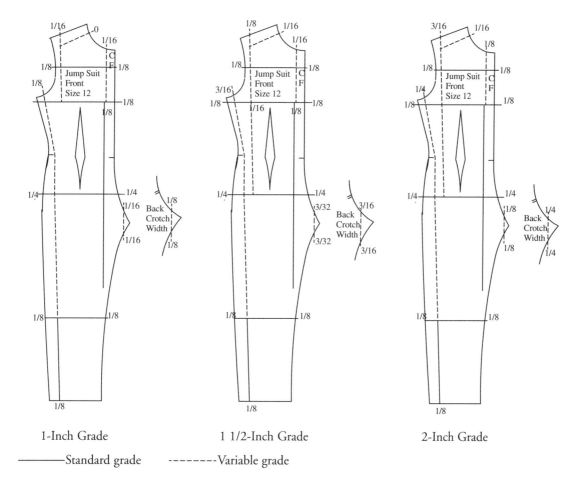

Figure 7.9 Grade Distributions for Jumpsuit

tation of the pattern. This combination of tables would not be possible if the pattern orientation had not been established at the waistline/center front intersection for both the pants and the bodice. The cardinal points and pattern orientation for a jumpsuit are given on Figure 7.10. Table 7.7 should be completed using previously developed grade rules where possible.

The jumpsuit back is graded using the same method of referring to bodice back and pant back grade rules. Many dress designs are also developed and graded using this method of combining bodice and skirt patterns and their grade rule tables. A foundation in flat patternmaking enables a pattern grader to readily apply similar grade rules to design variations. Understanding how a pattern is developed is essential to good pattern grading.

What you should know to grade the jumpsuit:

1. How a jumpsuit pattern is developed.
2. Grade rules and distribution of the grade for the basic bodice and pants (Figure 7.9).

3. Pattern orientation of the jumpsuit and the 0,0 reference point (Figure 7.10).
4. Location of cardinal points for the jumpsuit (Table 7.10).
5. New grade rules are required when there is a sign change or a movement change within a grade rule.

SURPLICE BODICE

In a surplice design, the garment has an asymmetric diagonal neckline in which one side laps over the other or a diagonal seamline simulates the lap line. Although the surplice design is not the combination of two different basic patterns, it is the combination of the right and left sides of the same pattern. When two sides of a garment are combined, as in this case, the grade distributions remain in their same location. The grade rules and pattern orientation may need to change so that the left and right side of the garment can be graded as one unit.

The surplice bodice shown in Figure 7.11, has two different pattern pieces both of which are cut with the

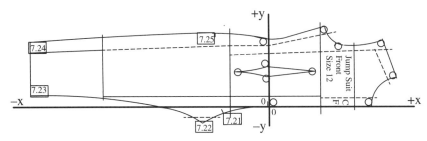

Five new grade rules for jumpsuit front

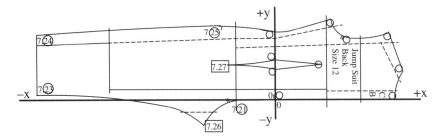

Two additional grade rules for jumpsuit back

Figure 7.10 Orientation for Grading Jumpsuit

fabric face up. It is also possible to make a surplice bodice in which the right front actually laps over the left front. The right and left fronts are cut alike with one being cut **face-up** and one **face-down** on the fabric. In this case, the grade rules written for the left surplice front would not be necessary.

The grade rules for this example are applications of previously developed grade rules. The grade distribution is given in Figure 7.11, and the orientation in Figure 7.12. The pattern orientation and cardinal points are given on Table 7.8. It is important to note the pattern orientation of the bodices so the correct *x,y* coordinates are recorded.

Computerized systems allow grade rules to be designated as opposites. (See Sleeve in Chapter 5, page 65, for further explanation.)

What you should know to grade the surplice bodice:

1. How a surplice bodice pattern is developed.
2. Grade rules and distribution of the grade for the basic bodice.
3. Pattern orientation of the surplice bodice and the 0,0 reference point.
4. Location of cardinal points for surplice bodice (Table 7.8).
5. New grade rules are required when there is a sign change or a movement change within a grade rule.

EFFECTS OF GRADING ON GARMENT STYLE AND PROPORTION

It is recommended that patterns be graded no more than two sizes beyond the master pattern to assure the best possible fit of a graded pattern. However, the importance of maintaining the **style sense** and proportion of a garment design is also a factor in that recommendation. Even slight changes in garment proportions can be perceived visually when patterns are graded two sizes or more from the master size

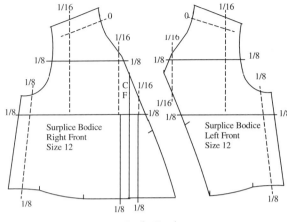

1-Inch Grade

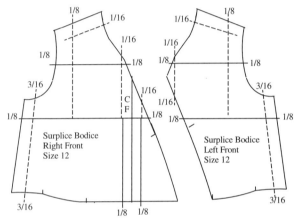

1 1/2-Inch Grade

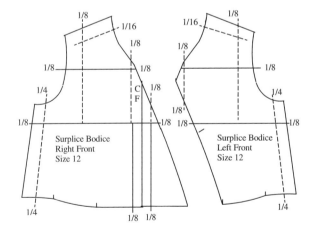

2-Inch Grade

———— Standard grade

--------Variable grade

Figure 7.11 Grade Distributions for Surplice Bodice

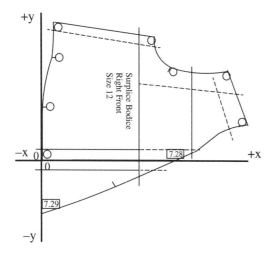

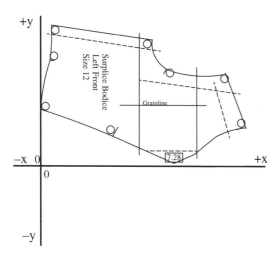

Figure 7.12 Orientation for Surplice Bodice

block (Bye & DeLong, 1994; Murphey, 1993; Solinger, 1988).

A problem in visual perception is created when the proportion in a garment is distorted so as to be noticeable (Bye & DeLong, 1994). Types of design distortions may be categorized as a garment's horizontal proportions (width of a yoke at a shoulder area of a shirt, width of yoke in pants or skirt, and width of cuffs of a sleeve); in its vertical proportions (princess seamlines that are not graded proportionally and non-proportional front button plackets); or in the proportions of garment details (size of patch pockets and width of collars).

In simplified grading systems, yokes, collars, and bands are examples of patterns pieces that generally are not graded in width (depth). To illustrate how the design proportion in a garment could be affected, consider the horizontal proportion of a midriff yoke in a bodice. If a yoke that is five inches wide top to bottom in the sample size is not graded in width (top to bottom) and the bodice portion is graded 1/4 inch in length per size, the size 22 bodice becomes 1 1/4 inches longer than the master size, but the yoke does not change from its original five inches. The proportion of the bodice length to the yoke depth is not the same as in the master size (Figure 7.13).

The successful pattern grader should have a knowledge of patternmaking, aesthetics, and mathematics. Understanding the relationship between these three areas is beyond the scope of this text, but further reading in Bye & DeLong, and Solinger is recommended.

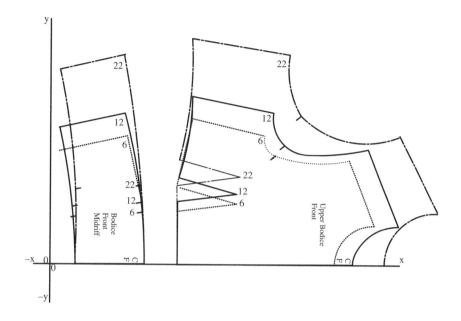

Figure 7.13 Proportional Changes in Grading Process

PATTERN GRADING
SUMMARY

The fundamentals of pattern grading using the basic pattern blocks introduced in Chapter 5 are applied to most design variations. Consideration of the effects of pattern grading on maintaining the style sense of the garment design across all graded sizes should be a factor in grading decisions. When a wide range of sizes is graded from a master pattern, problems can occur that relate to the proportion of design elements within a garment.

Poor fit and change in proportion are reasons the authors recommend that no more than two sizes on each side of the master pattern be graded when a simplified grading system is used. (When a range wider than five sizes is needed, a sample size in the low size range and a second sample size in the upper size range is suggested.) By limiting the grading range, there is better control of fit, style sense, and garment proportion.

If a manufacturer chooses to grade across a large size range from a single sample size knowing that style sense and proportion problems occur, the authors recommend that the size of these design details be graded with each change in grade (i.e., at the 1-inch, the 1 1/2-inch, and the 2-inch grade transitions).

EXERCISES

1. Grade the following design variations. A copy of a Grade Rule Table is available in Appendix D.
   a. Bodice with neckline yoke
   b. Waistband
   c. Gored skirt
2. To illustrate the problem of proportion in grading, cut out a patch pocket that would be the appropriate for one size. Place the pocket on different size individuals. Is the size appropriate for all individuals? Is it less appropriate for larger or smaller persons? At what sizes might you grade the pocket and are length and width grades needed?
3. Look at the instructions for grading the bodice with midriff yoke. How might you change the grade distribution in order to allow for the yoke to be graded proportionally?

REFERENCES

Armstrong, H. H. (1995). *Patternmaking for fashion design* (2nd ed.). New York: Harper Collins.

Bye, E. K., & DeLong, M. (1994). A visual sensory evaluation of the results of two pattern grading methods. *Clothing and Textiles Research Journal, 12*(4), 1–7.

Murphey, I. C. (1993). *A case study of the influence of pattern grading systems on the fit and style sense of two low-neckline, fitted bodices.* Unpublished doctoral dissertation, Virginia Tech, Blacksburg.

Solinger, J. (1988). *Apparel Manufacturing Handbook* (2nd ed.). Columbia, SC: Bobbin Blenheim Media Corp.

Table 7.1 Grade Rule Table: Princess Bodice Front

Pattern Piece: Princess Bodice Front
Unit: Inches   **Denominator:** 1/32
Size Range: Misses 6–22
Master Size: Misses 12
Grade Rules: 7.1–7.10

Note: New grade rule is needed for bust point

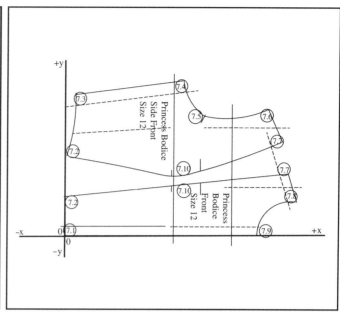

Size	Rule 7.1		Rule 7.2		Rule 7.3		Rule 7.4		Rule 7.5		Rule 7.6	
	X	Y	X	Y	X	Y	X	Y	X	Y	X	Y
6												
8												
10												
12	0	0	0	0	0	0	0	0	0	0	0	0
14												
16												
18												
20												
22												

Size	Rule 7.7		Rule 7.8		Rule 7.9		Rule 7.10	
	X	Y	X	Y	X	Y	X	Y
6								
8								
10								
12	0	0	0	0	0	0	0	0
14								
16								
18								
20								
22								

Table 7.2 Grade Rule Table: Full-Roll Collar

Pattern Piece: Full-Roll Collar
Unit: Inches   **Denominator:** 1/32
Size Range: Misses 6–22
Master Size: Misses 12
Grade Rules: 7.1, 7.11, 7.12

Note: The collar is not graded in width.

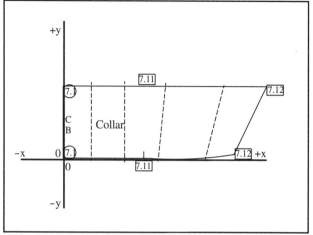

Size	Rule 7.1		Rule 7.11		Rule 7.12	
	X	Y	X	Y	X	Y
6						
8						
10						
12	0	0	0	0	0	0
14						
16						
18						
20						
22						

Table 7.3 Grade Rule Table: Circle Skirt—Manual Grading

Pattern Piece: Circle Skirt
Unit: Inches   **Denominator:** 1/32
Size Range: Misses 6–22
Master Size: Misses 12
Grade Rules: 7.13, 7.14, 7.15, 7.16

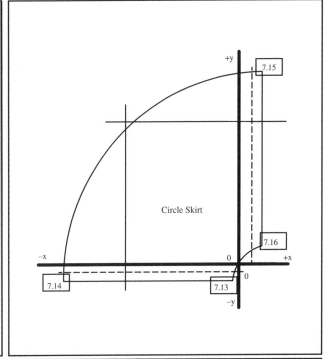

Size	Rule 7.13		Rule 7.14		Rule 7.15		Rule 7.16	
	X	Y	X	Y	X	Y	X	Y
6								
8								
10								
12	0	0	0	0	0	0	0	0
14								
16								
18								
20								
22								

Table 7.4 PS 42-70 Waist Circumference Specifications

Size	Waist Circumference	Radius
6	22 1/2	3 9/32 (3.581)
8	23 1/2	3 3/34 (3.740)
10	24 1/2	3 29/32 (3.899)
12	26	4 1/8 (4.138)
14	27 1/2	4 3/8 (4.376)
16	29	4 5/8 (4.615)
18	31	4 15/16 (4.934)
20	33	5 1/4 (5.252)
22	35	5 9/16 (5.570)

Note: Fractions are rounded to the nearest 32nd of an inch. Decimals are given in parentheses. Measurements are in inches.

Table 7.5 Grade Guide for Circle Skirt Waist

Size	6–8	8–10	10–12	12–14	14–16	16–18	18–20	20–22
Waist	5/32 (0.159)	5/32 (0.159)	1/4 (0.239)	1/4 (0.239)	1/4 (0.239)	5/16 (0.319)	5/16 (0.319)	5/16 (0.319)
Length	3/8 (.375)	3/8 (.375)	3/8 (.375)	3/8 (.375)	3/8 (.375)	3/8 (.375)	3/8 (.375)	3/8 (.375)

Note: Fractions are rounded to the nearest 32nd of an inch. Decimals are given in parentheses. Measurements are in inches.

Table 7.6 Grade Rule Table: Circle Skirt—Computer Grading

Pattern Piece: Circle Skirt—Computer grading
Unit: Inches **Denominator:** 1/32
Size Range: Misses 6–22
Master size: Misses 12
Grade Rules: 7.18–7.21

Size	Rule 7.18		Rule 7.19		Rule 7.20		Rule 7.21	
	X	Y	X	Y	X	Y	X	Y
6								
8								
10								
12	0	0	0	0	0	0	0	0
14								
16								
18								
20								
22								

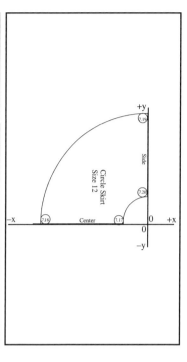

Table 7.7 Grade Rule Table: Jumpsuit

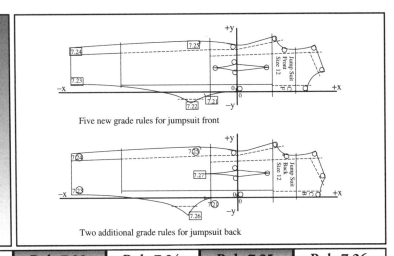

Pattern Piece: Jumpsuit
Unit: Inches   Denominator: 1/32
Size Range: Misses 6–22
Master Size: Misses 12
Note: See grade rules for basic bodice and pants Chapter 5.

Five new grade rules for jumpsuit front

Two additional grade rules for jumpsuit back

Size	Rule 7.21		Rule 7.22		Rule 7.23		Rule 7.24		Rule 7.25		Rule 7.26	
	X	Y	X	Y	X	Y	X	Y	X	Y	X	Y
6												
8												
10												
12	0	0	0	0	0	0	0	0	0	0	0	0
14												
16												
18												
20												
22												

Size	Rule 7.27		Rule		Rule		Rule		Rule		Rule	
	X	Y	X	Y	X	Y	X	Y	X	Y	X	Y
6												
8												
10												
12	0	0	0	0	0	0	0	0	0	0	0	0
14												
16												
18												
20												
22												

Table 7.8 Grade Rule Table: Surplice Bodice

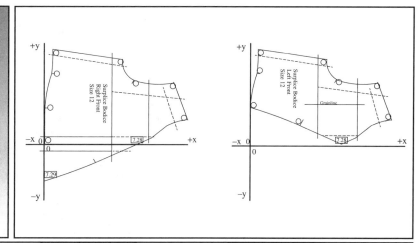

Pattern Piece: Surplice Bodice
Unit: Inches **Denominator:** 1/32
Size Range: Misses 6–22
Master size: Misses 12
Grade Rules:

Size	Rule 7.16		Rule 7.28		Rule		Rule		Rule		Rule	
	X	Y	X	Y	X	Y	X	Y	X	Y	X	Y
6												
8												
10												
12	0	0	0	0	0	0	0	0	0	0	0	0
14												
16												
18												
20												
22												

Size	Rule		Rule		Rule		Rule		Rule		Rule	
	X	Y	X	Y	X	Y	X	Y	X	Y	X	Y
6												
8												
10												
12	0	0	0	0	0	0	0	0	0	0	0	0
14												
16												
18												
20												
22												

Grading with

Multiple *x,y* Axes

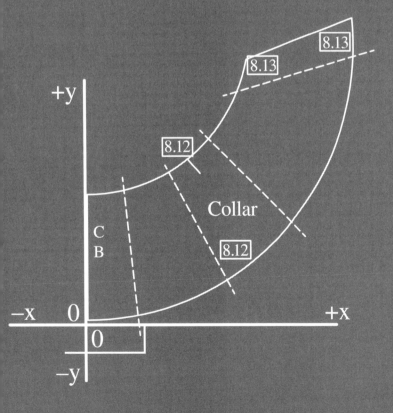

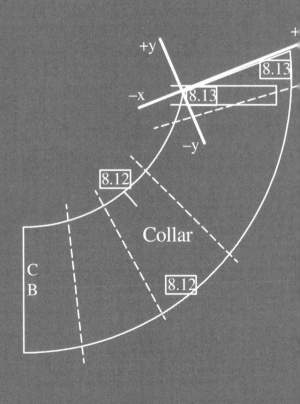

Introduction

Grading manually or by computer requires

the movement of cardinal points in x and y directions on a Cartesian graph. The Cartesian graph was introduced in Chapter 3, and a single set of x,y axes was discussed. The procedure for moving the pattern along the axes is illustrated in Chapter 4, and grading examples of the basic blocks and other basic styles are given in Chapters 5, 6, and 7.

Some garment styles have pattern pieces in which the use of only one set of x,y axes would distort the style sense and, in some cases, the fit of the garment. To prevent these problems, only a portion of the pattern is graded along the original axes, while other seams or cardinal points are moved in relation to another set of x,y axes. These additional x,y axes are referred to as **alternate grade reference axes**. Some draped patterns may be so complex that several alternate axes are needed to retain the style sense and fit across a size range (Ganete, 1991). The 0,0 point of the original x,y axes remains the reference point for all grade rules because it defines the areas of grade distribution across the body, but specific areas of the pattern are graded using the alternate grade reference axes for specified cardinal point movement. In order to write grade rules, each set of x,y axes must be identified. This is necessary for correct movement of the pattern along the appropriate axes for specific cardinal points.

Orientation of Multiple Grade Reference Axes

To determine the necessity of additional x, y axes, the shape of the pattern piece in relation to the human body must be analyzed. The basic blocks discussed in Chapter 5 are the pattern grader's representation of the shape and grade distributions of the human body. If a style line on the pattern piece forms an acute angle to the grade reference line (x axis) used in the corresponding basic block, alternate grade reference axes may be necessary to efficiently grade the seam. For example, the center back collar seam on a shawl collar style falls along the vertical center back of the body. When the shawl collar bodice front pattern (Figure 8.1a) is compared to the bodice back basic block (Figure 5.21), it is apparent that the center back of the

shawl collar is at an acute angle to the center back of the body. Therefore, an alternate grade reference axis is required to grade the center back of the collar. An alternate grade reference axis is also required when a style line is curved in such a manner that grading with a single grade reference axis would distort the curve in the graded sizes. This occurs when the intersections of the curved seamline are not aligned with the original x, y axes in the same manner as the corresponding seamline intersections on the basic block.

The orientation of the alternative x, y axes is also dependent upon the area of the body that the pattern is for and on the grade distribution for that area. The placement of the alternate grade reference axes corresponds to the orientation of the grade distributions for

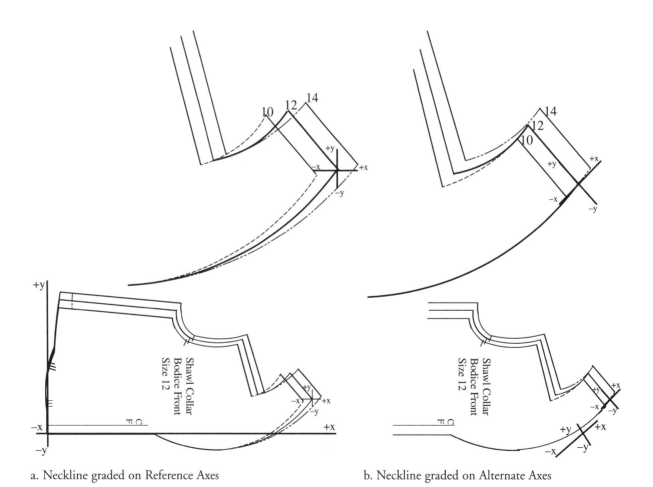

a. Neckline graded on Reference Axes   b. Neckline graded on Alternate Axes

■ **Figure 8.1** Neckline Graded by One and Two Sets of Axes

the position where the garment edge or seam lies against the body. For the shawl collar bodice, the center back neckline seam lies parallel to the center back of the body. The center back of the body is parallel to the *x* axis on the conventional (original) Cartesian graph. Therefore, the alternate grade reference axis is placed parallel to the center back collar seam of the shawl collar bodice front (Figure 8.1b).

The alternate grade reference axes for a specific area of a garment are parallel to the conventional (original) axes when the garment is worn by the consumer. This logic can be used to determine the necessity for and orientation of alternate grade reference axes for styles that are not illustrated in this text.

The new orientation of the alternate grade reference axes allows the pattern to be graded using information from grade guides, specification charts, or grade distributions to determine the grade rules. Sometimes existing grade rules may be applied by simply identifying the alternate grade reference axes. The flared skirt described in this chapter can use the same rules as the basic block skirt. In other cases, patterns may require new grade rules. The shawl collar, for example, is an extension to the front bodice, and the flat collar combines the front and back neckline grade distributions. Therefore, these patterns must have new grade rules.

Computer Applications Using Multiple *x,y* Axes

Computerized grading systems are designed to allow for the use of multiple grade reference axes. Although some computer systems may limit the total number allowed per pattern piece, only very complicated styles require the use of more than two or three total grade reference axes. The original grade reference line (the *x* axis) must be entered with each pattern piece. Additional alternate grade reference lines may be entered during the digitizing process or created after the pattern piece is in the computer. Each alternate grade reference line must be identified; this is usually by a number.

Each cardinal point on a pattern moves in reference to the original grade reference line unless designated otherwise. If an alternate grade reference line is appropriate, the cardinal point must be designated as such, with the specific alternate grade reference line identified by number. Refer to individual computer manuals for detailed instructions on the use of alternate grade reference lines.

The garment designs discussed in this chapter are a shawl collar bodice, a flat collar, briefs with a straight crotch, and a flared skirt. Each of these patterns requires the use of two *x,y* axes, and the location of each axis is explained. Grade rule tables are divided with a section for each set of axes. Care should be taken to write the *x* and *y* movements for each grade rule in the appropriate section of the table. Figure 8.1a illustrates the original *x,y* axes with related grade rules; figure 8.1b shows the alternate reference axes and the associated grade rules.

SHAWL COLLAR BODICE

The pattern for the shawl collar style is a combination of the collar pattern and the bodice front pattern. The pattern includes the grade distributions for the bodice front and for the back collar or neckline. See Figure 8.2 for the grade distributions; note how the grade is similar to the grades for the basic bodice front (Figure 5.2) and the collar (Figure 7.3).

The body of the shawl collar pattern is graded the same as the basic bodice front, with the original *x* axis parallel to the center front. The *x,y* coordinates are also the same as those used for the basic bodice front (Table 5.1). Table 8.1 has two additional rules and two alternate grade reference axes. Grade Rules 8.9, 8.10, and 8.11 have been added to the bodice area of the shawl collar to maintain the shape of the collar and to establish the break point for the first button (Figure 8.3). These three grade rules are length variations and are plotted as *x* coordinates only.

If the collar is graded by moving the slopers along the original *x,y* axes at the center front location, the

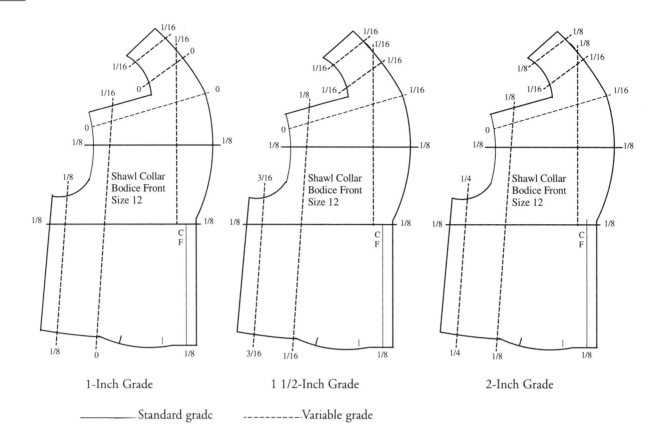

Figure 8.2 Grade Distributions for Shawl Collar Bodice Front

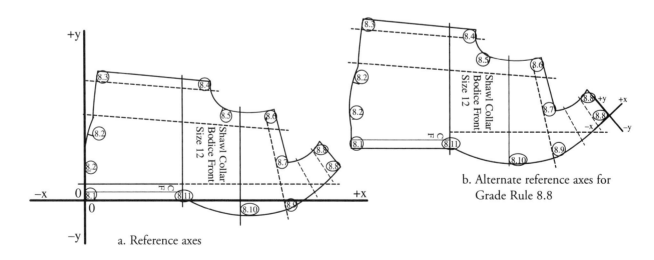

Figure 8.3 Orientation for Shawl Collar Bodice Front

rounded outer edge of the collar and the neck edge would become straighter in the larger sizes and more curved for smaller sizes, thus distorting the style of the garment (Figure 8.1a). In order to maintain the curve of the master pattern neck in all sizes, the cardinal points at the center back of the collar must be graded along the axes that are perpendicular and parallel to the center back of the collar. This is necessary because the center back of the collar is aligned with the center back of the body.

A new grade rule is needed for the center back of the collar and will be applied to both cardinal points. The 0,0 reference point for the pattern is still at the intersection of the waistline and center front. When grading from size 12 to size 14, the movement on the *x* axis must include the additive length of the center front (1/4″), plus the front neck length (1/16″), plus the back neck length and width (1/8″). This point is plotted by using the alternate grade reference axes in which the ruler is placed perpendicular to the new *x* axis (See Figure 4.5). The movement along the *x* axis is 7/16 inch. The movement along the *y* axis includes only the front neck width of 1/16 inch. The new Grade Rule 8.8 is (14,2) and is written on the Alternate Grade Reference Line, Table 8.1.

FLAT COLLAR

The grade distributions in the collar are a combination of the front and back neckline grades. Therefore, the distributions of the grade in the flat collar (Figure 8.4) is the same as the full-roll collar (Figure 7.3).

Two sets of axes are used to grade the flat collar because of the pattern shape. A flat collar or partial-roll collar is characterized by the curved neckline and the acute angle of the style line on the front edge. The distinct curve of these patterns make the use of a single set of *x, y* axes inappropriate, because the curve would flatten as the size is increased or become more curved as the master pattern is decreased in size. Figure 8.5 shows this distortion on a collar graded on only one

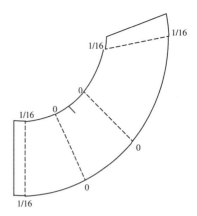

1-Inch Grade

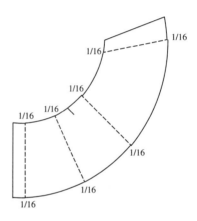

1 1/2-Inch Grade

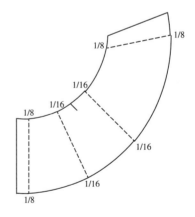

2-Inch Grade

------------Variable Grade

Figure 8.4 Grade Distributions for Flat Collar

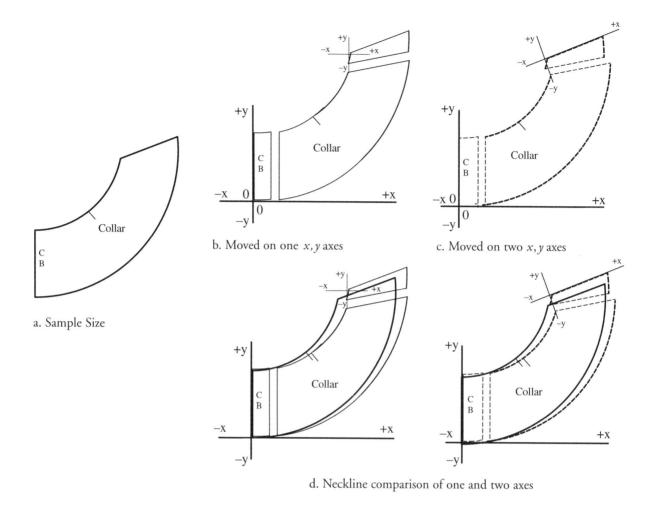

a. Sample Size

b. Moved on one *x, y* axes

c. Moved on two *x, y* axes

d. Neckline comparison of one and two axes

Figure 8.5 Flat Collar Graded on One and Two *x, y* Axes

set of *x, y* axes at the center back as compared to the use of two sets of axes.

The axes are located at the center back and center front of the pattern (Figure 8.6). The center back axes are at the same location as the axes in a full-roll collar, and Grade Rule 8.12 reflects the grade from the back neckline distribution. The alternate grade reference axes are parallel to the center front. Grade Rule 8.13 is an additive grade and must include the grade distribution of both the front and back necklines. The addition of the neckline grades for a size 14 graded from the sample size 12 is 4/16 inch with *x, y* coordinates of 0, 8 (Table 8.2).

It is important to note that the collar is not graded in width. This decision may need to be explored as larger or smaller sizes are graded. See discussions in Chapter 1 and Chapter 7 on the validity of this choice.

BRIEFS WITH STRAIGHT CROTCH

The briefs with straight crotch style require two sets of axes because of the curve of the waistline and the leg opening and the angle of the side seam in relation to the center front axis line. If only the original axes are used, the angle of the leg **sweep** for larger sizes becomes flatter, while the smaller sizes become more flared. The fit of the leg would be affected in both cases. The distribution of the grade in the briefs (Figure 8.7) is the same distribution seen in the pants (Figure 5.42). The straight crotch incorporates the 1/8″ grade that was seen in the crotch of the pants and becomes part of the length grade. The orientation of the original axes is at the center front/waistline intersection (Figure 8.8). Grade Rules 8.14, 8.15, and 8.16 are assigned based on this original set of axes.

The alternate grade reference axes are positioned at the side seam/waistline intersection so that the *x* axis is parallel to the side seam. The grade rules are the same as the *x, y* coordinates for Grade Rules 3 and 4 on the pants; but, because of the new axes, the points are identified differently (Table 8.3).

FLARED SKIRT

The grade distributions for the flared skirt style (Figure 8.9) is similar to the briefs (Figure 8.7) in both shape and grade. In the flared skirt, as in the briefs, the hem, side seam, and waistline of the pattern become distorted if only a single set of axes located at the center front is used. The curve of the hemline and the waist requires grade rules that maintain the curved shape as the pattern is graded. The location and num-

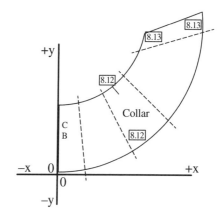

a. Reference Axes

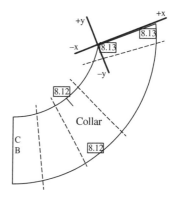

b. Alternate Reference Axes

Figure 8.6 Orientation for Flat Collar

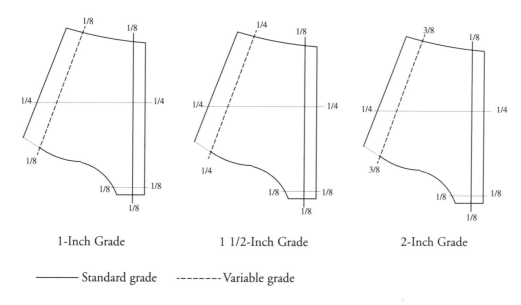

1-Inch Grade

1 1/2-Inch Grade

2-Inch Grade

———— Standard grade   ------- Variable grade

Figure 8.7 Grade Distributions for Briefs With Straight Crotch Seam

ber of rules may vary based on the amount of curve. For the flared skirt example, the cardinal points are identified and grade rule numbers assigned.

The alternate grade reference axes in the flared skirt is positioned at the waistline/side seam intersection because of the hip curve of the side seam (Figure 8.10).

This location is different from the alternate grade reference axes used in the briefs. Either location is appropriate because the grade rules are determined by the grade distributions from the 0,0 point of the original x, y axes. Both alternate grade reference lines reflect the grade distribution location in the basic skirt block (Table 8.4).

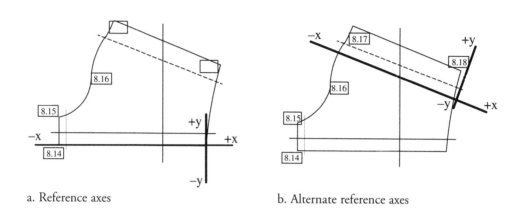

a. Reference axes   b. Alternate reference axes

Figure 8.8 Orientation for Briefs With Straight Crotch

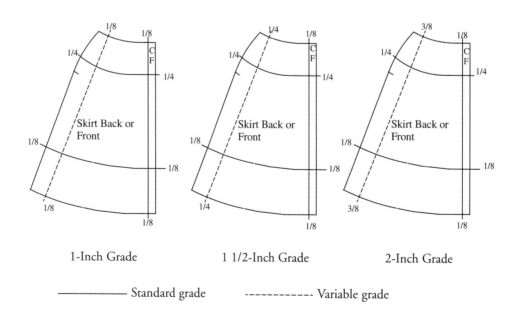

1-Inch Grade   1 1/2-Inch Grade   2-Inch Grade

——————— Standard grade   - - - - - - - - - Variable grade

Figure 8.9 Grade Distributions for Flared Skirt

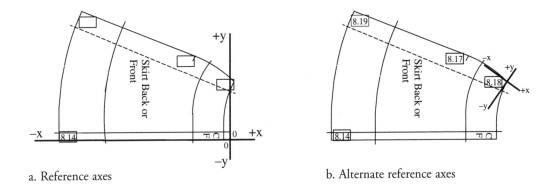

a. Reference axes   b. Alternate reference axes

■ **Figure 8.10** Orientation of Flared Skirt on Two Sets of Axes

PATTERN GRADING
SUMMARY

Multiple *x,y* axes are required for patterns with complex shaped style lines to avoid distortion of the original style of the garment. This distortion occurs most often when a pattern has style lines that are curved or form acute angles that are not aligned with the grade reference line used on corresponding basic pattern blocks. When the curve or pattern shape is not approximately parallel or perpendicular to the original *x,y* axes, then an alternate grade reference line is oriented so that the curve or pattern area has *x,y* axes that allow the pattern to maintain its original shape or grade, corresponding to basic block grade distributions.

In some instances, the use of alternate grade reference axes allows previously written grade rules to be applied to specified cardinal points. For example, the grade rules for the basic bodice front shoulder can be used for the cowl neck top, where alternate grade reference axes are used, because the cowl shoulder is set at a diagonal to the original *x,y* axes (Figure 8.11). Grade

rules are written from the original axes 0,0 point of reference, and therefore, the basic grade rules are the same for the cowl shoulder even though a new axes orientation is used.

There are too many different garment designs to explain each design variation; however, in addition to the cowl neckline style, examples of other garment styles that may require a second set of grade reference lines include a skirt waist yoke, a contour waistband, and a midriff bodice yoke.

Working out a grade distribution guide and determining alternate grade reference axes for each of these styles would be a good exercise to increase understanding of the grading process. Even when additional *x,y* axes are used for a pattern, the authors still recommend that a pattern be graded no more than two sizes up or down from the sample size. The use of alternate grade reference axes does not guarantee that the shape or fit of the pattern can be maintained over a large size range.

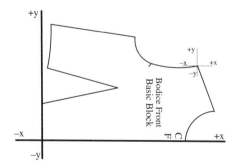

a. Grade reference axes at shoulder for basic block

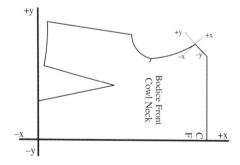

b. Alternate grade reference axes at shoulder for cowl neck

Figure 8.11 Alternate Reference Axes for Cowl Neck Bodice

EXERCISES

1. Why is an alternate grade reference line necessary for some patterns?

2. What are some basic characteristics of patterns that might need an alternate grade reference line? Find examples of design or patterns that might need two axes.

3. Grade the flat collar using a single grade reference line (grade rules for the full-roll collar can be used). Compare the results of grading the collar with one set of x, y axes and with 2 sets.

4. Draw in the grade distribution lines on the cowl neck style (Figure 8.11). Write grade rules for all cardinal points from size 12 to 14 and from size 12 to 10. (Table 8.5)

5. Find a multisized commercial pattern which might need two sets of axes for grading. Was the pattern graded using two sets of axes?

6. If a computer grading system is available, determine if multiple axes grading is possible. How are the two sets of axes identified and what are the grade rules written for the computer?

REFERENCE

Ganete, J. (1991). *Introduction to Apparel Grading, Video Series Workbook.* Torrance, CA: Joe Ganete, Inc.

Table 8.1 Grade Rule Table: Shawl Collar Using Two Axes

Pattern Piece: Shawl Collar	Reference Axes
Unit: Inches Denominator: 1/32	
Size Range: Misses 6–22	
Reference Size: Misses 12	
Grade Rules: 8.1–8.11	
Notes: New grades rules have been written for each cardinal point. The 8 refers to the chapter number. Grade Rule 8.8 is listed on the Alternate Grade Reference Line axis.	

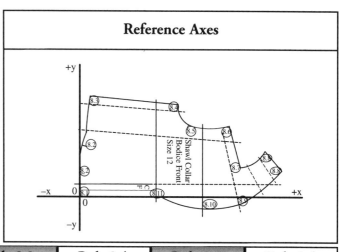

Size	Rule 8.1		Rule 8.2		Rule 8.3		Rule 8.4		Rule 8.5		Rule 8.6	
	X	Y	X	Y	X	Y	X	Y	X	Y	X	Y
6												
8												
10												
12	0	0	0	0	0	0	0	0	0	0	0	0
14												
16												
18												
20												
22												

Size	Rule 8.7		Rule 8.9		Rule 8.10		Rule 8.11	
	X	Y	X	Y	X	Y	X	Y
6								
8								
10								
12	0	0	0	0	0	0	0	0
14								
16								
18								
20								
22								

■**Table 8.1** *(continued)* Grade Rule Table: Shawl Collar Using Two Axes

Alternate Grade Reference Axes		Size	Rule 8.8		Rule	
			X	Y	X	Y
		6				
		8				
		10				
		12	0	0	0	0
		14	14	2		
		16				
		18				
		20				
		22				

Table 8.2 Grade Rule Table: Flat Collar Using Two Axes

Pattern Piece: Flat Collar	**Unit:** Inches	**Denominator:** 1/32	
Size Range: Misses 6–22	**Reference size:** Misses 12		

Reference Axes		Size	Rule 8.12		Rule	
			X	Y	X	Y
		6				
		8				
		10				
		12	0	0	0	0
		14				
		16				
		18				
		20				
		22				

Alternate Grade Reference Axes		Size	Rule 8.13		Rule	
			X	Y	X	Y
		6				
		8				
		10				
		12	0	0	0	0
		14				
		16				
		18				
		20				
		22				

Table 8.3 Grade Rule Table: Brief with Straight Crotch Using Two Axes

Pattern Piece: Brief with Straight Crotch		Unit: Inches		Denominator: 1/32	
Size Range: Misses 6–22		Reference Size: Misses 12			

Reference Axes	Size	Rule 8.14		Rule 8.15		Rule 8.16	
		X	Y	X	Y	X	Y
	6						
	8						
	10						
	12	0	0	0	0	0	0
	14						
	16						
	18						
	20						
	22						

Alternate Grade Reference Axes	Size	Rule 8.17		Rule 8.18		Rule	
		X	Y	X	Y	X	Y
	6						
	8						
	10						
	12	0	0	0	0		
	14						
	16						
	18						
	20						
	22						

Table 8.4 Grade Rule Table: Flared Skirt Using Two Axes

Pattern Piece: Flared Skirt	Unit: Inches	Denominator: 1/32
Size Range: Misses 6–22	Reference Size: Misses 12	

	Size	Rule 8.14		Rule 8.15		Rule 8.16	
Reference Axes		X	Y	X	Y	X	Y
	6						
	8						
	10						
	12	0	0	0	0		
	14						
	16						
	18						
	20						
	22						

	Size	Rule 8.17		Rule 8.18		Rule	
Alternate Grade Reference Axes		X	Y	X	Y	X	Y
	6						
	8						
	10						
	12	0	0	0	0		
	14						
	16						
	18						
	20						
	22						

■**Table 8.5** Grade Rule Table Using Two Axes

Pattern Piece:	Unit: Inches	Denominator: 1/32
Size Range: Misses 6–22	Reference size: Misses 12	

Reference Axes		Size	Rule		Rule		Rule	
			X	Y	X	Y	X	Y
		6						
		8						
		10						
		12	0	0	0	0		
		14						
		16						
		18						
		20						
		22						
Alternate Grade Reference Axes		Size	Rule		Rule		Rule	
			X	Y	X	Y	X	Y
		6						
		8						
		10						
		12	0	0	0	0		
		14						
		16						
		18						
		20						
		22						

9

Grading Stretch

Garments

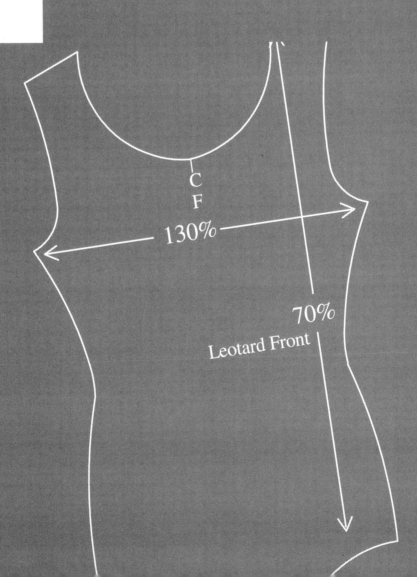

C
F

130%

70%

Leotard Front

Introduction

Grading garments made of stretch fabrics differs from grading garments made of rigid fabrics when the garments utilize the stretch as part of their fit and function. Garments in this category are actually cut smaller than the body dimensions for the size they are designed to fit. Swimwear, leotards, and unitards are examples of garments that fall into this category (Figure 9.1). These garments are referred to as *stretch garments* in this text. Fabrics that have enough stretch and recovery to utilize the stretch in the fit and function of this type of garment contain some percentage of an elastomeric fiber. Spandex is the most commonly used elastomeric fiber. The percentage of the elastomeric fiber may be as low as 5 percent if the structure of the fabric allows enough stretch to be used in a stretch garment.

Knit fabrics with elastomeric fibers, which are suitable for stretch garments, may also be used in some garments merely for **comfort stretch**. These garments are cut at least as large as the body dimensions and may even have additional ease in order to create the style lines the same way that nonstretch garments have both fitting ease and **styling ease**. Knit fabrics that do not contain elastomeric fibers may also have a considerable amount of stretch or give, but they lack the ability to recover to the original size during wear. These fabrics are not suitable for stretch garments, but they do provide comfort and flexibility of fit to the consumer. Garments that utilize fabric stretch for comfort only should be graded like garments manufactured from rigid (nonstretch) fabrics.

Figure 9.1 Stretch Garment

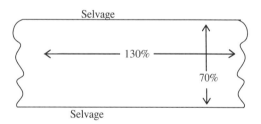

Stretch fabric A

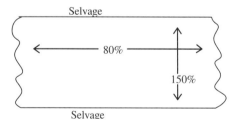

Stretch fabric B

Figure 9.2 Percentages of Stretch in Stretch Fabrics

STRETCH GARMENT FIT

Appropriate fit of the sample size must be established before the stretch garment is graded. In order to maintain a consistent garment fit across a size range, only a percentage of the difference in body dimensions is used when grading the stretch garment. This percentage is referred to as a **conversion factor**. The degree of stretch utilized in the garment fit and the percentage of stretch inherent in the fabric are both considered when deciding upon the percentage of each body dimension that will be used to establish the conversion factor for grading.

The percentage that a fabric will stretch and still recover to the original size is called the **stretch factor**. Stretch fabrics often have differing amounts of stretch in the lengthwise and crosswise directions (Figure 9.2). Also, some stretch fabrics have the greater amount of stretch in the crosswise direction, whereas some have the greater stretch in the lengthwise direction. Fabric specifications provided by the fabric manufacturer usually give the percentage of stretch for each direction.

If specifications are not available, the fabric can be tested using a stretch gauge. The stretch gauge is a ruler that is marked with percentages of stretch. The stretch gauge is usually at least 15 inches long with the first 5 inches indicating the amount of fabric to be tested (stretched) and each half inch following indicating 10 percent of stretch. Fabric stretch is never tested along a cut or selvage edge. Instead, a section of fabric a few inches from the edge is folded either parallel or perpendicular to the selvage. The parallel fold gives the lengthwise stretch and the perpendicular fold gives the crosswise stretch. A 5-inch fold of fabric that stretches to 9 inches and recovers to 5 has 80 percent stretch; stretching to 10 inches indicates 100 percent stretch; stretching to 12 inches indicates 140 percent stretch, and so on. The stretched fabric must return (recover) to the original 5 inches. If it does not, then it should be stretched in smaller increments until it reaches the point where it will recover to the original size in order to determine the stretch factor. The recovery is as important as the expansion in determining the stretch factor for a fabric. Any conventional ruler can be marked as a stretch gauge; however, ready-made gauges are often available from manufacturers of stretch products.

Because each fabric usually has a different stretch factor for each direction, the conversion factor will differ for each fabric *and* for each direction in the fabric. This text does not provide specific conversion factors suitable for grading all stretch fabrics because of the many variations in fabric and design. Although examples are provided, the pattern grader must determine the conversion factor appropriate for each style and fabric being graded.

EVALUATION OF FIT

The amount of stretch in each direction of the fabric affects the fit of a stretch garment. The greater amount of stretch may be used either vertically or horizontally. The direction of the greatest stretch depends on the garment style and the end use for each garment and may vary from one manufacturer to another. Therefore, the sample size must be evaluated for fit each time a fabric with different stretch factors is used. Once the sample pattern has been adjusted to accommodate the stretch of the fabric, the grading process can be implemented.

CONVERSION FACTOR

The grade guides for either rigid or stretch garments are based on the body dimensions for the target market. However, in order to grade stretch garments, the pattern grader also needs information about the fabric itself. This includes such variables as the percentage of lengthwise and crosswise stretch of the fabric (the stretch factors) and whether the greatest stretch will occur horizontally or vertically when the garment is on the body. A conversion factor must be used to establish the grade guide for use with the stretch fabric. A conversion factor is the percentage of the body measurements that is applied in the horizontal (*x*) and vertical (*y*) directions in order to maintain the appropriate fit across the size range. When grading a narrow size range of three or four sizes, the differences in fit may not be apparent in some styles if a conversion factor is not used. However, when a wider size range is graded, the quality of fit may be sacrificed in the extreme sizes if a conversion factor is omitted from the grade.

Fit Experimentation

To help understand the relationship of stretch and fit, try cutting a piece of elastic exactly your wrist size, then overlap it 1 inch and feel how tight it is on your wrist. Next cut the same type of elastic exactly your waist size, then overlap it 1 inch and feel how tight it is on your waist. As illustrated by this experiment, a specified increment (in this case, 1 inch) produces a different fit on a smaller area than on a larger area. This same principle applies to grading stretch fabrics that incorporate stretch into the fit of the garment. **If a conversion factor is not used, the sizes smaller than the sample size will have a tighter fit and the sizes larger than the sample size will have a looser fit**. The quality of fit deteriorates as the size range gets larger, with the extreme sizes having the poorest fit.

The conversion factors used in this text are for the purpose of explanation only; they will not work for all stretch fabrics or styles. They are given to provide the pattern grader a starting point from which to develop the necessary grade and to serve as a basis for completing practice grading problems. The stretch factors of the fabric may be used to establish a conversion factor if the pattern grader has no guidelines from previously successfully graded garments using the same fabric. The problems illustrated in this text use 10 percent of the fabric stretch to establish the conversion factor for adapting the grade guide to stretch fabrics. It is important to remember that this conversion factor is not appropriate for all fabrics or for all garments. The end-use of the garment and the preferences of the target customers are additional factors that must be considered in addition to fabric stretch when determining a conversion factor.

Another method of determining the conversion factor is to compare key width and length dimensions (bust, hip, vertical trunk) of the appropriately fitting finished stretch garment to the actual body dimensions of the corresponding body locations. This is the preferred method for actual manufacturing because it is based on the satisfactory fit of the garment. Using this method, the garment dimension is divided by the body dimension to determine the conversion factor percentage appropriate for the fabric and style. Since there are two key horizontal measurements (bust and hips), an average of the two will produce a usable percentage. The waist is not used as a key horizontal measurement because a stretch garment often does not fit as tightly through the waist as it does through the bust and hip. This is due to the relative shape of a one-piece garment, such as a leotard, to the shape of the body.

The conversion procedure often begins with available information such as size specifications, a grade guide, or a grade rule table for a similar style garment made of rigid fabric. If a grade guide or grade rule table exists for both the sizing specifications and style lines of the garment, the pattern grader may use the conversion factor directly on the grade guide or the grade rule table. It is not necessary to go back to the sizing specifications to develop a new grade guide or new grade rules. The existing one may be adapted for each stretch fabric.

PROCEDURE FOR GRADING STRETCH GARMENTS

Step 1: Mathematical Conversions

Size specifications from the PS 42-70 in Table A.1 are used as the basis for adapting the grade rules to the stretch fabric (Table 9.1). Corresponding grade rules developed in Chapters 3 and 5 are used for adapting a grade rule table for this exercise.

The following grading exercise starts with the size specifications in order that the pattern grader may see

the entire process. The garment being graded is a leotard made from fabric that has a 70 percent stretch factor in the vertical direction and 130 percent stretch factor in the horizontal direction as it is worn on the body (Figure 9.3). Converting size specifications, grade guides, and grade rule tables for use with stretch garments requires the use of some basic mathematical principles. This text uses 10 percent of the stretch factor to develop the conversion factor. The first step is to find 10 percent of the 130 percent horizontal stretch factor. The percentage of horizontal stretch is 13 percent (0.10 × 1.30). The conversion factor is then calculated by subtracting this 13 percent from the body measurement, giving a conversion factor of 87 percent (100% − 13% = 87%). Therefore, only 87 percent of the body measurement is used in the horizontal direction when grading a stretch garment made with the example fabric.

The vertical stretch factor for the fabric in our example is 70 percent. Ten percent of 70 percent is 7 percent. Therefore, only 93 percent of the body measurement is used for the garment (100% − 7% = 93%). These conversion factors are used with size specifications to develop grade guides for stretch fabrics. The ease of converting grade rules for rigid fabrics to grade rules for stretch fabric may be increased by using decimal forms of the grades. Both decimals and fractions are included in most of the tables.

The measurements listed in Table 9.1 for the abbreviated PS42-70 Size Specifications used for this example are all *horizontal girth measurements only*. Therefore, only the horizontal conversion factor for the measurements listed is used. The vertical conversion factor will be used when developing or adapting grade rules. (*All measurements must be included if a grade guide for stretch garments is to be complete.*) The measurements are multiplied by 0.87 to produce 87 percent of the measurement. The resulting product is rounded to the nearest 32nd of an inch. Fractions and decimal equivalents are given in all tables.

The incremental differences between sizes in the conversion table (Table 9.1) are given in decimal form in

Table 9.2. When this guide is compared to the guide developed directly from an established grade guide (Table 9.3), only negligible differences are observed.

Step 2: Grade Guide

Table 9.3 contains a previously developed grade guide for rigid fabrics that can be used to apply the conversion factors for stretch fabric. The direction of the greatest stretch is one of the variables that the grader must ascertain before beginning the grading process. The total girth grades of 1, 1 1/2, and 2 inches are changed to 7/8, 1 5/16, and 1 3/4. Length grades, which are not listed in this table, change by a different conversion factor due to the different amount of stretch.

Grade Distribution Calculated from Grade Rule Table

A table of grade rules allows the grader to define the distribution of the grade across the length and width of the body. Figure 9.4 visually illustrates the distribution of the total width and length grades that would be used for rigid fabric for a 1-inch, a 1 1/2-inch, and a 2-inch grade. Using the appropriate conversion factors for total length and width grades, the grade distribution in stretch fabrics can be determined. However, the grade distribution for stretch fabric is not as critical as for rigid fabrics since the fabric stretch accommodates the changes in the body curves. The total width grades are multiplied by the conversion factor of 0.87 and the total length grades by 0.93. Then the difference can be distributed as the grader deems appropriate for the style as long as the above-the-waist distributions stay above the waist and the below-the-waist distributions stay below the waist.

Step 3: Grade Rule Table

Table 9.4 is a grade rule table for rigid fabrics that contains a set of values for a range of sizes for each grade rule. The conversion factors (0.93 × *x* values and 0.83 × *y* values) were used on the values in Table 9.4 to develop the grade rules in Table 9.5. Notice that changes are not systematic between sizes in Table 9.5 as they

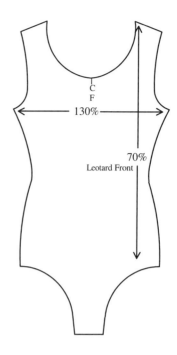

Figure 9.3 Two-Way Stretch in Leotard

are in Table 9.3, where changes are determined based on 7/8-, 1 5/16-, and 1 3/4-inch total girth grades.

Either method produces essentially the same results. If a grade guide is developed from size specifications rather than by converting an existing grade guide, some increments may vary by a 32nd of an inch due to rounding of decimals when converting them to fractions.

Grading from a grade guide instead of a grade rule table will result in systematic changes within 7/8-, 1 5/16-, and 1 3/4-inch grades, whereas the differences between sizes when working from the grade rule table are not consistent. This variance will not noticeably affect the fit of a stretch garment; however, corresponding seams and pieces must be graded using a consistent method of developing the grade guide.

Step 4: Grading Procedure

Stretch garments must be oriented in the same manner as all previously graded garments when converting grades from a grade rule table used for rigid fabrics. These rules must be converted for stretch fabrics using the conversion factors established for the designated style and fabric. The converted rules will require a new number or, if the same number is retained, they will need to be in a separate grade rule table so that they are not confused with grade rules for rigid fabrics. It is recommended that separate grade rule tables be established for rigid and stretch fabrics.

The orientation of the leotard to be graded (Figure 9.5) shows that converting the existing grade rules requires that the x increments (vertical on the body) use the conversion factor of 93 percent and y increments (horizontal on the body) use the conversion factor of 87 percent. Some areas of the leotard will require additional grade rules to be developed from the full range of sizing specifications (see Appendix A).

The numbering for examples in this chapter will begin with Grade Rule 9.1, which is always at the 0,0 point of reference at the intersection of the x,y axes (Figure 9.5). Grade Rule 9.2 represents the crotch length plus hip length (x); y is 0 since it is a center body line. Grade Rule 9.3 reflects the crotch length plus hip length (x) and crotch width (y), and Rule 9.4 is the hip length (x) and the hip width (y). The numbering continues in a clockwise direction and all grades are additive between 0,0 point of reference and the cardinal point for which the grade rule is assigned. When the leotard has a jewel neckline, Grade Rule 9.9 will have a different value because the entire bodice front length is being incorporated in it. A scoop neckline may vary with style, but the graded location will usu-ally be at three-quarters of the bodice center front length.

Multiplying the existing grade rules using the conversion factors involves multiplying all x increments by 93 percent and all y increments by 87 percent. The resulting products are rounded to the nearest whole number, because the increments in the grade rule table represent the numerator for the common denominator of 32. Table 9.5 illustrates the converted grade rules from Table 9.4 for use with stretch garments. If the garment being graded is to be offered in **alpha sizes** rather than **numeric sizes**, then the grade rule table will have to be collapsed into the appropriate sizes using the same methods that are used for grade rule tables developed for rigid fabrics. This concept is discussed in detail in Chapter 11.

Step 5: Fit and Style Sense Evaluation

Once the grade rule table has been established for a specific stretch fabric, it can be tested on a basic garment. A **size run** of the style is constructed so the pattern grader and design staff may evaluate the fit and the style sense. The conversion factors are then adjusted to reflect any changes necessary in the basic fit. The grade rule table is then modified to correspond to the change in the conversion factors. The conversion factors established for this garment may be used with other styles manufactured from fabrics with the same stretch factors.

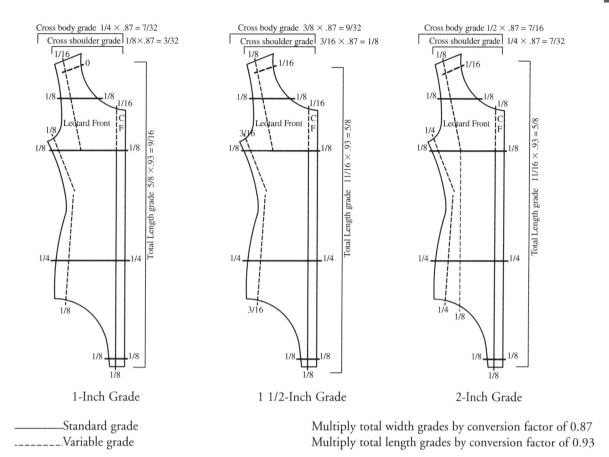

—————Standard grade
---------Variable grade

Multiply total width grades by conversion factor of 0.87
Multiply total length grades by conversion factor of 0.93

Figure 9.4 Total Grade Distributions for Rigid Fabric: Basis for Stretch Fabric Grade Conversion

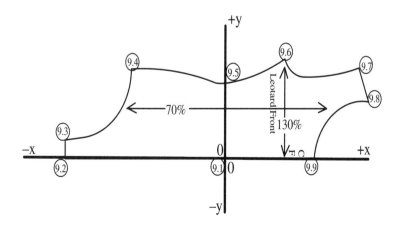

Figure 9.5 Orientation of Basic Leotard

PATTERN GRADING
SUMMARY

Stretch garments utilize fabric stretch and recovery in the fit and function of the garments and are actually cut smaller than body dimensions. Because the fabric stretch compensates for the difference in the body dimensions and the garment dimensions, the garments must be graded using only a percentage of the body dimensions. This percentage is referred to as a conversion factor. Specifications, grade guides, or grade rule tables for rigid fabric garments may be used as a basis for developing grade rules on patterns for stretch garments as long as the conversion factor is applied.

A stretch factor is the percentage a fabric will stretch and still recover to the original size. The stretch factor for each direction of the fabric must be determined in order to calculate the conversion factor required. The fabric stretch factors discussed in this chapter are for illustration only, because there is variation among fabrics in percentage of stretch in each direction and the direction in which the greatest stretch is found.

Before converting grading information for rigid fabrics to stretch fabrics, appropriate fit of the sample size must be established. This step should be taken each time a different stretch fabric is used. Once stretch factors are determined, then the conversion factors are established to convert grading information for rigid fabrics to usable information for stretch fabrics. A size run of the graded style should be constructed so that the pattern grader and design staff may evaluate the fit and style sense.

EXERCISES

1. The length and width grade distribution in the jumpsuit made from rigid fabric are illustrated by the horizontal and vertical lines in Table 7.7. Horizontal lines indicate grade distribution for length and the vertical lines indicate grade distribution for width. Using information in this chapter and the grade rule, develop a grade rule table for grading a half-pattern for stretch fabric. Use 10% of stretch factors of **125% in the length** direction and **120% in the width** direction.

   Suggested Steps: *Note the use of decimals instead of fractions for the calculations*

   1. Determine the conversion factor for each fabric direction. Length _____.
      Width _____.
   2. On Figure 9.6, fill in the converted length and width grade values that reflect the stretch factor of the fabric. See Figure 9.6 below.
   3. Use Figure 9.7 to number the cardinal points and indicate lengthwise grain. New grade rules must be used since the conversion factors are different from any other grade rules written in this chapter.
   4. Multiply each grade rule used from Table 7.1 and 7.7 by the appropriate conversion factor. Record the converted grade rules in Table 9.6. See Table 9.6 for converted grade rules. The x values have been multiplied by .875 and the y values by .91. A new grade rule 9.19 is developed since the neckline is lower and the center front length changes by 1/8 inch and not 1/4 inch.

2. On Figure 9.8 fill in the grade distribution for 7/8, 1 5/16, and 1 3/4 inch grades. The

length and width distributions must equal the total length and width grades.

3. Measure a ready-made stretch garment such as a leotard, bike pants, or stretch leggings.

Compare these measurements to the body dimensions for the respective size and determine the conversion factors necessary to grade the garment.

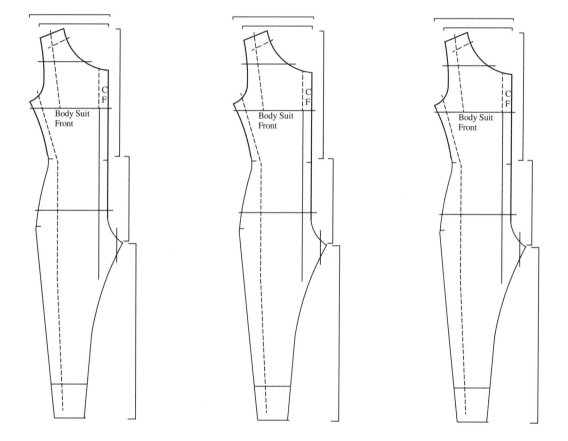

Conversion factors are not the same for width and length grades.

■**Figure 9.6** Converted Grades for Stretch Fabric

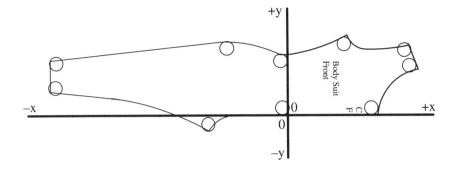

Figure 9.7 Grade Rule Numbers to Be Assigned on Body Suit

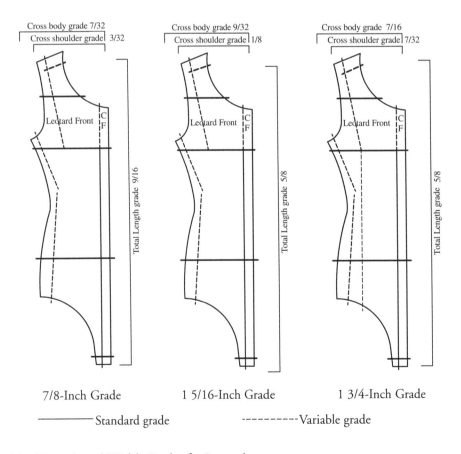

Cross body grade 7/32 | Cross shoulder grade 3/32 — Leotard Front C F — Total Length grade 9/16 — 7/8-Inch Grade

Cross body grade 9/32 | Cross shoulder grade 1/8 — Leotard Front C F — Total Length grade 5/8 — 1 5/16-Inch Grade

Cross body grade 7/16 | Cross shoulder grade 7/32 — Leotard Front C F — Total Length grade 5/8 — 1 3/4-Inch Grade

———— Standard grade   - - - - - - Variable grade

Figure 9.8 Total Length and Width Grades for Leotard

Table 9.1 PS 42-70 Size Specifications for Misses Sizes 6 to 22 Converted for 130 Percent Horizontal Stretch Fabric

Size	6	8	10	12	14	16	18	20	22
PS 42-70 Size Specifications for Misses Sizes									
Bust	31 1/2 (31.5)	32 1/2 (32.5)	33 1/2 (33.5)	35 (35.0)	36 1/2 (36.5)	38 (38.0)	40 (40.0)	42 (42.0)	44 (44.0)
Waist	22 1/2 (22.5)	23 1/2 (23.5)	24 1/2 (24.5)	26 (26.0)	27 1/2 (27.5)	29 (29.0)	31 (31.0)	33 (33.0)	35 (35.0)
Hips	33 1/2 (33.5)	34 1/2 (34.5)	35 1/2 (35.5)	37 (37.0)	38 1/2 (38.5)	40 (40.0)	42 (42.4)	44 (44.0)	46 (46.0)
Conversion to 87 Percent of PS 42-70 Size Specifications for Misses Sizes									
Bust	27 13/32 (27.405)	28 9/32 (28.275)	29 5/32 (29.145)	30 15/32 (30.45)	31 3/4 (31.755)	33 1/6 (33.06)	34 1/2 (34.8)	36 (36.54)	38-9/32 (38.28)
Waist	19 9/16 (19.575)	20 7/16 (20.445)	31 5/16 (21.315)	22 5/8 (22.62)	23 15/16 (23.925)	25 7/32 (25.23)	26 31/32 (26.97)	28 23/32 (28.71)	30-7/16 (30.45)
Hips	29 5/32 (29.145)	30 (30.015)	30 27/32 (30.885)	32 3/16 (32.19)	33 1/2 (33.495)	34 1/2 (34.8)	36 17/32 (36.54)	38 9/32 (38.28)	40 1/32 (40.02)

Note: Measurements are in inches.

Table 9.2 Grade Guide Developed From Size Specification Conversion Table 9.1 (in decimal form only)

Size	6–8	8–10	10–12	12–14	14–16	16–18	18–20	20–22
Bust	.87	.87	1 .305	1 .305	1 .305	1 .74	1 .74	1 .74
Waist	.87	.87	1 .305	1 .305	1 .305	1 .74	1 .74	1 .74
Hips	.87	.87	1 .305	1 .305	1 .305	1 .74	1 .74	1 .74

Table 9.3 Grade Guide for Misses Sizes 6 to 22 Converted for 130 Percent Horizontal Stretch Fabric

Size	6–8	8–10	10–12	12–14	14–16	16–18	18–20	20–22
PS 42-70 Incremental Grade Guide for Misses Sizes								
Bust	1	1	1 1/2	1 1/2	1 1/2	2	2	2
Waist	1	1	1 1/2	1 1/2	1 1/2	2	2	2
Hips	1	1	1 1/2	1 1/2	1 1/2	2	2	2
Conversion to 87 Percent of PS 42-70 Incremental Grade Guide for Misses Sizes								
Bust	7/8 (.875)	7/8 (.875)	1 5/16 (1.3125)	1 5/16 (1.3125)	1 5/16 (1.3125)	1 3/4 (1.75)	1 3/4 (1.75)	1 3/4 (1.75)
Waist	7/8 (.875)	7/8 (.875)	1 5/16 (1.3125)	1 5/16 (1.3125)	1 5/16 (1.3125)	1 3/4 (1.75)	1 3/4 (1.75)	1 3/4 (1.75)
Hips	7/8 (.875)	7/8 (.875)	1 5/16 (1.3125)	1 5/16 (1.3125)	1 5/16 (1.3125)	1 3/4 (1.75)	1 3/4 (1.75)	1 3/4 (1.75)

Note: Measurements are in inches.

Table 9.4 Selected Grade Rules for Grading Rigid Fabrics from Table 5.1 Bodice Front

Pattern Piece: Bodice Front with waist dart

Units: Inches   **Denominator:** 1/32

Size Range: Misses 6–22

Master Size: Misses 12

Grade Rules:

Notes: Values in parenthesis are the decimal form of the fractions in the table.

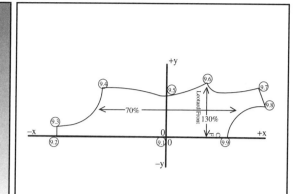

Size	Rule 1		Rule 3		Rule 4		Rule 6		Rule 7	
	X	Y	X	Y	X	Y	X	Y	X	Y
6	0	0	0	−28 (−.875)	−12 (−.375)	−28 (−.875)	−24 (−.75)	−14 (−.4375)	−26 (−.8125)	−6 (−.1875)
8	0	0	0	−20 (−.625)	−8 (−.25)	−20 (−.625)	−16 (−.375)	−10 (−.3125)	−18 (−.5625)	−4 (−.125)
10	0	0	0	−12 (−.375)	−4 (−.125)	−12 (−.375)	−8 (−.25)	−6 (−.1875)	−10 (−.3125)	−2 (−.0625)
12	0	0	0	0	0	0	0	0	0	0
14	0	0	0	12 (.375)	4 (.125)	12 (.375)	8 (.25)	6 (.1875)	10 (.3125)	2 (.0625)
16	0	0	0	24 (.75)	8 (.25)	24 (.75)	16 (.5)	12 (.375)	20 (.625)	4 (.125)
18	0	0	0	40 (1.25)	12 (.375)	40 (1.25)	24 (.75)	20 (.625)	30 (.9375)	12 (.25)
20	0	0	0	56 (1.75)	16 (.5)	56 (1.75)	32 (1.0)	28 (.875)	40 (1.25)	12 (.375)
22	0	0	0	72 (2.25)	20 (.625)	72 (2.25)	40 (1.25)	36 (1.125)	50 (1.125)	16 (.5)

■ Table 9.5 Selected Rules Converted for Grading Stretch Garments (*x* times 0.93 and *y* times 0.87)

Pattern Piece: Bodice Front with waist dart

Units: Inches   **Denominator:** 1/32

Size Range: Misses 6–22

Master Size: Misses 12

Grade Rules:

Notes: Values in parenthesis are the decimal form of the fractions in the table.

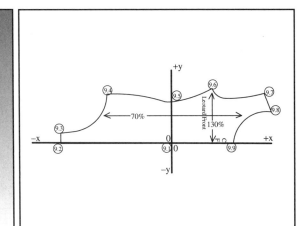

Size	Rule 1		Rule 3		Rule 4		Rule 6		Rule 7	
	X	Y	X	Y	X	Y	X	Y	X	Y
6	0	0	0	−24 (−.75)	−11 (−.3438)	−24 (−.75)	−22 (−.6875)	−12 (−.375)	−24 (−.75)	−5 (−.1563)
8	0	0	0	−19 (−.5938)	−7 (−.2188)	−19 (−.5938)	−15 (−.4688)	−9 (−.2813)	−17 (−.5313)	−4 (−.125)
10	0	0	0	−10 (−.3125)	−4 (−.125)	−11 (−.3438)	−7 (−.2188)	−5 (−.1563)	−9 (−2813)	−2 (−.625)
12	0	0	0	0	0	0	0	0	0	0
14	0	0	0	10 (.3125)	4 (.125)	11 (.3438)	7 (.2188)	5 (.1563)	9 (.2813)	2 (.0625)
16	0	0	0	21 (.6563)	7 (.2188)	21 (.6563)	15 (.4688)	10 (.3125)	19 (.5938)	4 (.125)
18	0	0	0	35 (1.0948)	11 (.3438)	35 (1.0948)	22 (.6875)	17 (.5313)	28 (.875)	7 (.2188)
20	0	0	0	49 (1.5313)	15 (.4688)	49 (1.5313)	30 (.9375)	24 (.75)	37 (1.1563)	10 (.3125)
22	0	0	0	63 (1.9688)	19 (.5938)	63 (1.9688)	37 (1.1563)	31 (.9688)	47 (1.4688)	14 (.4375)

■**Table 9.6** Grade Rule Table Stretch Body Suit

Pattern Piece: Body Suit
Units: Inches   **Denominator:** 1/32
Size Range: Misses 6–22
Master Size: Misses 12

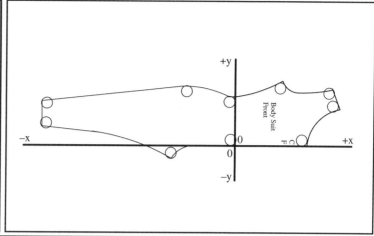

Size	Rule		Rule		Rule		Rule		Rule		Rule	
	X	Y	X	Y	X	Y	X	Y	X	Y	X	Y
6												
8												
10												
12	0	0	0	0	0	0	0	0	0	0	0	0
14												
16												
18												
20												
22												

Size	Rule		Rule		Rule		Rule		Rule		Rule	
	X	Y	X	Y	X	Y	X	Y	X	Y	X	Y
6												
8												
10												
12	0	0	0	0	0	0	0	0	0	0	0	0
14												
16												
18												
20												
22												

10

Grading from

Garment Specifications

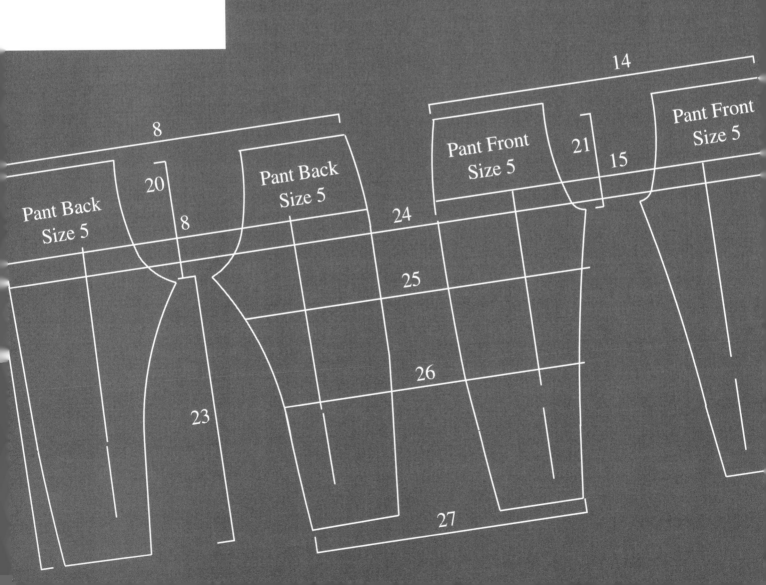

Introduction

Apparel manufacturers may engage in contract work in which they do the pattern grading, cutting, and sewing for several different firms. Lands' End, L. L. Bean, J. C. Penney, and Wal-Mart are examples of retailers that use contractors to manufacture their apparel products. The retailers usually supply the contractor with **garment specifications** that indicate the finished garment dimensions for each size. If garment specifications are not supplied, size specifications (body dimensions) must be analyzed to develop appropriate garment specifications.

In some cases more than one retailer may use the same contractor for a particular product, but it would be unlikely that any two retailers would provide identical sets of size specifications for the contracted garment. Most manufacturers covet contracts from large retail firms, and their precise use of specifications to develop a grade guide can help ensure repeat orders. Therefore, a careful study of size specifications is important in preparing a grade guide, a grading system, and garment specifications.

Size specifications supplied to the manufacturer must include all garment measurements necessary to determine how the grade is distributed in the garment. If they do not, additional information should be obtained from the contracting firm before a grading system is established. Ideally, a size run is made for each size in the size range in order to perfect the fit before finalizing the size specifications.

Garment specification tables indicate the finished garment dimensions, not body dimensions. They are developed for each garment style that is manufactured and generally include a flat sketch with measurement locations. Table 10.1 is an example of information contained in a set of specifications for a girl's skirt. Specifications for a full-body garment should include back and front width measurements of bust, waist, and hips; back and front body width measurements at the mid-armscye; and back and front neck width measurements from shoulder to shoulder. Length measurements should include shoulder, overarm and underarm sleeve, shoulder to bust, armscye depth, crotch depth, center front to waist, nape of back neck to waist, and skirt and pant lengths. The differences in these measurements between adjacent sizes in the size range are used to determine the grade guide and the grading system necessary for the grading process.

DEVELOPMENT OF A GRADE GUIDE FROM GARMENT SPECIFICATIONS

Garment specifications in Table 10.2 are adapted from *The ABC's of Grading* and are for basic garment blocks (Scheier, 1974); Table 10.3 contains the subsequent grade guide that indicates the difference in the measurements between adjacent sizes. Garment specifications give the dimensions of the finished garment in each size, and they are used as a quality control standard for garment dimension inspection. However, they must also be used to develop a grade guide for determining the grade distributions in the patterns.

Specifications for Key Garment Areas

The grade distributions within a garment may not be obvious from a review of the specifications. Therefore, a logical approach to analyzing the specifications will simplify the development of a grade guide. The following procedure is necessary to develop a grading system.

- Determine the circumference grade for the bust, waist, and hips.
- Determine the width grade distributions for the neck, shoulder, armscye, arms, legs, and hips.
- Determine the length grade distributions for the neck, armscye, bodice side seam, neck to bust point, and torso, arms, and legs.

Calculation Formula

A review of the formula for working with data in specification tables is appropriate at this point. Width grades in Table 10.3 are divided by 2 to determine the grade for some of the cardinal points on the pattern because half-patterns are graded (refer to Figure 3.4). Length grades are not divided since the pattern pieces represent the actual body length. If circumference measurements are given in the chart, they are divided by 4.

The back and front contours of the female body differ dramatically from one another; therefore, the dimension of the back and front garment sections are usually listed separately in garment specifications. However, when developing a simplified grade guide from the garment specifications, the total dimension of back and front garment areas is used. For example, the back waist width and the front waist width are added together to produce the waist circumference, which determines if the grade is a 1-inch, a 1 1/2-inch, or a 2-inch grade in a simplified grading system (Table 10.4).

Step 1: Total Circumference Grade

The garment specifications in Table 10.2 are different from the PS 42-70 and the ASTM D 5585 specifications. The bust, waist, and hip circumference grades specify the *total grade* between sizes and are determined from the size specifications. In Figure 10.1, measurements 2 and 4 from the size specifications are used for the bust circumference; measurements 5 and 6 are used for the waist circumference; and measurements 7 and 8 are used for the hip circumference. The bust, waist, and hip circumferences change uniformly between sizes, and in simplified grading systems the back and front of each area (bust, waist, hips) change by the same amount between sizes. Table 10.4 gives the total circumference measurements for the three areas and shows the incremental grade between adjacent sizes. A 1-inch grade is used for sizes up to size 12; a 1 1/2-inch grade is used between sizes 12 and 16; and a 2-inch grade is used between sizes 16 and 18. The grade guide developed from the specifications in this chapter is different from a grade guide based on the PS 42-70 specifications. Grade guides are reflective of the garment or body dimensions they are derived from, but the method of developing the grade guide is consistent for any set of specifications.

Step 2: Width Grade Distribution

After the total grade between adjacent sizes has been established, the distribution of the total grade within each pattern piece must be determined for a 1-inch grade, a 1 1/2-inch grade, and a 2-inch grade.

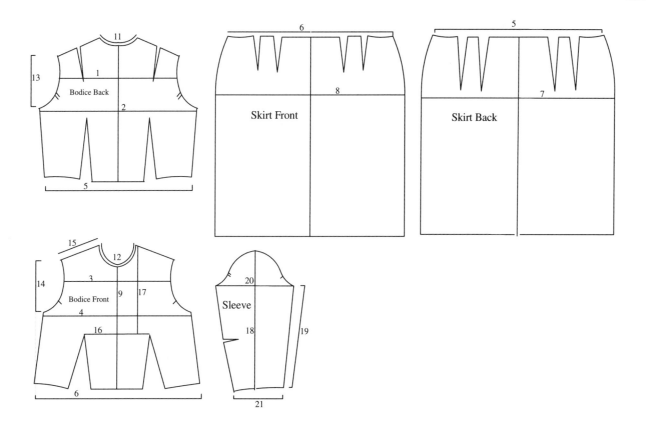

a. Dress Locations

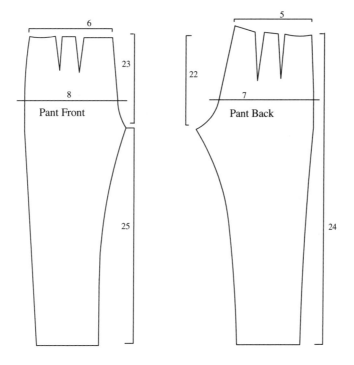

b. Pant Locations

Figure 10.1 Garment Measurement Locations

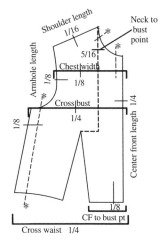

1-Inch Grade

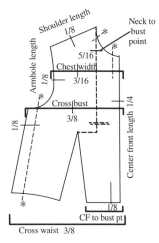

1 1/2-Inch Grade

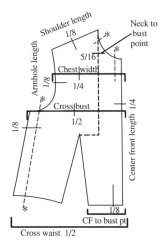

2-Inch Grade

——————Standard Grade   --------Variable Grade

■Figure 10.2 Grades Specified on Grade Guide

The width measurements in Table 10.5 are for the combined right and left sides of the garment; but when grading a pattern piece, only a half-pattern is used. Because the back and front garment dimensions of the bust, waist, and hips are added to determine the total circumference grade between sizes, the total grade must be divided by 4 to arrive at the cross bust, waist, and hip grades for a half-pattern piece. For a total grade of 1 inch, the cross grade for the half-pattern is 1/4 inch; for the 1 1/2-inch total grade, the cross grade is 3/8 inch; and for the 2-inch total grade, the cross grade is 1/2 inch (Figure 10.2).

Figure 10.2 illustrates the grades for half-patterns based on the grade guide for the bodice front. The same grades are applicable to the bodice back. The asterisks identify grades that must be calculated from more than one measurement.

Cross Bust Grade Distribution

Areas of width distribution for the bodice are the neck, shoulder, armscye width, and bust point to bust point. Table 10.5 gives specifications for garment width dimensions and contains the grade between adjacent sizes for each area.

Shoulder Grade

The shoulder changes by 1/16 inch in the 1-inch grade and by 1/8 inch in the 1 1/2-inch and 2-inch grades (Figure 10.2). The shoulder length measurement is not divided; however, the other measurements in Tables 10.5 represent the full body width and are divided by 2 in the grade guide.

Neck Width Grade

The neck width grade can be established by beginning with the back width and chest width to determine the cross shoulder grade. The cross shoulder grade includes the shoulder length grade plus the neck width grade. Therefore, by calculating the difference in the cross shoulder grade and the shoulder length grade, the neck width grade is determined (Table 10.6) (Figure 10.3).

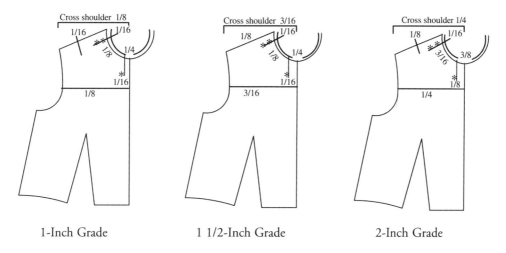

| 1-Inch Grade | 1 1/2-Inch Grade | 2-Inch Grade |

*Front neck width equals cross shoulder minus shoulder length.

**Front neck length equals half the neck measurement minus neck width.

Figure 10.3 Neck Grades

Armscye Width Grade

The remainder of the cross bust/waist grade goes into the armscye width, which is calculated by subtracting the cross shoulder grade from the cross body grade (Table 10.7). Recognizing the relationship between grades in different body locations facilitates the grade rule development process. **Note that in this grading system the armscye width grade is always equal to the cross shoulder grade, and they are each equal to one-half of the cross bust grade** (Figure 10.4).

Cross Waist Grade Distribution
Center Front to Bust Point Grade

The distribution for the cross bust grade has been determined, but not for the cross waist. The total cross waist grade has been established—1/4 inch for the 1-inch grade, 3/8 inch for the 1 1/2-inch grade, and 1/2 inch for the 2-inch grade. The bust point to bust point information from the grade guide shows the change is 1/4 inch between sizes. When that 1/4 inch width grade is divided by 2, it is a standard 1/8 inch for the 1-inch, the 1 1/2-inch, and the 2-inch grades (Figure 10.5).

Dart to Side Seam Grade

The change between the dart and side seam is calculated by subtracting one-half of the bust point to bust point (bust point to center front) change from the cross waist grade (Figure 10.5). Generally the 1/8-inch width grade between center front and bust point is standard, but the change between the bust dart and side seam varies between the 1-inch, the 1 1/2-inch, and the 2-inch grades.

Step 3: Length Grade Distributions

Table 10.8 contains the specifications for the length measurements. The grade distributions for length are given or can be determined by calculations from other measurements. Specifications for center back and center front lengths, back and front armscye depths, and shoulder to bust point are used to establish the distributions for length in the bodice pattern. Changes in the length grades between sizes are the same for the front and back pattern pieces just as the width changes were. Figure 10.6 shows where the length measurements were taken and Figure 10.7 illustrates where the

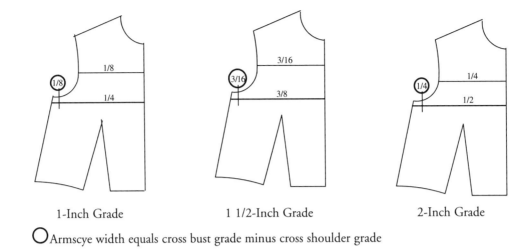

1-Inch Grade   1 1/2-Inch Grade   2-Inch Grade

◯ Armscye width equals cross bust grade minus cross shoulder grade

■Figure 10.4 Calculated Armscye Width Grade

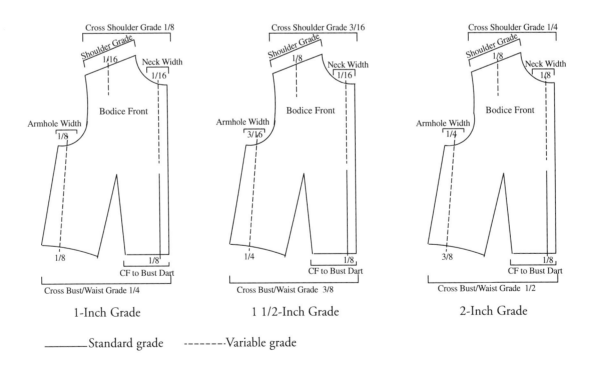

1-Inch Grade   1 1/2-Inch Grade   2-Inch Grade

_____ Standard grade   - - - - - - - Variable grade

■Figure 10.5 Width Distributions for 1-, 1 1/2-, and 2-Inch Grades

increases/decreases are made in the pattern piece. Because the length changes are standard grades, they are the same whether using a 1-inch, a 1 1/2-inch, or a 2-inch grade.

Note that changes occurred with most of the width grades between the 1-inch, the 1 1/2-inch, and the 2-inch grades; therefore, most width grades are variable grades. Unlike width grades, the length grades generally do not change across the 1-inch, the 1 1/2-inch, and the 2-inch grades, so they are referred to *as standard grades*. **Memorizing the grades that are variable and those that are standard greatly expedites the development of a grading system and the writing of grade rules for cardinal points.**

Center Front and Center Back Length Grades

The grade guide (Table 10.3) indicates that changes in both the center front and center back lengths are 1/4 inch between sizes. This 1/4-inch length grade is distributed in the armscye and the underarm seam.

Armscye Depth Grade and Underarm Seam Grade

The amount of length that goes into the armscye is specified by the armscye depth change and is 1/8 inch between all sizes for both the back and front (Figure 10.7). The remaining 1/8-inch change goes into the pattern under the armscye in the underarm seam. The exact location in the underarm seam is dependent upon the bust point location.

Shoulder to Bust Point Grade

The shoulder to bust point length change is 5/16 inch between all sizes (Table 10.3) (Figure 10.2). The distribution of the shoulder to bust point grade includes the neck length grade. Therefore, the neck length grade must be determined before the shoulder to bust point grade can be distributed.

Neck Length Grade

The grade guide for a half-pattern in Table 10.5 specifies the neck grade for the bodice, and indicates how the grade is divided between the neck length and neck

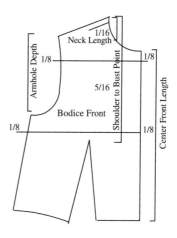

1-Inch Grade

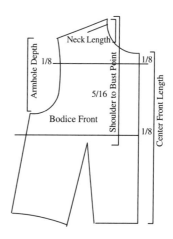

1 1/2-Inch Grade

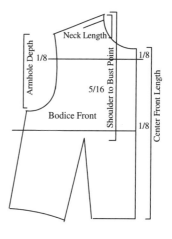

2-Inch Grade

——— Standard grade

Figure 10.6 Length Distributions for 1-, 1 1/2-, and 2-Inch Grades

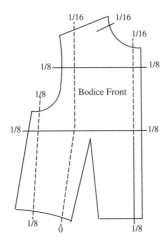

1-Inch Grade

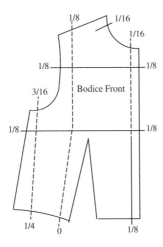

1 1/2-Inch Grade

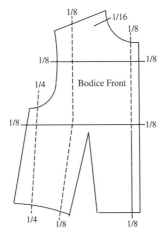

2-Inch Grade

————————Standard grade

■Figure 10.7 Bodice Length and Width
Distributions

width. The changes in the neck width were discussed in the width grade distributions (Figures 10.3 and 10.5) The neck area of the body changes in both width and length, so a simple calculation of subtracting the neck width grade from the total half-pattern neck grade determines the neck length grade (Figure 10.6). It is a standard 1/16 inch for the 1-inch, the 1 1/2-inch, and the 2-inch grades (Figure 10.7).

Underarm Seam Grade

The 1/16 inch in the neck length grade and the 1/8 inch in the armscye depth (length) grade account for only 3/16 inch of the grade between shoulder and bust point. Therefore, an additional 1/8 inch must be added between the bust point level and the underarm/side seam intersection in order to maintain the correct shoulder to bust point change. This encompasses the total grade distribution for the area between the armscye and the waist; therefore, no additional length grade distribution is necessary between the bust point and the waist. The 1/8-inch grade distribution is made on the back pattern piece in approximately the same location under the armhole. Figure 10.7 illustrates the locations of both length and width grades on the bodice pattern.

Step 4: Sleeve Specifications for Length and Width

Four measurements for sleeves are given in the sizing specifications in Table 10.2. Table 10.9 contains the dimensions for each size and the grade between sizes. The length grades are standard across all sizes, whereas the girth grades are variable between the 1-inch, 1 1/2-inch, and 2-inch grades. The girth changes in the sleeve affect the length of the sleeve cap seamline; the sleeve cap seamline must change the same as the total change in the back and front armscye seams. Figure 10.5 illustrates the variable grades in the armhole width between the 1-inch, the 1 1/2-inch, and the 2-inch total grades. The sleeve length grade is a standard 1/4 inch across all sizes.

Corresponding seams of different pattern pieces that will be joined in the construction process

must be changed the same amounts in the pattern grading process. Therefore, the armscye length grade in the sleeve cap is the same as the corresponding armscye length grade in the bodice back and front (Figure 10.8). The sleeve cap length grade is a standard 1/8 inch for the 1-inch, the 1 1/2-inch, and the 2-inch grades.

The difference in the overarm and underarm sleeve lengths is the length grade for the sleeve cap. The remaining 1/8-inch sleeve length is distributed in the underarm seam. This 1/8 inch is divided between the areas above and below the elbow dart. If a sleeve pattern has no elbow dart, the change may be made arbitrarily between the underarm and wrist.

Figure 10.9 shows the variable changes in the biceps and wrist girth in relation to the bodice back and front. When working with the flat, two-dimensional sleeve pattern, the biceps girth change may be treated as a pattern width change. In this case, the sleeve pattern represents the total biceps girth (sleeve width), so the **measurement is not divided** as it was for the bodice patterns, where only one-half the body width was represented. Although part of the sleeve width is distributed in the sleeve cap, the total change across the width of the sleeve must equal the change made in the armscye width of the back and bodice front. It is important that some of the width is placed in the sleeve cap to maintain the shape of the curve on the cap line.

Step 5: Skirt/Pants Specifications for Width and Length Grade Distributions

The grade guide (Table 10.3) is used to determine the grade distribution for the skirt/pants. The waist and hip measurements were listed in Table 10.4; for convenience they are also in Table 10.10. Table 10.10 gives the measurements for the total girth instead of listing the back and front widths separately. The grade guide for the skirt/pant measurements is included with the specification table.

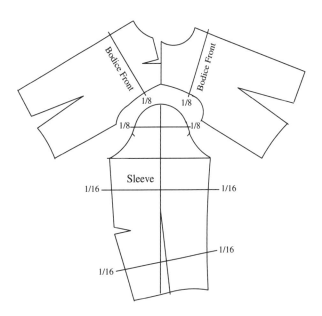

Figure 10.8 Sleeve Length Distributions for 1-, 1 1/2-, and 2-Inch Grades

The size breaks between the 1-inch, the 1 1/2-inch, and the 2-inch grades are the same as in Table 10.4. Therefore, the one-dart skirt or pant is graded the same as the bodice waist. In a two-dart pattern the cross grade is distributed in three areas instead of the two areas that are found in the bodice distribution (Figure 10.5). The cross waist width distribution for the skirt and pants from the center front to the dart is the same as for the bodice; a standard 1/8 inch for the 1-inch, the 1 1/2-inch, and the 2-inch grades. However, the grade distribution between the first dart and the side seam is variable with the amount dependent upon whether a 1-inch, a 1 1/2-inch, or a 2-inch grade is used; the remaining distribution is divided with equal amounts on each side of the second dart (Figure 10.10).

An additional crotch width grade goes into the pants. As noted at the bottom of Table 10.10, this change is calculated based on the cross hip grade, and because the cross hip grade varies for the 1-inch, the 1 1/2-inch, and the 2-inch grades, the crotch width grade is variable (Figure 10.11). An additional note at the bottom of Table 10.10 states that the bottom leg grade

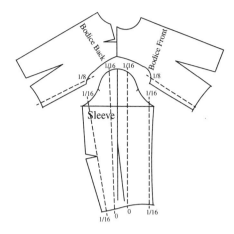

1-Inch Grade

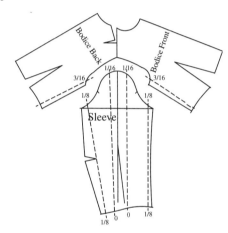

1 1/2-Inch Grade

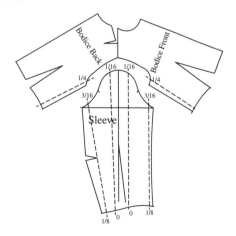

2-Inch Grade

------------Variable grade

■**Figure 10.9** Sleeve Width Distributions for 1-,
1 1/2-, and 2-Inch Grades

(leg width grade) depends upon the style of the pants. A straight-leg pant may be graded the same as the hip—3/8 inch for a 1 1/2-inch grade—whereas, half of the hip grade is appropriate for the leg width of a tapered leg pant. The use of this distinction in grading styles is at the discretion of the pattern grader and the desired design proportion. The grade for the skirt sweep (width across the lower edge of the skirt) is the same as the cross waist/hip grade which is 1/4 inch for the 1-inch grade, 3/8 inch for the 1 1/2-inch grade, and 1/2 inch for the 2-inch grade.

The length grades for the skirt and pant are standard, just as the length grades were standard for the bodice. Tables 10.10 and 10.3 shows a 1/4-inch change between sizes for the outer leg length. The back and front **rise** (crotch depth) also changes by 1/4 inch; therefore, we can deduce that the entire length change is between the crotch and the waist. The inseam length change verifies the placement of the length grade because the change is zero between all sizes. On the skirt and pants back, where the waist darts terminate near the fullest part of the hips, at least part of the length should be placed so that the dart is lengthened (Figure 10.11). Refer to Figures 5.33 and 5.43 to see how the basic block was graded.

Some specifications for pants may also give the garment dimensions for the knee and the leg opening widths as well as for additional length to be placed in the inseam. Sometimes the specified length in skirts increases up to size 16 or 18, but not in sizes beyond these.

The sizing specifications must be examined thoroughly so that subtle details are not missed when developing the grade guide. If any questions remain after studying the specifications, the company that supplied the specifications should be contacted to clarify information.

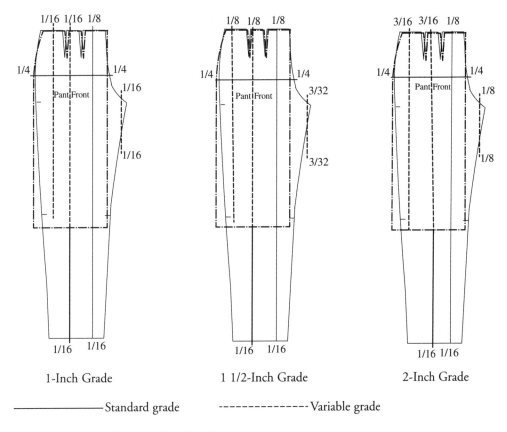

1-Inch Grade

1 1/2-Inch Grade

2-Inch Grade

——————Standard grade   - - - - - - - - - -Variable grade

■Figure 10.10 Grade Distributions for Skirt/Pant Front

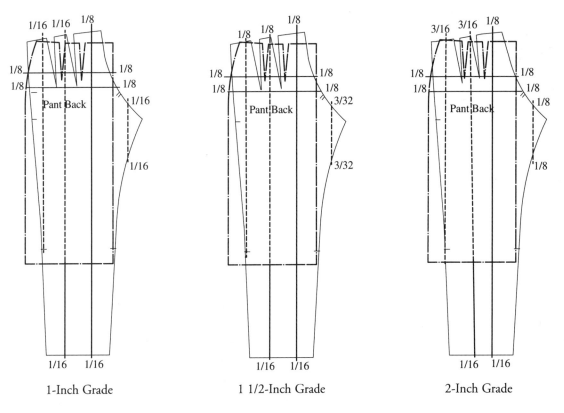

1-Inch Grade

1 1/2-Inch Grade

2-Inch Grade

■Figure 10.11 Grade Distributions for Skirt/Pant Back

PATTERN GRADING
Summary

Size specifications are written specifically for each garment style. They reflect finished garment dimensions, not body dimensions and are an important tool for quality control. They are essential for companies that contract their work to outside manufacturers and wish to maintain consistency throughout their product lines. Size specifications differ for the front and back of most garments because they reflect finished garment dimensions, but the total circumference measurements must be considered when developing the grade guide. Therefore, size specifications must be analyzed in order to develop a grading system that encompasses circumference, length, and width grades.

In addition to reflecting changes in body dimensions, pattern grade guides must be written so that corresponding seams of adjoining pattern pieces match on all graded sizes. Learning the areas that contain variable grades and those that contain standard grades greatly expedites the development of grading systems and grade rules. Generally, width and horizontal circumference measurements are variable grades, whereas length and vertical circumferences are standard grades. Some exceptions to this general rule do exist; an example is the neck length grade, which is a variable grade.

Specifications for skirt length, pant length, and pant width may vary depending upon the desired design proportion. Sizing specifications may also reflect the proportion of other design details and should be examined thoroughly to determine all areas of a garment that may need grading.

Exercises

The principles of developing grade guides from size specifications are also applicable to children's and men's grading, when size specifications are available for them. Although the grade distribution may vary between body types, the grading concepts are the same.

Grading From Specifications: Child's Garment
To apply the principles discussed in this chapter, develop a grade guide from size specifications for a child's garment. Table 10.11 contains a set of size specifications for select measurements of children's garments sizes 3 to 6X, adapted from *The ABC's of Grading* (Scheier, 1974). Tables and figures are provided to help the reader develop the grade guide and a grade rule table for the child's garment. Figures 10.12 and 10.13 illustrate the locations on basic garment blocks that the measurements represent. Use the following steps.

Step 1: Total Circumference Grade
The grader should first calculate the total circumference grade to determine the grade between sizes. To facilitate this step, use Table 10.12 to determine the total circumference measurements and grades between sizes for the child's garment.

Step 2: Width Grade Distribution
The width distribution is calculated from measurements for different locations in the garment. In Table 10.13 indicate the measurements to determine the grades between sizes. The number and type of these measurements may vary. It should be remembered

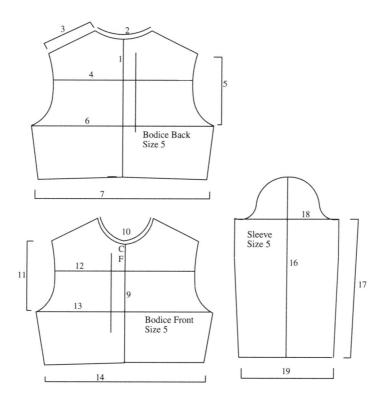

Figure 10.12 Upper Body Measurement Locations

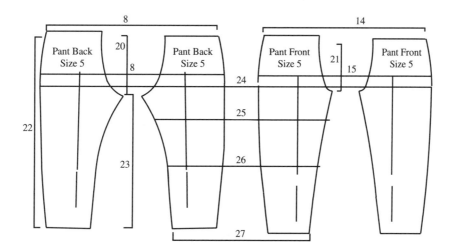

Figure 10.13 Lower Body Measurement Locations

that the more measurements provided, the more accurate the grade distribution will be.

Step 3: Total Length Grade

The length grades are taken as total differences and do not have to be divided for half-patterns. Use Table 10.14 to record the length measurements and grades.

Step 4: Sleeve Specifications for Length and Width

Complete Table 10.15 to determine the width and length grade distributions for the sleeve.

Step 5: Pants Measurements for Width and Length

The grade distributions for the child's pants are determined by completing Table 10.16.

Step 6: Development of Grade Rule Table

Once the distributions have been calculated, label the grade distribution lines on the half-patterns for the child's basic garment blocks in Figure 10.14. The width and circumference grades are standard for the child's garment, but length grades are variable between the size 6 and size 6X. Grade distributions for half-patterns must be calculated by dividing circumference measurements by 4 and width measurements by 2. Table 10.17 is provided so the grader may compile the measurements into one chart.

Regardless of differences in how different body types change, the concepts used to write grade rules and to grade the pattern for any body type are the same. In Figure 10.15 a child's garment is illustrated and

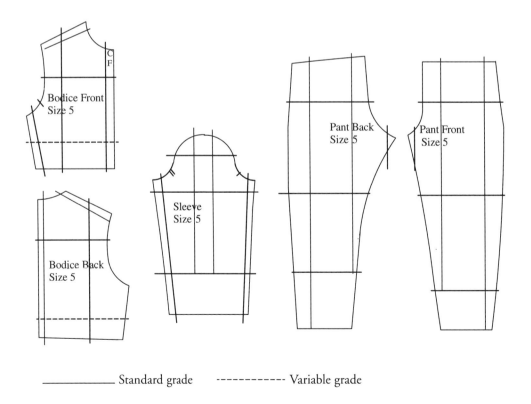

_____ Standard grade   ----------- Variable grade

Figure 10.14 Grade Distributions for Child's Pattern

Figure 10.16 shows the pattern pieces in that garment. Write grade rules in the Grade Rule Table 10.18 using size 5 as the sample size pattern. Grade rules are based on the orientation of pattern pieces in Figure 10.17. If the pattern is graded as an extension of this exercise, master blocks must be developed for each pattern piece.

When the children's grade guide is completed, compare it to the grade guide for misses sizes to determine differences in the way the body changes between sizes of the two groups.

1. Which body type changes most in the length grades?
2. Which body type changes most in the width grades? Notice length grades between sizes 6 and 6X.

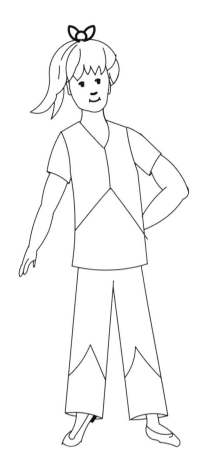

Figure 10.15 Child's Garment

REFERENCE

Scheier, M. (1974). *The ABC's of grading*. Bronxville, NY: Murray Scheier.

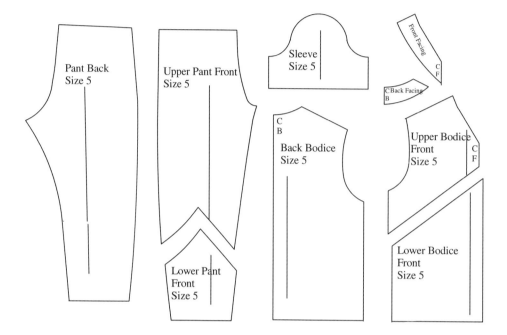

Figure 10.16 Child's Pattern Pieces for Grade Rule Application

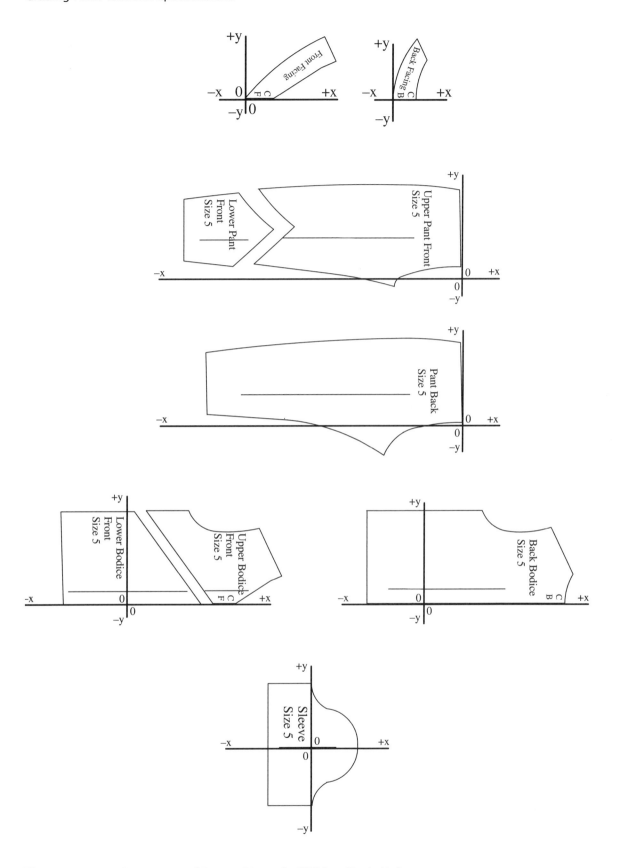

Table 10.1 Specifications for a Girl's A-line Skirt

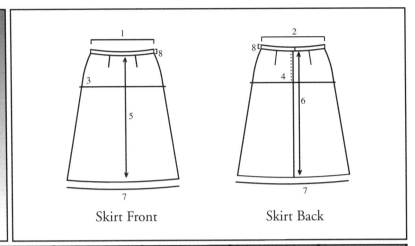

Style: 1234 Spring	
Description: A–line silhouette; straight waistband; zipper in center back seam	
Sizes: 7 through 14	
Fabric: 432 Corduroy Content: 50% cotton, 50% polyester	

Skirt Front   Skirt Back

Size	7	8	10	12	14
1. Front waistline	12 1/8	12 5/8	13 1/8	13 5/8	14 1/8
2. Back waistline	12 3/8	12 7/8	13 3/8	13 7/8	14 3/8
3. Front hip	14 1/4	14 3/4	15 3/8	16	16 3/4
4. Back hip	15 3/4	16 1/4	16 7/8	17 1/2	18 1/4
5. Front length	17	18	19 1/2	21	22 1/2
6. Back length	17	18	19 1/2	21	22 1/2
7. Front and back sweep	21	22	24	26	28
8. Waistband width	7/8	7/8	7/8	7/8	7/8

Note: Measurements are in inches.

■**Table 10.2** Garment Specifications for Misses' Sizes 6 to 18

Size	6	8	10	12	14	16	18
Width Measurements							
1. Back width at mid-armscye	13 1/8	13 3/8	13 5/8	13 7/8	14 1/4	14 5/8	15 1/8
2. Full back body width	16	16 1/2	17	17 1/2	18 1/4	19	20
3. Chest width at mid-armscye	12 3/8	12 5/8	12 7/8	13 1/8	13 1/2	13 7/8	14 3/8
4. Full front body width	18	18 1/2	19	19 1/2	20 1/4	21	22
5. Back waist width	11 1/4	11 3/4	12 1/4	12 3/4	13 1/2	14 1/4	15 1/4
6. Front waist width	12 1/4	12 3/4	13 1/4	13 3/4	14 1/2	15 1/4	16 1/4
7. Back hip width	17 1/2	18	18 1/2	19	19 3/4	20 1/2	21 1/2
8. Front hip width	17 1/2	18	18 1/2	19	19 3/4	20 1/2	21 1/2
9. Center back waist length	15 3/4	16	16 1/4	16 1/2	16 3/4	17	17 1/4
Upper Body Length Measurements							
10. Center front waist length	14 1/4	14 1/2	14 3/4	15	15 1/4	15 1/2	15 3/4
11. Back neck measurement	5 1/2	5 3/4	6	6 1/4	6 1/2	6 3/4	7 1/8
12. Front neck measurement	8 1/2	8 3/4	9	9 1/4	9 1/2	9 3/4	10 1/8
13. Back armhole depth	7	7 1/8	7 1/4	7 3/8	7 1/2	7 5/8	7 3/4
14. Front armhole depth	6	6 1/8	6 1/4	6 3/8	6 1/2	6 5/8	6 3/4
15. Shoulder length	4 7/8	4 15/16	5	5 1/16	5 3/16	5 5/16	5 7/17
16. Bust point to bust point	6 3/4	7	7 1/4	7 1/2	7 3/4	8	8 1/4
17. Shoulder to bust point	8 7/16	8 3/4	9 1/16	9 3/8	9 11/16	10	10 5/16
18. Overarm length	22 1/4	22 1/2	22 3/4	23	23 1/4	23 1/2	23 3/4
19. Underarm length	16 5/8	16 3/4	16 7/8	17	17 1/8	17 1/4	17 3/8
Girth Measurements							
20. Biceps girth	12	12 1/4	12 1/2	12 3/4	13 1/8	13 1/2	14
21. Wrist girth	6 7/8	7	7 1/8	7 1/4	7 1/2	7 3/4	8
Lower Body Length Measurements							
22. Pants back rise (waist to crotch level)	11 5/8	11 7/8	12 1/8	12 3/8	12 5/8	12 7/8	13 1/8
23. Pants front rise (waist to crotch level)	10 7/8	11 1/8	11 3/8	11 5/8	11 7/8	12 1/8	12 3/8
24. Outer leg seam (waist to ankle)	41 1/2	41 3/4	42	42 1/4	42 1/2	42 3/4	43
25. Inseam (crotch to ankle)	30 1/4	30 1/4	30 1/4	30 1/4	30 1/4	30 1/4	30 1/4

Notes: Measurements are for patterns with ease allowances but no seam allowances. Measurements are in inches. Size 18, added by authors, includes a 2-inch grade. Crotch level grade equals the hip grade plus a quarter of the hip grade. Bottom leg grade depends upon the style of the pant.
Source: Adapted from *THE ABC's of Grading.*

Table 10.3 Grade Guide for Misses' Sizes 6 to 18 Calculated From Table 10.2

Size	6–8	8–10	10–12	12–14	14–16	16–18
Width Measurements						
1. Back width at mid–armscye	1/4	1/4	1/4	3/8	3/8	1/2
2. Full back body width	1/2	1/2	1/2	3/4	3/4	1
3. Chest width at armscye	1/4	1/4	1/4	3/8	3/8	1/2
4. Full front body width	1/2	1/2	1/2	3/4	3/4	1
5. Back waist width	1/2	1/2	1/2	3/4	3/4	1
6. Front waist width	1/2	1/2	1/2	3/4	3/4	1
7. Back hip width	1/2	1/2	1/2	3/4	3/4	1
8. Front hip width	1/2	1/2	1/2	3/4	3/4	1
Upper Body Length Measurements and Neckline (Shoulder to Shoulder)						
9. Center back waist length	1/4	1/4	1/4	1/4	1/4	1/4
10. Center front waist length	1/4	1/4	1/4	1/4	1/4	1/4
11. Back neck measurement	1/4	1/4	1/4	1/4	1/4	3/8
12. Front neck measurement	1/4	1/4	1/4	1/4	1/4	3/8
13. Back armscye depth	1/8	1/8	1/8	1/8	1/8	1/8
14. Front armscye depth	1/8	1/8	1/8	1/8	1/8	1/8
15. Shoulder length	1/16	1/16	1/16	1/8	1/8	1/8
16. Bust point to bust point	1/4	1/4	1/4	1/4	1/4	1/4
17. Shoulder to bust point	5/16	5/16	5/16	5/16	5/16	5/16
18. Overarm length	1/4	1/4	1/4	1/4	1/4	1/4
19. Underarm length	1/8	1/8	1/8	1/8	1/8	1/8
Girth Measurements						
20. Biceps girth	1/4	1/4	1/4	3/8	3/8	1/2
21. Wrist girth	1/8	1/8	1/8	1/4	1/4	1/4
Lower Body Length						
22. Pant back rise (waist to crotch level)	1/4	1/4	1/4	1/4	1/4	1/4
23. Pant front rise (waist to crotch level)	1/4	1/4	1/4	1/4	1/4	1/4
24. Outer leg seam (waist to ankle)	1/4	1/4	1/4	1/4	1/4	1/4
25. Inseam (crotch to ankle)	0	0	0	0	0	0

Notes: Measurements are in inches. Crotch level grade equals the hip grade plus one quarter of the hip grade. Bottom leg grade depends upon the style of the pant.

Table 10.4 Total Circumference for Bust, Waist, and Hips to Determine 1-, 1 1/2-, and 2-Inch Grades and Grade Guide

Total Circumference Measurements							
Size	**6**	**8**	**10**	**12**	**14**	**16**	**18**
Bust measurement 2[a]	16	16 1/2	17	17 1/2	18 1/4	19	20
Bust measurement 4[a]	18	18 1/2	19	19 1/2	20 1/4	21	22
Total bust circumference	**34**	**35**	**36**	**37**	**38 1/2**	**40**	**42**
Waist measurement 5[a]	11 1/4	11 3/4	12 1/4	12 3/4	13 1/2	14 1/4	15 1/4
Waist measurement 6[a]	12 1/4	12 3/4	13 1/4	13 3/4	14 1/2	15 1/4	16 1/4
Total waist circumference	**23 1/2**	**24 1/2**	**25 1/2**	**26 1/2**	**28**	**29 1/2**	**31 1/2**
Hip measurement 7[a]	17 1/2	18	18 1/2	19	19 3/4	20 1/2	21 1/2
Hip measurement 8[a]	17 1/2	18	18 1/2	19	19 3/4	20 1/2	21 1/2
Total hip circumference	**35**	**36**	**37**	**38**	**39 1/2**	**41**	**43**

Grade Guide for Bust, Waist, and Hip						
Size	**6–8**	**8–10**	**10–12**	**12–14**	**14–16**	**16–18**
Bust	1	1	1	1 1/2	1 1/2	2
Waist	1	1	1	1 1/2	1 1/2	2
Hips	1	1	1	1 1/2	1 1/2	2

Note: Measurements are in inches.

[a]Numbers refer to measurements in Figure 10.1.

Table 10.5 Garment Specifications and Grade Guide for Bodice Width

Measurements from Specification Table 10.2							
Size	6	8	10	12	14	16	18
Shoulder 15[a]	4 7/8	4 15/16	5	5 1/16	5 3/16	5 5/16	5 7/16
Back width 1[a]	13 1/8	13 3/8	13 5/8	13 7/8	14 1/4	14 5/8	15 1/8
Chest width 3[a]	12 3/8	12 5/8	12 7/8	13 1/8	13 1/2	13 7/8	14 3/8
Full back body width 2[a]	16	16 1/2	17	17 1/2	18 1/4	19	20
Full front body width 4[a]	18	18 1/2	19	19 1/2	20 1/4	21	22
Back waist width 5[a]	11 1/4	11 3/4	12 1/4	12 3/4	13 1/2	14 1/4	15 1/4
Front waist width 6[a]	12 1/4	12 3/4	13 1/4	13 3/4	14 1/2	15 1/4	16 1/4
Back neck 11[a]	5 1/2	5 3/4	6	6 1/4	6 1/2	6 3/4	7 1/8
Front neck 12[a]	8 1/2	8 3/4	9	9 1/4	9 1/2	9 3/4	10 1/8
Bust point to bust point 16[a]	6 3/4	7	7 1/4	7 1/2	7 3/4	8	8 1/4

Grade Guide for Half-Pattern						
Size	6–8	8–10	10–12	12–14	14–16	16–18
Shoulder	1/16	1/16	1/16	1/8	1/8	1/8
Back width	1/4÷2=1/8	1/4÷2=1/8	1/4÷2=1/8	3/8÷2=3/16	3/8÷2=3/16	1/2÷2=1/4
Chest width	1/4÷2=1/8	1/4÷2=1/8	1/4÷2=1/8	3/8÷2=3/16	3/8÷2=3/16	1/2÷2=1/4
Full back width	1/2÷2=1/4	1/2÷2=1/4	1/2÷2=1/4	3/4÷2=3/8	3/4÷2=3/8	1÷2=1/2
Full front width	1/2÷2=1/4	1/2÷2=1/4	1/2÷2=1/4	3/4÷2=3/8	3/4÷2=3/8	1÷2=1/2
Back waist width	1/2÷2=1/4	1/2÷2=1/4	1/2÷2=1/4	3/4÷2=3/8	3/4÷2=3/8	1÷2=1/2
Front waist width	1/2÷2=1/4	1/2÷2=1/4	1/2÷2=1/4	3/4÷2=3/8	3/4÷2=3/8	1÷2=1/2
Back neck	1/4÷2=1/8	1/4÷2=1/8	1/4÷2=1/8	1/4÷2=1/8	1/4÷2=1/8	3/8÷2=3/16
Front neck	1/4÷2=1/8	1/4÷2=1/8	1/4÷2=1/8	1/4÷2=1/8	1/4÷2=1/8	3/8÷2=3/16
Bust point to bust point	1/4÷2=1/8	1/4÷2=1/8	1/4÷2=1/8	1/4÷2=1/8	1/4÷2=1/8	1/4÷2=1/8

Distribution of Neck Width and Length Grades						
Neck width[b]	1/16	1/16	1/16	1/16	1/16	1/8
Neck length[c]	1/16	1/16	1/16	1/16	1/16	1/16
[b]Neck width equals chest or back width minus shoulder length.						
[c]Neck length equals back or front neck minus neck width.						

Armscye Width Grade						
Armscye width[d]	1/8	1/8	1/8	3/16	3/16	1/2

Note: Measurements are in inches.

[a]Numbers refer to measurements in Figure 10.1.

[b]Neck width equals chest or back width minus shoulder length.

[c]Neck length equals back or front neck minus neck width.

[d]Armscye width (full back or front width minus chest or back width).

Table 10.6 Neck Width Grade Calculations

Body Location Grades	1-Inch Grade	1 1/2-Inch Grade	2-Inch Grade
Cross shoulder grade	1/8	3/16	1/4
Shoulder length grade	−1/16	−1/8	−1/8
Neck width grade	1/16	1/16	1/8

Note: Measurements are in inches.

Table 10.7 Armscye Width Grade Calculations

Body Location Grades	1-Inch Grade	1 1/2-Inch Grade	2-Inch Grade
Cross bust grade	1/4	3/8	1/2
Cross shoulder grade	−1/8	−3/16	−1/4
Armscye width grade	1/8	3/16	1/4

Note: Measurements are in inches.

Table 10.8 Garment Specifications and Grade Guide for Bodice Length

Measurements from Specification Table 10.2							
Size	6	8	10	12	14	16	18
Center back waist length 9[a]	15 3/4	16	16 1/4	16 1/2	16 3/4	17	17 1/4
Center front waist length 10[a]	14 1/4	14 1/2	14 3/4	15	15 1/4	15 1/2	15 3/4
Back armhole depth 13[a]	7	7 1/8	7 1/4	7 3/8	7 1/2	7 5/8	7 3/4
Front armhole depth 14[a]	6	6 1/8	6 1/4	6 3/8	6 1/2	6 5/8	6 3/4
Shoulder to bust point 17[a]	8 7/16	8 3/4	9 1/16	9 3/8	9 11/16	10	10 5/16
Grade Guide for Bodice Length Measurements							
Size	6–8	8–10	10–12	12–14	14–16	16–18	
Center back waist length	1/4	1/4	1/4	1/4	1/4	1/4	
Center front waist length	1/4	1/4	1/4	1/4	1/4	1/4	
Back armhole depth	1/8	1/8	1/8	1/8	1/8	1/8	
Front armhole depth	1/8	1/8	1/8	1/8	1/8	1/8	
Shoulder to bust point	5/16	5/16	5/16	5/16	5/16	5/16	

Note: Measurements are in inches.
[a]Numbers refer to measurements in Figure 10.1.

■Table 10.9 Garment Specifications and Grade Guide for Sleeve

Measurements From Specification Table 10.2							
Size	6	8	10	12	14	16	18
Overarm length 18[a]	22 1/4	22 1/2	22 3/4	23	23 1/4	23 1/2	23 5/8
Underarm length 19[a]	16 5/8	16 3/4	16 7/8	17	17 1/8	17 1/4	17 3/8
Biceps girth 20[a]	12	12 1/4	12 1/2	12 3/4	13 1/8	13 1/2	14
Wrist girth 21[a]	5 7/8	7	7 1/8	7 1/4	7 1/2	7 3/4	8
Grade Guide for Sleeve							
Size	6–8	8–10	10–12	12–14	14–16	16–18	
Overarm length	1/4	1/4	1/4	1/4	1/4	1/4	
Underarm length	1/8	1/8	1/8	1/8	1/8	1/8	
Biceps girth	1/4	1/4	1/4	3/8	3/8	1/2	
Wrist girth	1/8	1/8	1/8	1/4	1/4	1/4	

Note: Measurements are in inches.
[a]Numbers refer to measurements in Figure 10.1.

■Table 10.10 Garment Specifications and Grade Guide for Shirt/Pant

Measurements From Specification Table 10.2							
Size	6	8	10	12	14	16	18
Waist girth 5 + 6[a]	23 1/2	24 1/2	25 1/2	26 1/2	28	29 1/2	31 1/2
Hip girth 7 + 8[a]	35	36	37	38	39 1/2	41	43
Pants back rise 22[a]	11 5/8	11 7/8	12 1/8	12 3/8	12 5/8	12 7/8	13 1/8
Pants front rise 23[a]	10 7/8	11 1/8	11 3/8	11 5/8	11 7/8	12 1/8	12 3/8
Outer leg seam 24[a]	41 1/2	41 3/4	42	42 1/4	42 1/2	42 3/4	43
Inseam 25[a]	30 1/4	30 1/4	30 1/4	30 1/4	30 1/4	30 1/4	30 1/4
Grade Guide for Skirt/Pant							
Size	6–8	8–10	10–12	12–14	14–16	16–18	
Waist girth	1	1	1	1 1/2	1 1/2	2	
Hip girth	1	1	1	1 1/2	1 1/2	2	
Back and front rise	1/4	1/4	1/4	1/4	1/4	1/4	
Outer leg seam	1/4	1/4	1/4	1/4	1/4	1/4	
Inseam	0	0	0	0	0	0	

Note: Crotch level grade equals the hip grade plus one quarter of the hip grade at the cardinal point of intersection of inseam and crotch seam. The actual change in the crotch area is one quarter of the hip grade. Bottom leg grade depends upon the style of the pants. Measurements are in inches.
[a]Numbers refer to measurements in Figure 10.1.

■ Table 10.11 Specifications for Children's Sizes 3 to 6X

Size	3	4	5	6	6X
Body Specifications					
1. Center back waist length	9	9 1/2	10	10 1/2	10 3/4
2. Back neck (shoulder to shoulder)	5 1/4	5 1/2	5 3/4	6	6 1/4
3. Shoulder length	3 3/8	3 1/2	3 5/8	3 3/4	3 7/8
4. Across back (between armscyes)	9 7/8	10 1/4	10 5/8	11	11 3/8
5. Back armhole depth	5 1/4	5 3/8	5 1/2	5 5/8	5 3/4
6. Full back body width (side seam to side seam)	11 3/4	12 1/4	12 3/4	13 1/4	13 3/4
7. Back waistline width	10 1/2	11	11 1/2	12	12 1/2
8. Back hip width	12 1/2	13	13 1/2	14	14 1/2
9. Center front to waist length	8 1/4	8 3/4	9 1/4	9 3/4	10
10. Front neck (shoulder to shoulder)	6 1/4	6 1/2	6 3/4	7	7 1/4
11. Front armhole depth	5 1/8	5 1/4	5 3/8	5 1/2	5 5/8
12. Chest width (between armscyes)	9 1/4	9 5/8	10	10 3/8	10 3/4
13. Full front body width (side seam to side seam)	12	12 1/2	13	13 1/2	14
14. Front waistline width	11	11 1/2	12	12 1/2	13
15. Front hip width	12	12 1/2	13	13 1/2	14
Sleeve Specifications					
16. Overarm length (long sleeve)	12 1/2	13 1/4	14	14 3/4	15 1/2
17. Underarm length (long sleeve)	8 5/8	9 1/4	9 7/8	10 1/2	11 1/8
18. Biceps circumference	8	8 1/4	8 1/2	8 3/4	9
19. Wrist circumference	5 1/2	5 3/4	6	6 1/4	6 1/2
Two-Legged Sportswear Specifications					
20. Pants back rise (waist to crotch level)	8 3/8	8 5/8	8 7/8	9 1/8	9 3/8
21. Pants front rise (waist to crotch level)	8	8 1/4	8 1/2	8 3/4	9
22. Outer leg seam (waist to ankle)	22	23 1/2	25	26 1/2	28
23. Inseam (crotch to ankle)	13 1/4	14 1/2	15 3/4	17	18 1/4
24. Seat girth (about 1 1/2" up from crotch)	25	26	27	28	29
25. Thigh circumference	15 1/4	15 3/4	16 1/4	16 3/4	17 1/4
26. Knee circumference	14 1/2	15	15 1/2	16	16 1/2
27. Ankle circumference	13	13 1/4	13 1/2	13 3/4	14

Notes: Measurements are for patterns with ease allowances but no seam allowances. Measurements are in inches. Crotch level grade equals the hip grade plus one-quarter of the hip grade. Bottom grade depends on the style of pants.

Source: Adapted from *The ABC's of Grading.*

Table 10.12 Total Circumference Measurements and Grade Guide for Upper Body, Waist, and Hip

Circumference Measurements From Specification Table 10.11					
Size	3	4	5	6	6X
Back body width 6[a]					
Front body width 13[a]					
Total body circumference					
Back waist width 7[a]					
Front waist width 14[a]					
Total waist circumference					
Back hip width 8[a]					
Front hip width 15[a]					
Total hip circumference					
Grade Guide for Circumference Measurements					
Size		3–4	4–5	5–6	6–6X
Body					
Waist					
Hips					

Notes: Measurements are in inches.

[a]Numbers refer to measurements in Figure 10.1.

Table 10.13 Garment Specifications and Grade Guide for Bodice Width

Measurements From Specification Table 10.11					
Size	**3**	**4**	**5**	**6**	**6X**
Shoulder 3[a]					
Back width 4[a]					
Chest width 12[a]					
Full back body width 6[a]					
Full front body width 13[a]					
Back waist width 7[a]					
Front waist width 14[a]					
Back neck 2[a]					
Front neck 10[a]					
Grade Guide for Bodice Width					
Size		**3–4**	**4–5**	**5–6**	**6–6X**
Shoulder					
Back width					
Chest width					
Full back body width					
Full front body width					
Back waist width					
Front waist width					
Back neck					
Front neck					

Notes: Measurements are in inches.

[a]Numbers refer to measurements in Figure 10.1.

Table 10.14 Garment Specifications and Grade Guide for Bodice Length

Measurements From Specification Table 10.11					
Size	3	4	5	6	6X
Center back waist length 1[a]					
Center front waist length 9[a]					
Back armhole depth 5[a]					
Front armhole depth 11[a]					
Grade Guide for Length Dimensions					
Size		3–4	4–5	5–6	6–6X
Center back waist length					
Center front waist length					
Back armhole depth					

Notes: Measurements are in inches.

[a]Numbers refer to measurements in Figure 10.1.

Table 10.15 Garment Specifications and Grade Guide for Sleeve

Measurements From Specification Table 10.11					
Size	3	4	5	6	6X
Overarm length 16[a]					
Underarm length 17[a]					
Biceps girth 18[a]					
Wrist girth 19[a]					
Grade Guide for Sleeve					
Size		3–4	4–5	5–6	6–6X
Overarm length					
Underarm length					
Biceps girth					
Wrist girth					

Notes: Measurements are in inches.

[a]Numbers refer to measurements in Figure 10.1.

Table 10.16 Garment Specifications and Grade Guide for Pant

Measurements From Specification Table 10.11					
Size	3	4	5	6	6X
Waist girth 7 + 14[a]					
Hip girth 8 + 15[a]					
Pants back rise 20[a]					
Pants front rise 21[a]					
Outer leg seam 22[a]					
Inseam 23[a]					
Knee circumference 26[a]					
Ankle circumference 27[a]					
Grade Guide for Pant					
Size		3–4	4–5	5–6	6–6X
Waist girth					
Hip girth					
Pants back rise					
Pants front rise					
Outer leg seam					
Inseam					
Knee circumference					
Ankle circumference					

Notes: Crotch level grade equals the hip grade plus one quarter of the hip grade at the cardinal point of intersection of inseam and crotch seam. The actual change in the crotch area is one quarter the hip grade. Bottom leg grade depends upon the style of the pants. Measurements are in inches.

■**Table 10.17** Grade Guide for Writing Grade Rules for Children's Sizes 3 to 6X Halfpatterns

Measurements From Specification Table 10.11				
Sizes	3–4	4–5	5–6	6–6X
Full body cross grade at chest				
Full body cross grade at waist				
Full body cross grade at hips				
Cross shoulder grade				
Shoulder length grade				
Neck width grade				
Armhole width grade				
Center front and center back length grades				
Armhole depth (length) grade				
Neck grade				
Neck length grade				
Overarm length grade				
Underarm length grade				
Bicep grade				
Wrist grade				
Pants front and back rise				
Outer leg length				
Inseam length				
Thigh grade				
Knee grade				
Ankle grade				

Notes: Crotch level grade equals hip grade plus one-quarter of the hip grade. Grade Rule Sheet.

Table 10.18 Grade Rule Table: Children's Garment Sizes 3 to 6X

Pattern Piece:
Unit: Inches   **Denominator:** 1/32
Size Range: Children's 3 to 6X
Master Size: Size 5
Grade Rules:
Notes:

Size	Rule		Rule		Rule		Rule		Rule		Rule	
	X	Y	X	Y	X	Y	X	Y	X	Y	X	Y
3												
4												
5	0	0	0	0	0	0	0	0	0	0	0	0
6												
6X												

Size	Rule		Rule		Rule		Rule		Rule		Rule	
	X	Y	X	Y	X	Y	X	Y	X	Y	X	Y
3												
4												
5	0	0	0	0	0	0	0	0	0	0	0	0
6												
6X												

Size	Rule		Rule		Rule		Rule		Rule		Rule	
	X	Y	X	Y	X	Y	X	Y	X	Y	X	Y
3												
4												
5	0	0	0	0	0	0	0	0	0	0	0	0
6												
6X												

11

Alphanumeric Grading

from Specifications

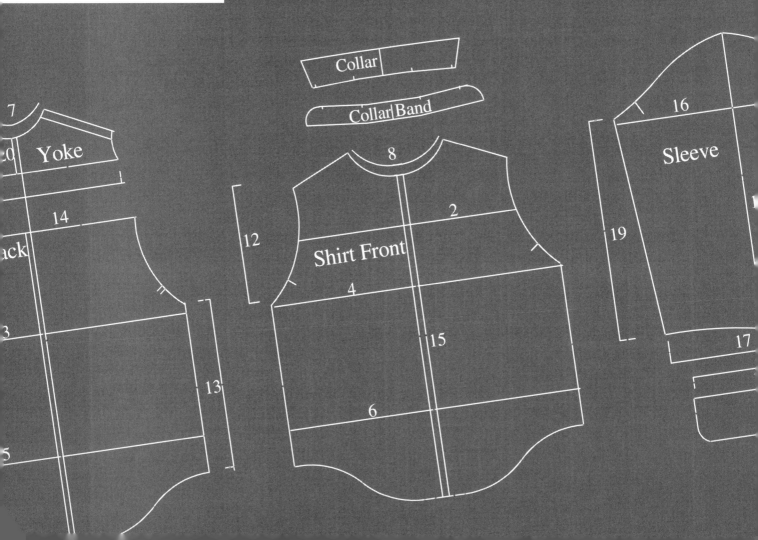

Introduction

An efficient, cost-effective size range for a garment should consist of as few sizes as possible, yet still provide a good fit for the target market. Smaller size ranges allow a manufacturer to build greater stock in each size without increasing the total stock keeping units (SKUs). This increases the efficiency of production management and distribution, as well as the ability to supply retailers with requested merchandise.

Close-fitting garments require a wide size range, in which there is a difference of 1 inch, 1 1/2 inches, or 2 inches between the total circumference of adjacent sizes, whereas loose-fitting garments require fewer sizes. Examples of wide size ranges are PS 42-70 with sizes 6 to 22 (Appendix A), ASTM D 5586 with sizes 6 to 22 (Appendix B), and ASTM D 5585 with sizes 2 to 20 (Appendix C). A full size run of these ranges would include nine or ten sizes. However, a full size run for loose-fitting garments could be collapsed into a range of five sizes (extra small, small, medium, large, and extra large) that still remains a satisfactory fit for the same population. For very loose fitting garments a three-size range of small, medium, and large is feasible. The alphanumeric size nomenclature for the collapsed size range consists of letters or a combination of letters and numbers.

ASTM D 5585 Standard Table of Body Measurements for Adult Female Misses Figure Type, Sizes 2-20 (Appendix C) is used to illustrate the procedure for collapsing a numerical size range. The ten numeric sizes are collapsed to three sizes, small, medium, and large.

DEVELOPING AN ALPHANUMERIC GRADE GUIDE FROM A NUMERICAL GRADE GUIDE

Step 1: Specify Sizes to Collapse Based on Specifications, Grade Guide, and Grade Distribution in Half-Pattern

The numerical sizes to include in each of the alphanumeric sizes small, medium, and large is a decision made by the manufacturer. For the purpose of illustrating the development of an alphanumeric grade guide from a numerical grade guide, sizes 2, 4, and 6 make up size small; sizes 8, 10, 12, and 14 are included in size medium; and sizes 16, 18, and 20 are in size large. Measurement information for upper body dimensions from Table C.1 (Appendix C) are given in Table 11.1.

Table 11.2 contains the numerical differences between sizes (grade guide) for each of the body areas, and Figure 11.1 shows the distributions of the grades. Table 11.3 contains grades for a half-pattern that was developed by dividing girth grades by 4, width grades by 2, and by calculating grades for neck width and length and for armscye width. Review Chapter 10 for calculating grades and distributing the grades in half-patterns.

Step 2: Collapsing Sizes

When collapsing numerical sizes into a smaller number of alphanumeric sizes, the garments must provide an acceptable fit for all sizes in the target market. Customers who normally purchase sizes 2, 4, or 6 will find their fit in size small. However, since the garment must be large enough for size 6 customers, women who wear size 2 and 4 will find more ease in a size small garment than size 6 women will. Numerical sizes 8, 10, 12, and 14 are included in size medium. Size medium garments must fit size 14 customers, so smaller customers will find more fitting ease in a size medium garment. Size large includes numerical sizes 16, 18, and 20 and must be large enough for size 20 customers, which results in greater ease for size 16 cus-

tomers. Alphanumeric sized garments are very loose fitting, so the extra ease experienced by customers in the low end of the size range may be considered styling ease and have a negligible effect on customer satisfaction.

Garment specifications for the three-size range of small, medium, and large are the same as the specifications for the *largest* numeric size in each range, that is, size 6 for small; size 14 for medium; and size 20 for large.

Table 11.4 is an example of collapsing the shoulder grades of the numerical sizes from size small to size medium and from size medium to size large. Notice that the grades between sizes 2 and 4 and 4 and 6 in Table 11.3 are not included in Table 11.4 or in Table 11.5. Those grades are disregarded because the size small garment must have the dimensions of a numerical size 6.

Once the concept of summation of the increments is understood, the grader may use a simplified shortcut to determine the amount of the grade from the Size Specifications (Table 11.1). The shortcut to determine the grade increment involves subtracting the smallest numeric measurement from the largest numeric measurement. For example, the shoulder length for the size 6 of 5 1/16 inches is subtracted from the size 14 shoulder length of 5 7/16 inches to equal 3/8 inch (5 7/16″ − 5 1/16″ = 6/16″ = 3/8″). This is the same as the number seen in Table 11.4 for the small to medium shoulder length grade. When size specifications are used to collapse grades, the divisions of girth and width grades, the calculations of the neck width and length grades, and the calculation of the armscye width grades must be made. See Chapter 10, Table 10.6 and 10.7 for calculations.

Step 3: Analysis of Collapsed Grades

The decision to collapse the grades in the above example results in a total circumference 5-inch grade from small to medium and a 5 1/2-inch grade from medium to large. The last column in Table 11.5 shows the difference in the two total circumference grades.

The differences are larger in the length grades than in the width grades, because length grades are standard and four sizes were collapsed into size medium, whereas only three sizes were collapsed into size large. To simplify the grading process, a manufacturer might choose to use only one total circumference grade.

Grading across the sizes with a 5-inch grade would reduce the dimensions of the size large, whereas a 5 1/2-inch grade would reduce the dimensions of the size small. A thorough analysis of the collapsed grades is necessary to determine the most efficient grading system.

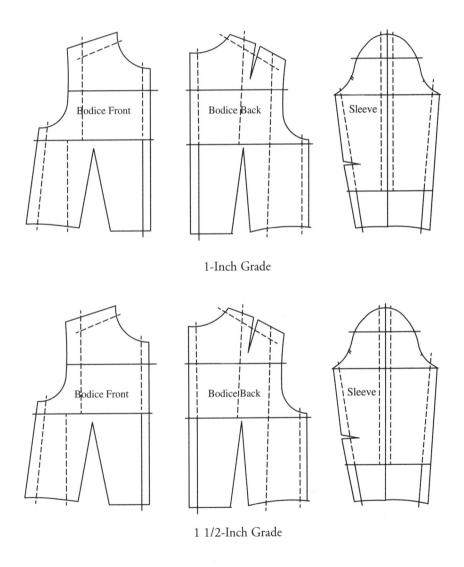

Figure 11.1 Grade Distributions for Bodice and Sleeve

PATTERN GRADING

SUMMARY

The relaxed fit of many garments allows manufacturers to reduce the number of sizes in a product line. Collapsing the number of sizes required to fit the target population increases the efficiency of production. Depending upon the style of the garment and the intended target market, production of a three-to-five size range may be adequate. Collapsed size ranges are identified by letters or a combination of letters and numbers to indicate the size and are referred to as *alphanumeric sizing*. Three size ranges usually include small (S), medium (M), and large (L). Five size ranges usually include extra xmall (XS), and extra large (XL) as well as S, M, and L.

Each garment in an alphanumeric size must fit the largest consumer in the specified size. In the example given in this chapter, a garment graded to fit a small (sizes 2–6) must fit the size 6 while a medium (sizes 8–14) must fit the size 14. The method of grading is the same as used in numeric grading, but the grade encompasses the changes for all sizes between the upper ends of the alphanumeric sizes. Therefore, grading from a small to a medium is the same as grading from a size 6 to a 14 in a numeric size range. Consumers who fall between these sizes must choose the size that best fits them. Alphanumeric sizing systems can be used successfully only on garments designed to be very loose fitting; otherwise, the style sense would not be maintained for all customers.

EXERCISES

Grading Men's Shirt Into Alphanumeric Sizes Small, Medium, Large, and Extra Large

Table 11.6 provides specifications for the dimensions for men's dress shirt sizes 14 to 17 1/2. Specifications are based on Vogue Pattern 4004 and on Hanford's (1980) instructions for grading mens wear and a 2-inch grade across all sizes. The men's shirt size nomenclature represents the neck size. Figure 11.2 shows the measurement locations on the pattern pieces that correspond to the body areas listed in the specifications.

Step 1: Complete Grade Guide

Fill in Table 11.7 with incremental differences between sizes to complete a grade guide for the shirt.

Step 2: Distribution of Grades for Half-Pattern

Determine the distributions of total grades in Table 11.8. Make appropriate divisions for girth and width grades for half-patterns. Calculate neck and armscye grades.

Step 3: Collapse Sizes

Collapse the sizes to show incremental differences between alphanumeric sizes small, medium, large, and extra large in Table 11.9. Sizes 14 and 14 1/2 should be collapsed into size small; sizes 15 and 15 1/2 into size medium; sizes 16 and 16 1/2 into size large; and sizes 17 and 17 1/2 into size extra large. The dimensions of each alpha numeric size (small, medium, large, and extra large) must fit the largest consumers in that size grouping.

Step 4: Create Grade Rule Table

From the collapsed incremental grade guide for the half-pattern (Table 11.9), write grade rules in Table 11.10 for grading sizes small, large, and extra large from the master size medium. To facilitate the development of the grade rule table, draw variable (broken) and standard (solid) grade lines on all pattern pieces in Figure 11.3 and label each with the appropriate half-pattern grade from Table 11.8. Number the cardinal points in the conventional clockwise direction from the 0,0 point of reference on the Cartesian graph beginning with the shirt front. Next number the cardi-

nal points on the shirt yoke and back and then the sleeve, cuff, and collars. Reassign grade rule numbers whenever possible to minimize the number of grade rules. The grade rules for all sizes at each cardinal point are determined relative to size medium.

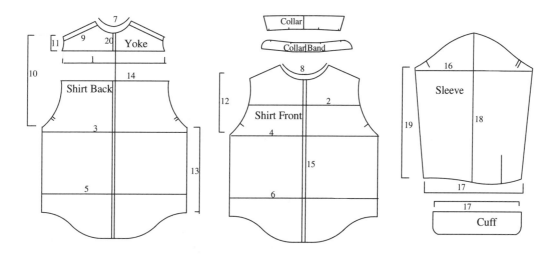

Figure 11.2 Measurement Locations for Men's Shirt

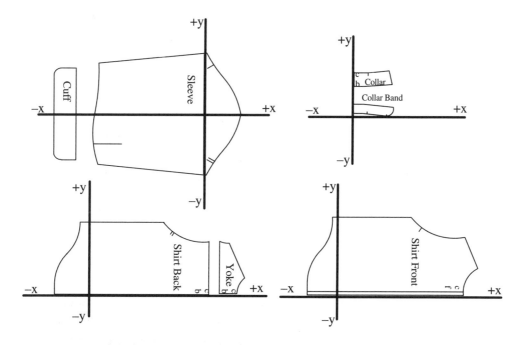

Figure 11.3 Orientation for Shirt Pattern Pieces

REFERENCE

Handford, J. (1980). *Professional pattern grading for women's, men's and children's apparel.* Redondo Beach, CA: Plycon Press.

Table 11.1 Upper Body Measurements From Table C.1 ASTM Standard for Misses Sizes 2 to 20

Size	2	4	6	8	10	12	14	16	18	20
1. Bust	32	33	34	35	36	37 1/2	39	40 1/2	42 1/2	43 1/2
2. Waist	24	25	26	27	28	29 1/2	31	32 1/2	34 1/2	36 1/2
6. Neck base	13 1/2	13 3/4	14	14 1/4	14 1/2	14 7/8	15 1/4	15 5/8	16 1/8	16 5/8
7. Armscye[a]	13 3/4	14 1/4	14 3/4	15 1/4	15 3/4	16 3/8	17	17 5/8	18 3/8	19 1/8
8. Upper arm[b]	10	10 1/4	10 1/2	10 3/4	11	11 3/8	11 3/4	12 1/8	12 5/8	13 1/8
10. Wrist	5 5/8	5 3/4	5 7/8	6	6 1/8	6 1/4	6 3/8	6 1/2	6 5/8	6 3/4
26. Front waist length	13 1/2	13 3/4	14	14 1/4	14 1/2	14 3/4	15	15 1/4	15 1/2	15 3/4
27. Back waist length	15 1/2	15 3/4	16	16 1/4	16 1/2	16 3/4	17	17 1/4	17 1/2	17 3/4
30. Back width	13 7/8	14 1/8	14 3/8	14 5/8	14 7/8	15 1/4	15 5/8	16	16 1/2	17
31. Chest width	12 7/8	13 1/8	13 3/8	13 5/8	13 7/8	14 1/4	14 5/8	15	15 1/2	16
32. Shoulder length	4 15/16	5	5 1/16	5 1/8	5 3/16	5 5/16	5 7/16	5 9/16	5 .31/4	5 15/16
34. Overarm length	22 15/16	23 1/8	23 5/16	23 1/2	23 11/16	23 7/8	24 1/16	24 1/4	24 7/16	24 5/8
35. Shoulder to elbow	13 1/4	13 3/8	13 1/2	13 5/8	13 3/4	13 7/8	14	14 1/8	14 1/4	14 3/8
39. Armscye depth	7 1/8	7 1/4	7 3/8	7 1/2	7 5/8	7 3/4	7 7/8	8	8 1/8	8 1/4

Note: Measurements are in inches.

[a]Armscye grade for a 1-inch grade is decreased by 1/2 inch in this chart instead of 3/8 inch in ASTM D 5585 because the cross bust distribution cannot be made with a 3/8 inch grade difference.

[b]Upper arm grade for a 2-inch grade is decreased by 1/2 inch in this chart instead of 5/8 inch in ASTM D 5585 because the sleeve would be too large for armscye.

Table 11.2 Grade Guide ASTM D 5585 Misses Sizes 2 to 20 (Derived from Table 11.1)

Size	2–4	4–6	6–8	8–10	10–12	12–14	14–16	16–18	18–20
1. Bust girth	1	1	1	1	1 1/2	1 1/2	1 1/2	2	2
2. Waist girth	1	1	1	1	1 1/2	1 1/2	1 1/2	2	2
6. Neck	1/4	1/4	1/4	1/4	3/8	3/8	3/8	1/2	1/2
7. Armscye	1/2	1/2	1/2	1/2	5/8	5/8	5/8	3/4	3/4
8. Upper arm	1/4	1/4	1/4	1/4	3/8	3/8	3/8	1/2	1/2
10. Wrist	1/8	1/8	1/8	1/8	1/8	1/8	1/8	1/8	1/8
26. Front waist length	1/4	1/4	1/4	1/4	1/4	1/4	1/4	1/4	1/4
27. Back waist length	1/4	1/4	1/4	1/4	1/4	1/4	1/4	1/4	1/4
30. Bodice back width	1/4	1/4	1/4	1/4	3/8	3/8	3/8	1/2	1/2
31. Chest width	1/4	1/4	1/4	1/4	3/8	3/8	3/8	1/2	1/2
32. Shoulder length	1/16	1/16	1/16	1/16	1/8	1/8	1/8	3/16	3/16
34. Overarm length	3/16	3/16	3/16	3/16	3/16	3/16	3/16	3/16	3/16
35. Shoulder to elbow	1/8	1/8	1/8	1/8	1/8	1/8	1/8	1/8	1/8
37. Bust pt to bust pt[a]									
38. Neck to bust point[a]									
39. Armscye depth	1/8	1/8	1/8	1/8	1/8	1/8	1/8	1/8	1/8

Note: Measurements are in inches.

[a]Because a very loose fitting garment would not contain darts, the grades from bust point to bust and from the shoulder to bust point are irrelevant in an alphanumeric grading guide.

Table 11.3 Distributions of Total Grade in Half-Pattern

Size	2–4	4–6	6–8	8–10	10–12	12–14	14–16	16–18	18–20
Girth Grades Divided by 4 to Derive Half-Pattern Grades									
1. Cross bust	1/4	1/4	1/4	1/4	3/8	3/8	3/8	1/2	1/2
2. Cross waist	1/4	1/4	1/4	1/4	3/8	3/8	3/8	1/2	1/2
6. Neck	1/16	1/16	1/16	1/16	3/32	3/32	3/32	1/8	1/8
Width Grades Divided by 2									
30. Bodice back width	1/8	1/8	1/8	1/8	3/16	3/16	3/16	1/4	1/4
31. Bodice front width	1/8	1/8	1/8	1/8	3/16	3/16	3/16	1/4	1/4
Length and Girth Grades Not Divided									
8. Upper arm	1/4	1/4	1/4	1/4	3/8	3/8	3/8	1/2	1/2
10. Waist	1/8	1/8	1/8	1/8	1/8	1/8	1/8	1/8	1/8
26. Front waist length	1/4	1/4	1/4	1/4	1/4	1/4	1/4	1/4	1/4
27. Back waist length	1/4	1/4	1/4	1/4	1/4	1/4	1/4	1/4	1/4
32. Shoulder length	1/16	1/16	1/16	1/16	1/8	1/8	1/8	3/16	3/16
34. Overarm length	3/16	3/16	3/16	3/16	3/16	3/16	3/16	3/16	3/16
35. Shoulder to elbow	1/8	1/8	1/8	1/8	1/8	1/8	1/8	1/8	1/8
39. Armscye depth	1/8	1/8	1/8	1/8	1/8	1/8	1/8	1/8	1/8
Calculated Grades									
Neck width	1/16	1/16	1/16	1/16	1/16	1/16	1/16	1/16	1/16
Neck length	0	0	0	0	1/32	1/32	1/32	1/16	1/16
Armscye width	1/8	1/8	1/8	1/8	3/16	3/16	3/16	1/4	1/4

Note: Measurements are in inches.

■Table 11.4 Collapsed Grades for Misses Alphanumeric Sizes Small, Medium, and Large

Shoulder length	Small to Medium Collapsing Sizes 6 to 14		Medium to Large Collapsing Sizes 14 to 20	
	Size	Amount	Size	Amount
	6 to 8	1/16	14 to 16	1/8
	8 to 10	1/16	16 to 18	3/16
	10 to 12	1/8	18 to 20	3/16
	12 to 14	1/8		
Total grade		3/8		1/2

Note: Measurements are in inches.

Table 11.5 Grades Guide for Misses Sizes Small, Medium, and Large

Size	Small	Medium[a]	Large	Differences in Cross Body Grades
	Sizes 2–6 5-inch Grade	Sizes 8–14	Sizes 16–20 5 1/2 -inch Grade	
Cross bust/waist	1 1/4	**0**	1 3/8	1/8
Cross shoulder	5/8	**0**	11/16	1/16
Shoulder length	3/8	**0**	1/2	1/8
Neck girth	5/16	**0**	11/32	1/32
Neck width	1/4	**0**	3/16	1/16
Neck length	1/16	**0**	5/32	3/32
Armscye width	5/8	**0**	11/16	1/16
Overarm length	3/4	**0**	9/16	3/16
Shoulder to Elbow	1/2	**0**	3/8	1/8
Armscye depth	1/2	**0**	3/8	1/8

Note: Measurements are in inches.

[a]Medium is the master size.

Table 11.6 Men's Dress Shirt Sizes 14 to 17 1/2

Size	14	14 1/2	15	15 1/2	16	16 1/2	17	17 1/2
1. Back shoulder width	17 1/4	17 3/4	18 1/4	18 3/4	19 1/4	19 3/4	20 1/4	20 3/4
2. Chest width	14 3/4	15 1/4	15 3/4	16 1/4	16 3/4	17 1/4	17 3/4	18 1/4
3. Back width (side seam to side seam)	23 1/2	24 1/2	25 1/2	26 1/2	27 1/2	28 1/2	29 1/2	30 1/2
4. Front width (side seam to side seam)	19 1/4	20 1/4	21 1/4	22 1/4	23 1/4	24 1/4	25 1/4	26 1/4
5. Back hip width	23 1/4	24 1/4	25 1/4	26 1/4	27 1/4	28 1/4	29 1/4	30 1/4
6. Front hip width	19	20	21	22	23	24	25	26
7. Back neck measurement	8	8 1/4	8 1/2	8 3/4	9	9 1/4	9 1/2	9 3/4
8. Front neck measurement	7 7/8	8 1/8	8 3/8	8 5/8	8 7/8	9 1/8	9 3/8	9 5/8
9. Shoulder length	5 5/8	5 13/16	6	6 3/16	6 3/8	6 9/16	6 3/4	6 15/16
10. Back armhole depth (including yoke)	7 7/8	8 1/16	8 1/4	8 7/16	8 5/8	8 13/16	9	9 3/16
11. Yoke length at armhole	1 1/8	1 1/4	1 3/8	1 1/2	1 5/8	1 3/4	1 7/8	2
12. Front armhole depth (center sleeve point)	7 7/8	7 9/16	7 3/4	7 15/16	8 1/8	8 5/16	8 1/2	8 11/16
13. Side seam (armhole to hem)	15 5/8	15 11/16	15 3/4	15 13/16	15 7/8	15 15/16	16	16 1/16
14. Center back length (including yoke)	29	29 1/4	29 1/2	29 3/4	30	30 1/4	30 1/2	30 3/4
15. Center front length	27	27 1/4	27 1/2	27 3/4	28	28 1/4	28 1/2	28 3/4
16. Biceps circumference	15 5/8	16 1/4	16 7/8	17 1/2	18 1/8	18 3/4	19 3/8	20
17. Wrist circumference	8	8 1/4	8 1/2	8 3/4	9	9 1/4	9 1/2	9 3/4
18. Overarm length	23 5/16	23 1/2	23 11/16	23 7/8	24 1/16	24 1/4	24 7/16	24 5/8
19. Underarm length[a]	19 1/2	19 1/2	19 1/2	19 1/2	19 1/2	19 1/2	19 1/2	19 1/2
20. Yoke length at center back	1 1/4	1 3/8	1 1/2	1 5/8	1 3/4	1 7/8	2	2 1/8

[a]Each sleeve size has alteration lines for 32-, 33-, 34-, and 35-inch lengths.

Note: Pattern measurements include ease allowances but not seam allowances. Measurements are in inches.

Source: Adapted from *Professional Pattern Grading for Women's, Men's, and Children's Apparel.*

Table 11.7 Incremental Grade Guide for Men's Shirt Sizes 14 to 17 1/2

Size	14 to 14 1/2	14 1/2 to 15	15 to 15 1/2	15 1/2 to 16	16 to 16 1/2	16 1/2 to 17	17 to 17 1/2
Cross shoulder width							
Shoulder lenth							
Neck width							
Cross body width							
Armhole width							
Center front length							
Center back length (including yoke)							
Yoke length at center back							
Front armhole length							
Back armhole length (including yoke)							
Side seam length							
Neck length							
Overarm length							
Underarm length							
Wrist circumference							
Bicep circumference							

Note: Measurements are in inches.

Table 11.8 Distributions of Total Grades in Half-Pattern

Size	14 to 14 1/2	14 1/2 to 15	15 to 15 1/2	15 1/2 to 16	16 to 16 1/2	16 1/2 to 17	17 to 17 1/2
Width Grades Divided by 2							
Back shoulder width							
Chest width							
Back width (side seam to side seam)							
Front width (side seam to side seam)							
Back hip width							
Front hip width							
Back neck measurement							
Front neck measurement							
Length and Girth Grade Not Divided							
Shoulder length							
Back armscye depth (including yoke from center sleeve point)							
Yoke length at armscye							
Front armscye depth							
Side seam (armscye to hem)							
Center back length (including yoke)							
Center front length							
Biceps girth							
Wrist girth							
Overarm length[a]							
Underarm length[a]							
Yoke length at center back							
Calculated Grades							
Neck width							
Neck length							
Armscye width							

[a]Each sleeve size has alteration lines for 32-, 33-, 34-, and 35-inch lengths.

Table 11.9 Collapsed Grade Distributions for Half-Patterns

Size	Small (14–14 1/2) to Medium (15–15 1/2)	Medium (15–15 1/2) to Large (16–16 1/2)	Large (16–16 1/2) to Extra Large (17–17 1/2)
Width Grades			
Back shoulder width			
Chest width			
Back width (side seam to side seam)			
Front width (side seam to side seam)			
Back hip width			
Front hip width			
Back neck measurement			
Front neck measurement			
Length and Girth Grade			
Shoulder length			
Back armscye depth (including yoke from center sleeve point)			
Yoke length at armscye			
Front armscye depth			
Side seam (armscye to hem)			
Center back length (including yoke)			
Center front length			
Biceps girth			
Wrist girth			
Overarm length[a]			
Underarm length[a]			
Yoke length at center back			
Calculated Grades			
Neck width			
Neck length			
Armscye width			

[a]Each sleeve size has alteration lines for 32″, 33″, 34″, and 35″ lengths.

Table 11.10 Grade Rule Table: Men's Shirt Sizes S to XL

Pattern Piece:
Units: Inches   **Denominator:** 1/32
Size Range: Men's S, M, L, XL
Master size: Men's M
Grade Rules:

Size	Rule		Rule		Rule		Rule		Rule		Rule	
	X	Y	X	Y	X	Y	X	Y	X	Y	X	Y
S												
M	0	0	0	0	0	0	0	0	0	0	0	0
L												
XL												

Size	Rule		Rule		Rule		Rule		Rule		Rule	
	X	Y	X	Y	X	Y	X	Y	X	Y	X	Y
S												
M	0	0	0	0	0	0	0	0	0	0	0	0
L												
XL												

Size	Rule		Rule		Rule		Rule		Rule		Rule	
	X	Y	X	Y	X	Y	X	Y	X	Y	X	Y
S												
M	0	0	0	0	0	0	0	0	0	0	0	0
L												
XL												

NOTES

Appendix A

Rationale for a Simplified Grading System Based on PS 42-70 Grade Guide

INTRODUCTION

The PS 42-70 Grade Guide included in the PS 42-70 *Voluntary Product Standard: Body Measurements for Sizing of Women's Pattern and Apparel* (U.S. Department of Commerce, 1971). The authors' simplified incremental grading system, in which the front and back body grade alike, is based upon the PS 42-70 Grade Guide and was derived after developing the complex system directly from the grade guide. Table A.1 lists the measurements in PS 42-70 Size Specifications and Table A.2 is the Grade Guide contained in the same document. Table A.3 contains grades from the PS 42-70 Grade Guide relative to the bodice and sleeve, and the grades for the skirt and pant are in Table A.4. The body locations are numbered in Tables A.3 and A.4 and correspond to numbered body locations in Figure A.1.

As discussed in Chapter 1, a large number of anthropometric survey measurements were necessary because of the complexity of the adult female body. In the PS 42-70 Grade Guide the front and back of the body change differently between sizes in several areas. The arc grades for the bust front and waist front are greater than half the girth grade; therefore, the back of the body in those areas change less (Table A.3). The back body width between the mid-armscyes grades differently than the front body between the armscyes.

Taylor and Shoben (1986) and Cooklin (1994) emphasize that a three-dimensional (complex) grading system results when a grade guide developed from survey data is followed. Not only are the back and the front of garments graded differently in a complex sys-

tem, but dart size may change to increase or decrease garment width and contour. Using this type of a system complicates the grading process; therefore, most grading systems have been simplified. However, Taylor and Shoben, and Cooklin agree that with each simplification, integrity is lost in the fit of the graded sizes. Even though the differences in the changes between the back and front of the body are small, each time the master pattern is graded to another size by a simplified system, those differences are additive. The wider the size range, the poorer the fit will be in the extreme sizes. The resulting problems of fit are more evident in close-fitting than in loose-fitting garments.

The complex grading system derived directly from the PS 42-70 data was considered before the PS 42-70 grading system was simplified. Therefore, the following complex system is the first step in the rationale for the authors' simplified system.

PS 42-70 COMPLEX GRADING SYSTEM

Grades were taken either directly from the PS 42-70 Grade Guide or were calculated based on grade guide information. The development of the system is discussed in two parts, the upper body (bodice front, bodice back, and sleeve) and the lower body (skirt and pant).

Step 1: Grades Specified in PS 42-70 Grade Guide for Upper Body
Bodice Front

The bust, waist, and hip girth grades indicate the sizes that require a 1-inch, a 1 1/2-inch, or a 2-inch grade (Table A.2). The bodice front length grades listed in the PS 42-70 Grade Guide that can be applied directly to the half-pattern for a 1-inch, a 1 1/2-inch, and a 2-inch grade are indicated in Figure A.2. The cross chest

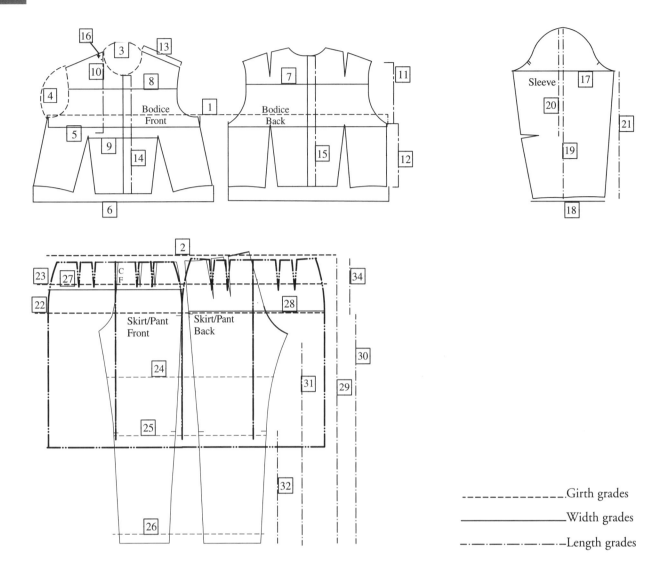

Figure A.1 Location of Body Grades

and the arc grades that are used for the cross bust and cross waist grades in the Grade Guide were divided by 2 for the half-pattern. Grades that had to be calculated are identified by asterisks.

Figure A.2 shows the neck to bust point grade distributions taken directly from the PS 42-70 Grade Guide. It is the only length grade on the bodice that is

variable, and it will be discussed with the grading of the darts.

Bodice Back

Figure A.3 illustrates the grades from PS 42-70 that can be applied to the bodice back. Back cross bust and cross waist grades were derived by subtracting the front cross grades from the girth grades for the same

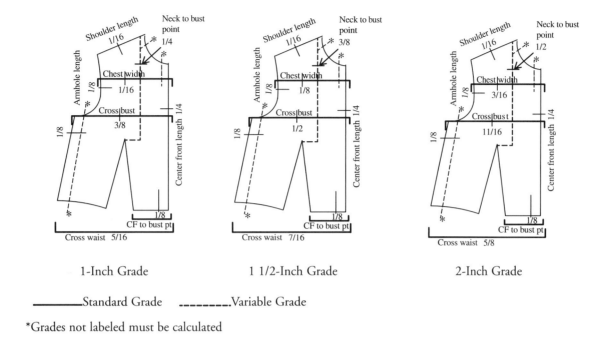

1-Inch Grade   1 1/2-Inch Grade   2-Inch Grade

————Standard Grade   ----------Variable Grade

*Grades not labeled must be calculated

Figure A.2 Grade Distributions Specified in PS 42-70 Grade Guide for Bodice Front

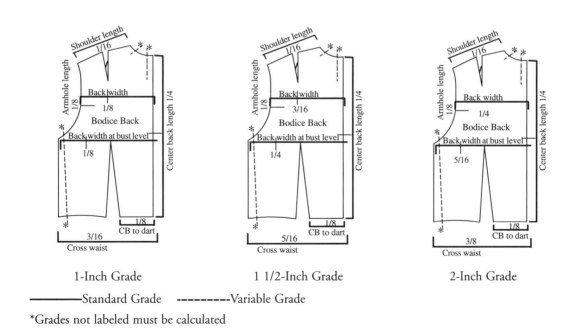

1-Inch Grade   1 1/2-Inch Grade   2-Inch Grade

————Standard Grade   ----------Variable Grade

*Grades not labeled must be calculated

Figure A.3 Grade Distributions Specified in PS 42-70 Grade Guide for Bodice Back

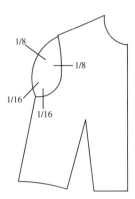

Armscye girth 3/8
Armscye length 1/8
Armscye width 1/16

1-Inch Grade

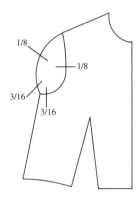

Armscye girth 5/8
Armscye length 1/8
Armscye width 3/16

1 1/2-Inch Grade

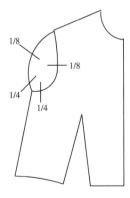

Armscye girth 3/4
Armscye length 1/8
Armscye width 1/4

2-Inch Grade

Figure A.4 Calculated Armscye Width Grade

body area. The neck to bust point grade on the bodice front is not needed on the back.

Comparison of Bodice Front and Bodice Back Cross Grades

The cross bust and waist grades are converted to half-pattern grades from the girth and arc grades in PS 42-70. The obvious differences between the bodice front and the bodice back are the waist, bust, and back/chest cross grades. The front grades are greater at the waist and bust levels, but less in the chest width than in the bodice back width.

Comparison of Bodice Front and Bodice Back Length Grades

The length grades in most areas are the same for the bodice front and back and are standard for the 1-, the 1 1/2-, and the 2-inch grades. The neck to bust length is not applicable to the bodice back. The shoulder length grade of 1/16 inch is the same for both front and back and is standard in all three total circumference grades.

Step 2: Calculated Grades
Armscye Width Grade

The armscye width grade can be calculated easily from the armscye girth and armscye length grades listed in the Grade Guide (Figure A.4). The armscye length changes by 1/8 inch; that is true for both the back and front and is standard for the 1-, the 1 1/2-, and the 2-inch grades. For each armscye girth grade, 1/4 inch (1/8" in back armscye length and 1/8" in front armscye length) can be subtracted and the remainder divided between the back and front underarm area to change the armscye width. For example, for a 1 1/2-inch grade the total armscye girth change is 5/8 inch; 5/8 inch minus 1/4 inch equals 3/8 inch. The remaining 3/8 inch is divided by 2 resulting in 3/16 inch in the back armscye width and 3/16 inch in the front.

Neck Grades

The distribution of the neck width and length grades is more complicated and the rationale is less conclusive. Taylor and Shoben (1986) state that the neck front increases/decreases more than the neck back and that when a high neck block is used for a large size range, the grade distribution becomes more critical. They also illustrate the front neck as having both length and width changes, whereas, the neck back changes only in width. However, the PS 42-70 Grade Guide indicates that the back and front necklines grade similarly to maintain shoulder slope and neckline shape. Additional research is needed to make a solid recommendation for the neck grades.

In the PS 42-70 Grade Guide the neck girth grade incorporates the neck width and length grades. To grade a half-pattern, one-fourth of the girth grade is distributed in the neck area; a portion is in the width and the remainder is in the length. The total half-pattern grade is 1/16 inch for the 1-inch grade, 3/32 inch for the 1 1/2-inch grade, and 1/8 inch for the 2-inch grade (Figure A.5).

Neck Width Grade

Neck width is generally calculated by subtracting the shoulder length grade from the cross shoulder grade (chest/back width between armscyes). However, in the 1-inch grade, the cross shoulder grade and the shoulder length grades are both 1/16 inch (Figure A.2); therefore, that calculation would result in no width grade in the neck. The authors made the decision to grade the neck width in the 1-inch grade by 1/32 inch (Figure A.5).

The calculation described above was used for the 1 1/2-inch grade; the cross shoulder grade (1/8 inch) minus the shoulder length grade (1/16 inch) leaves 1/16 inch for the neck width grade. The 2-inch cross shoulder grade (3/16 inch) minus the shoulder length grade (1/16 inch) results in a neck width grade of 1/8 inch. However, 1/8 inch is the total half-pattern neck grade, so nothing would be left for the neck length grade. The authors elected to use 3/32 inch for neck

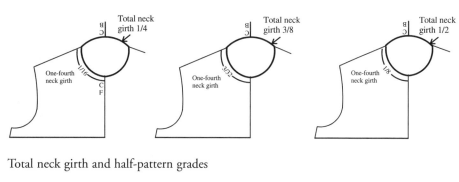

Total neck girth and half-pattern grades

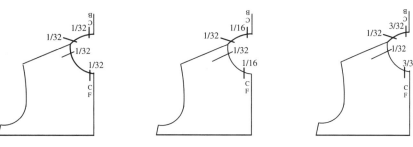

Bodice front and back neck width and length grades

1-Inch Grade   1 1/2-Inch Grade   2-Inch Grade

■ **Figure A.5** Neck Grades Rationale

width in the 2-inch grade. The neck width grades are applied to both the bodice front and the bodice back.

The neck width grade for the 1-inch and the 2-inch grades puts too much change in the cross shoulder width. This descrepancy may be compensated for in the dart grade to be discussed later.

Neck Length (Depth) Grade

The neck length grade is a simple calculation of subtracting neck width grade from the total neck grade for the half-pattern (Figure A.5). The length grade of 1/32 inch is the same for the bodice front and bodice back, and is standard for the 1-, the 1 1/2-, and the 2-inch grades.

The shoulder slope, the cross chest width, and the shoulder to bust point grades are all affected by the neck length grade. The shoulder slope degree grade is zero in the PS 42-70 Grade Guide, which means the shoulder lines in all sizes should remain parallel. The armscye length grade is a standard 1/8 inch and the side seam length is a standard 1/8 inch (Figure A.2). If the pattern is oriented on the Cartesian graph so that the 0,0 point of reference is at the center front/waistline (Figure 5.3), the shoulder/armscye point is changed by 1/4 inch (armscye length plus side seam length) along the *x* axis. The neck width plus the shoulder length grade affects the grade along the *y* axis at the shoulder/armscye point; whereas the neck width and length grades determine the neckline/shoulder point on the *x* and *y* axes (Figure A.6). Because the shoulder line changes 1/16 inch in length as the pattern is graded, the shoulder lines in the graded sizes do not remain perfectly parallel even without a neck length grade (Figure A.6a). When the neck length is included in the additive grade at the shoulder/neckline end, and the shoulder lines in the graded sizes become slightly wider apart at the neckline than at the armscye end, the shoulder lines are not parallel (Figure A.6b). Even though the shoulder lines do not remain parallel, the neck length grade of 1/32 inch is assigned to the 1-, the 1 1/2-, and the 2-inch grades to help retain the neckline shape.

Step 3: Dart Length Grade

Figure A.7 illustrates that the neck length to bust point grades are additive to include the standard 1/4-inch center front length and the neck length grade. The neck to bust point length grade in the PS 42-70 Grade Guide for a 1-inch grade is 1/4 inch, the 1 1/2-inch grade is 3/8 inch, and the 2-inch grade is 1/2 inch. However, only 1/32 inch is used in the neck length for all three total circumference grades (Figure A.5). The differences are compensated for by grading the dart length (Figure A.7).

The dart is lengthened by 1/32 inch to reduce the neck to bust point length to 1/4 inch for the 1-inch grade. The 1 1/2-inch grade neck to bust point length grade is 3/8 inch, so the dart point is lowered 3/32 inch to increase the length between the neck and bust point (Figure A.7). The 2-inch neck to bust point grade is 1/2 inch, which necessitates the dart being shortened by 7/32 inch.

Step 4: Bodice Dart Suppression Grades

Grades to create width and contour appear in the front bust dart and the back shoulder dart. The cross bust grade is greater than the cross waist for the bodice front in the 1-, 1 1/2-, and 2-inch grades, so grading through the dart take-up into the cross bust area compensates for the differences to increase the cross bust width (Figure A.7). (The decrease in the dart take-up for the 1-inch grade and the increase in the 2-inch grade helps to compensate for the change in the cross shoulder grade caused by the front neck width grade.)

The front cross waist grade is larger than the cross bust width grade on the bodice back, but that difference is compensated for by the waistline/side seam grade. However, the cross back grade between the armscyes is greater than the combined neck width and shoulder length grades (cross shoulder grade). The additional grade for the cross back is placed in the shoulder dart (Figure A.8). Figures A.7 and A.8 clearly indicate that the bodice back and front require a different set of grade rules, which creates a complex grading system.

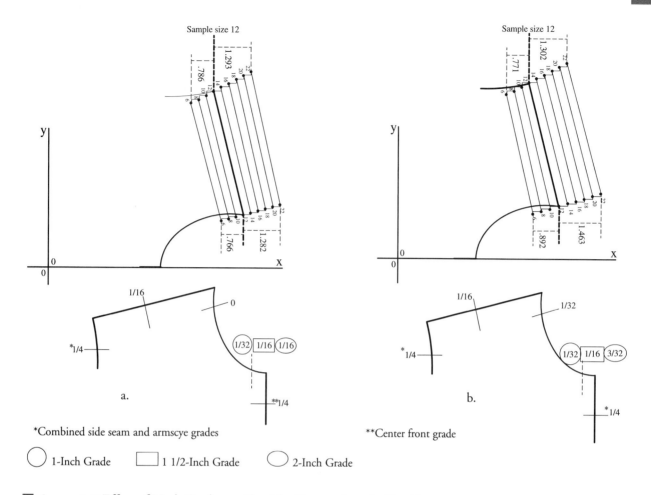

*Combined side seam and armscye grades

**Center front grade

○ 1-Inch Grade   ▭ 1 1/2-Inch Grade   ⬭ 2-Inch Grade

Figure A.6 Effect of Neck Grades on Shoulder Slope—Sample Size 12

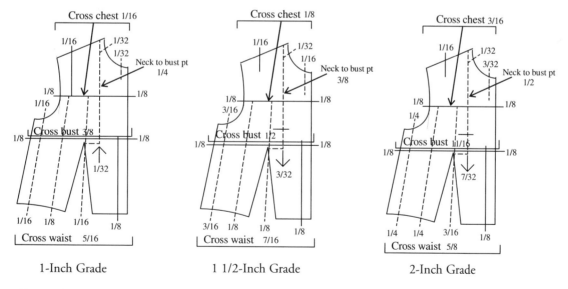

1-Inch Grade   1 1/2-Inch Grade   2-Inch Grade

Ø Lengthen or shorten bust dart to achieve Neck to Bust Point measurement.

Figure A.7 Complex Grade Distributions for Bodice Front

The areas in which the bodice back and front grade differently are illustrated in Figure A.9 for the 1-inch, the 1 1/2-inch, and the 2-inch grades.

Step 5: Complex Grading System for Sleeve Based on PS 42-70 Grade Guide

Table A.2 contains the grade increments necessary to develop a grading system for the sleeve. The grade distributions for the seam that joins the sleeve to the bodice include both length (capline) and width (upper arm) grades and must equal the total grade in the combined bodice front and back armscyes. A portion of the sleeve width distribution is placed in the sleeve capline in order to preserve the curve across the top of the sleeve (Figure A.10).

The 2-inch grade requires an additional adjustment. The upper arm grade for the 2-inch grade is 5/8 inch and the armscye girth is 3/4 inch in the PS 42-70 Grade Guide. When the front and back armscye length grades of 1/8 inch each are added to the upper arm girth grade of 5/8 inch, the resulting cap seamline of 7/8 inch is longer than the armscye girth of 3/4 inch. However, this additional 1/8 inch is necessary to accommodate the growth in the upper arm. It is added in the bias portion of the sleeve cap width— 1/16 inch to each the front and back, as shown in Figure A.10—and it must be treated as additional ease during the construction of the garment. If the graded pattern is for a loose-fitting sleeve, the additional 1/8 inch specified for the upper arm girth may possibly be eliminated without adversely affecting the fit of the

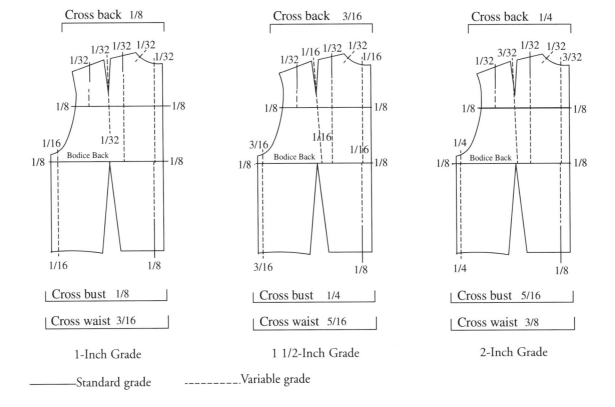

Figure A.8 Complex Grade Distributions for Bodice Back

garment. This sleeve/armscye 2-inch grade is an area that requires the pattern grader to individually evaluate each style in order to determine the best method of grading the sleeve.

The sleeve is graded 3/16 inch in length in the 1-inch, the 1 1/2-inch, and the 2-inch grades with 1/8 inch grade in the sleeve cap length to correspond with the armscye length. The other 1/16 inch is placed below the elbow. The grade for the sleeve opening at the lower edge may vary with the style of the sleeve.

Step 6: Complex Grading System for Skirt/Pant Based on PS 42-70 Grade Guide

Table A.1 contains lower body measurements taken from the PS 42-70 Table of Body Measurements for the Sizing of Women's Pattern and Apparel. Arc measurements are given for waist front, high hip front, and hip back. The difference between the arc measurements and the total girth measurements for the waist was discussed in the development of the complex grading system for the bodice. A complex grading sys-

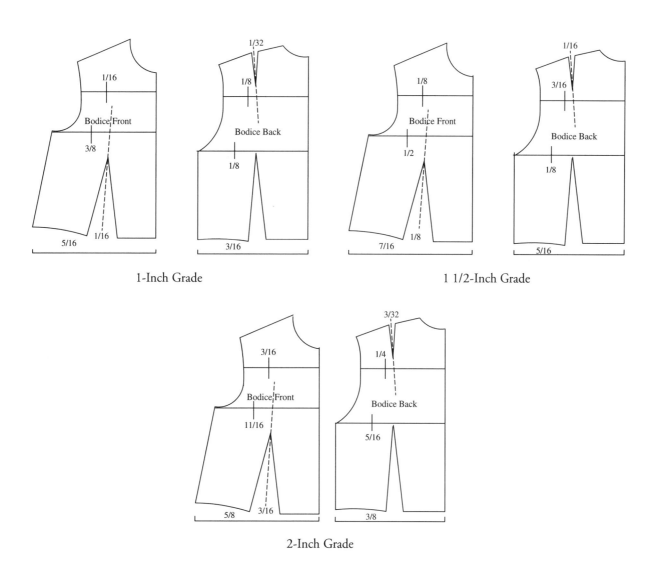

1-Inch Grade

1 1/2-Inch Grade

2-Inch Grade

Figure A.9 Differences Between Bodice Front and Back Complex Grades

tem for a skirt or pant entails grading the waist in the the same manner as the bodice. The skirt/pant front is larger than the back in waist, abdomen, and hip. Table A.4 shows grades taken from the PS 42-70 Grade Guide that are needed to develop a grading system for skirts and pants. The pant waist and hips are graded in width in the same manner as the skirt. However, the body girth at the crotch level requires an additional grade for the crotch width.

The PS 42-70 tables contain a vertical trunk measurement, but not a measurement that can be used directly to determine the crotch width grade. Price and Zamkoff (1996) and Handford (1980) use a standard 1/8 inch for both front and back crotch width grades. Taylor and Shoben (1986) use one-half of the cross hip grade for the back and for the front crotch width grade while Scheier (1974) recommends one-fourth of the cross hip grade for both back and front. Pattern drafting instructions generally specify that the back crotch width is one-half the hip width (for a half-pattern) and the front crotch width is one-fourth of the hip width (Armstrong, 1995). The authors elected to calculate the crotch width grade based upon the hip

width as cited by Scheier and Taylor, and Shoben, but to use the pattern drafting instructions as the basis for the calculation. Therefore, the back crotch grade is one-half of the hip width grade and the front crotch grade is one-fourth of the hip width grade (Figures A.11 and A12). The leg width grades are determined by the PS 42-70 Grade Guide, but will vary with the style of the pant.

SIMPLIFIED GRADING SYSTEM BASED ON PS 42-70 GRADE GUIDE
Step 1: Cross Grades for Half-Patterns

In a simplified grading system the total change in measurements is equally distributed around the body. Therefore, the front and back of a garment grade by the same increments. This allows the pattern grader to use only one set of grade rules for both the front and back of most garments.

Modifications of the complex grading system based on the PS 42-70 Grade Guide were made in the grade distribution for the 1-inch, the 1 1/2-inch, and the 2-

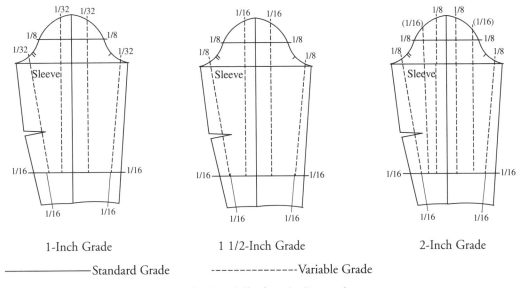

Numbers in parentheses indicate grades that differ from bodice grades.

■ Figure A.10 Complex Grade Distributions for Sleeve

inch grades. The cross bust and cross waist grades for the front and back were altered to equal a quarter of the girth grades so the bodice front and back are graded the same—1/4 inch for 1-inch grade; 3/8 inch for 1 1/2-inch grade; and 1/2 inch for 2-inch grade (Figure A.13). The chest width and the back width for each of the grades also grade alike and equal one-half of the cross bust grade.

Step 2: Modifications of a Complex Grade Guide to a Simplified Grade Guide

The 1-inch grade was modified in the underarm width, the armscye girth, and the neck circumference; the 1 1/2-inch grade was modified in the shoulder length and the neck circumference; and the 2-inch grade was modified in the shoulder length, the upper arm girth (upper arm width), and the neck circumference (Figure A.13). The shoulder/neck to bust point grade was modified for both the 1 1/2-inch grade (from 3/8″ to 5/16″) and the 2-inch grade (from 1/2″ to 5/16″). All of the other length grades remain the same in both systems. Table A.5 compares PS 42-70 bodice specifications with those of the simplified grading system. In Table A.6 the PS 42-70 Grade Guide and the simplified grade guide are compared in specific areas. The back width is the only area that is the same in both systems across sizes, but the shoulder/neck area is larger in the simplified system, so the fit across the back is different.

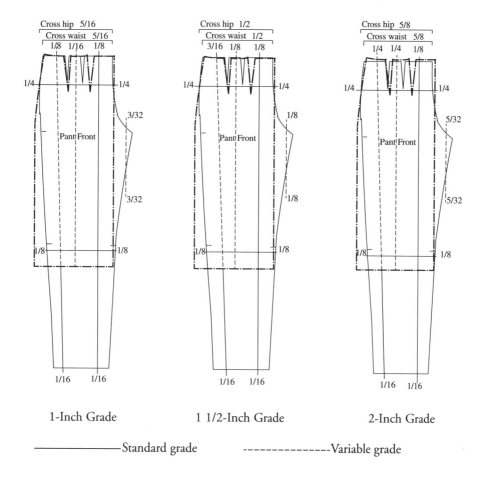

1-Inch Grade   1 1/2-Inch Grade   2-Inch Grade

————————Standard grade   --------------Variable grade

Figure A.11 Complex Grade Distributions for Skirt/Pant Front

Bodice Fit in the Simplified System

The width areas of the bodice front and back were modified to create a simplified grading system in which the back and front could be graded by the same set of grade rules. The bust and waist girth grades are not listed in Table A.6 because they do not change in the simplification of the PS 42-70 Grade Guide. However, both the front and the back at the bust level are affected considerably, with the front increasing/decreasing less in the simplified system and the back changing more. The location of the underarm seam moves closer to the front when graded to larger sizes by the simplified system. This could result in tightness across the front of the garment and excess ease across the back. The bust contour also increases as the larger sizes are graded by the PS 42-70 Grade Guide because the dart take-up is increased.

The greatest effect on fit in extreme sizes appears to be in the upper bodice area which includes the front chest, the shoulder, the upper arm girth, the neck, and the armscye. The back width grade in the PS 42-70 is greater than the chest width grade. Although, the back width grades are the same in the two systems, the shoulder dart take-up is graded in PS 42-70, which allows for the increase in the back width without affecting the shoulder length and neck. In the simplified system, the shoulder length and the neck width grade are greater as the pattern is graded to larger sizes. The front is affected more than the back, with the shoulder length, neck, and the chest width grades being greater across the front in the simplified system.

The armscye is affected in the 1-inch grade in the simplified system because the total armscye girth is de-

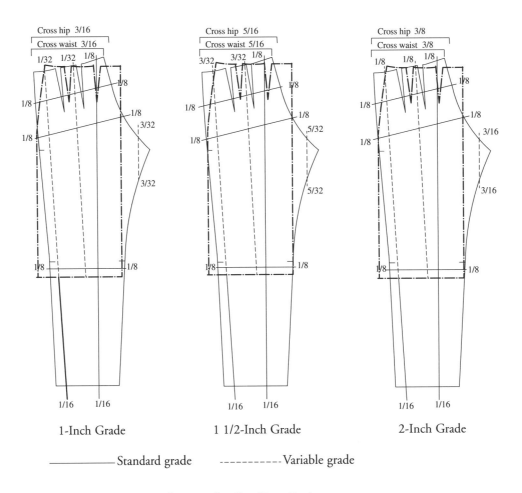

—————— Standard grade   - - - - - - - Variable grade

Figure A.12 Complex Grade Distributions for Skirt/Pant Back

creased by 1/2 inch instead of 3/8 inch, as in the PS 42-70. Tightness in the armhole might result.

The simplified system results in a grading process that is easier to follow, but the negative effects on garment fit in extreme sizes are blatant. It is understandable that poor garment fit is a widespread complaint. A comparison of garment fit across a size range between a complex grading system and a simplified system created from the same database is a worthy research topic. The technology of computer grading may make the use of a three-dimensional system feasible.

Step 3: Simplified Grading System for Sleeve

The simplified system is different from the complex system in the 1 inch and the 2 inch sleeve grades. The armscye girth grade in the PS 42-70 Grade Guide is 3/8″ for a 1 inch grade. However, the armscye width must be 1/8 inch (not the 1/16 inch applied in the complex system) to allow 1/4 inch in the cross bust grade, which results in a total of 1/2 inch armscye girth grade instead of 3/8 inch (Figure A.14). The result may be tightness in the armhole as the pattern is

graded to smaller sizes. (In the complex system the extra cross bust grade was placed through the dart take-up instead of in the armscye width). A similar problem exists with the 2 inch grade. In the PS 42-70 Grade Guide the upper arm width grade is 5/8″ and the armscye girth grade is 3/4″. However, when the length grade of 1/8″ on both the back and front of the sleeve is added to the sleeve width grade of 5/8″, the total sleeve seam grade of 7/8″ is greater than the armscye girth grade (3/4″). Rather than decreasing the sleeve by 1/8″ to fit into the armscye, which could result in tightness across the sleeve in the larger sizes (a common complaint), the additional 1/8″ in the sleeve can be eased across the bias section of the seam to fit the armscye. See discussion of the complex system sleeve grade in this Appendix.

Step 4: Simplified Grading System for Skirt and Pant
Skirt Grades

The skirt width grade distribution includes the waist, the hip, and the sweep. The waist on a one-dart (half-

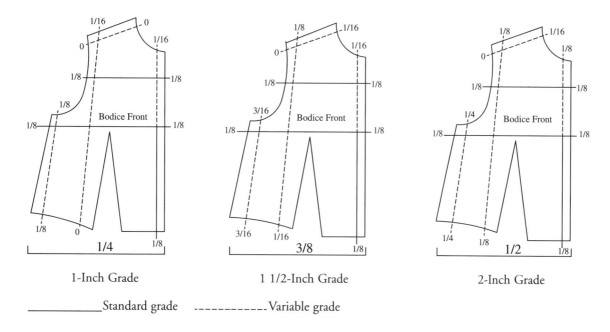

Figure A.13 Simplified System for Bodice Front and Back

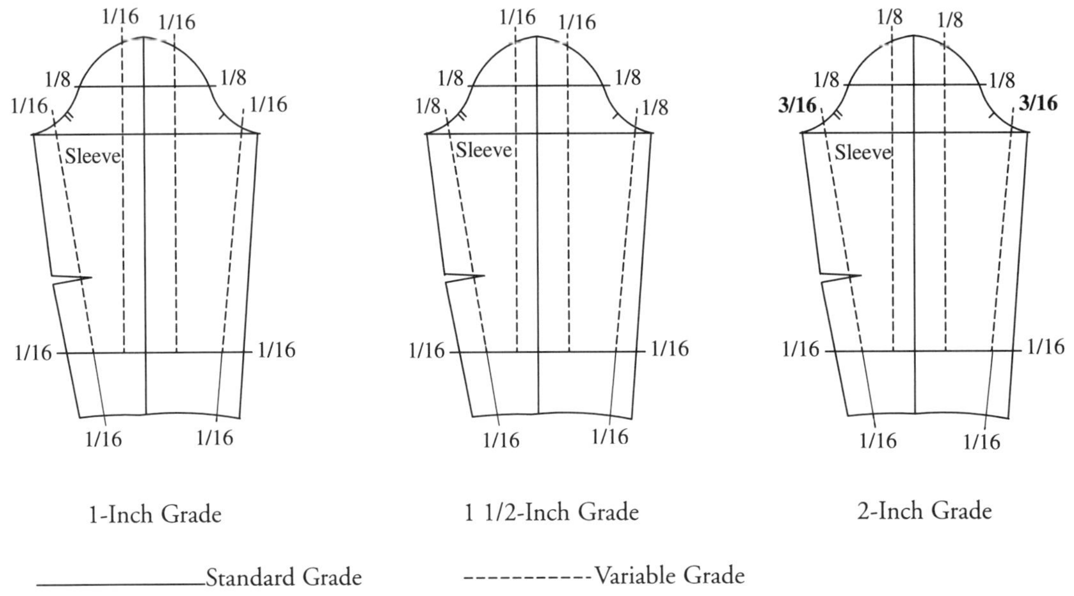
1/16 1/16
1/8 1/8
1/16 1/16
Sleeve
1/16 1/16
1/16 1/16
1-Inch Grade
1/16 1/16
1/8 1/8
1/8 1/8
Sleeve
1/16 1/16
1/16 1/16
1 1/2-Inch Grade
1/8 1/8
1/8 1/8
3/16 3/16
Sleeve
1/16 1/16
1/16 1/16
2-Inch Grade
Standard Grade
Variable Grade

Figure A.14 Simplified Grade Distributions for Sleeve

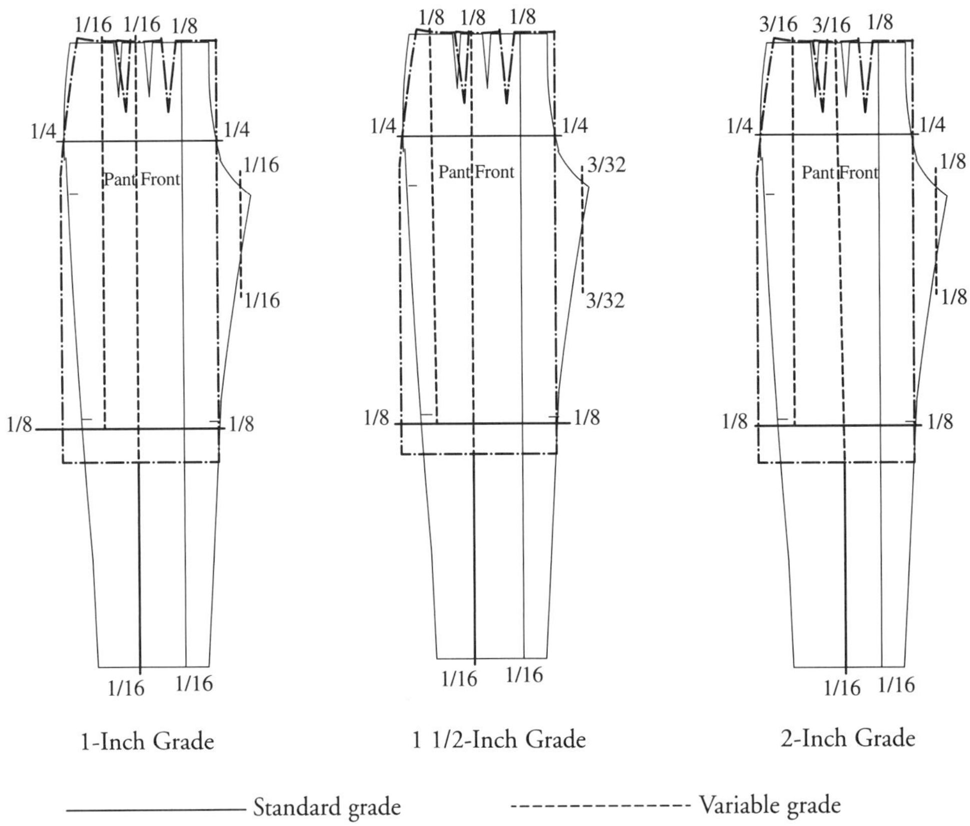
1/16 1/16 1/8
1/4 1/4
1/16
Pant Front
1/16
1/8 1/8
1/16 1/16
1-Inch Grade
1/8 1/8 1/8
1/4 1/4
3/32
Pant Front
3/32
1/8 1/8
1/16 1/16
1 1/2-Inch Grade
3/16 3/16 1/8
1/4 1/4
1/8
Pant Front
1/8
1/8 1/8
1/16 1/16
2-Inch Grade
Standard grade
Variable grade

Figure A.15 Simplified Grade Distributions for Skirt/Pant Front

pattern) skirt pattern is graded in the same manner as the basic bodice waist. The standard 1/8 inch grade between the center front/back and the dart is applied to the skirt waistline. In a two-dart lower body garment (Figures A.15 and A16), half of the remainder of the waist grade is placed on each side of the second dart. The skirt hip and sweep have the same cross grade as the waist. Except for the standard width grade of 1/8 inch between the center front/back and first dart, the grade is variable; therefore, it is different for the 1-inch, the 1 1/2-inch , and the 2-inch grades. The length grade is distributed between the waist and hip and between the hip and lower edge. The waist to hip grade in the PS 42-70 is a standard 1/4 inch. It is the same for both a complex and a simplified grading system for a skirt. An additional 1/8-inch grade is added below the hip line or the knee.

Pant Grades

Waist and hips are graded in width the same as the skirt. However, the body girth at the crotch level requires an additional grade for the crotch width.

The PS 42-70 table contains no measurement that can be used directly to determine the crotch width grade. The authors elected to calculate the crotch width grade based upon the hip width as cited by Scheier (1974) and Taylor and Shoben (1986), but to use the drafting principle as the basis for the calculation as was used in the complex grading system. Therefore, the back crotch grade is one-half of the hip

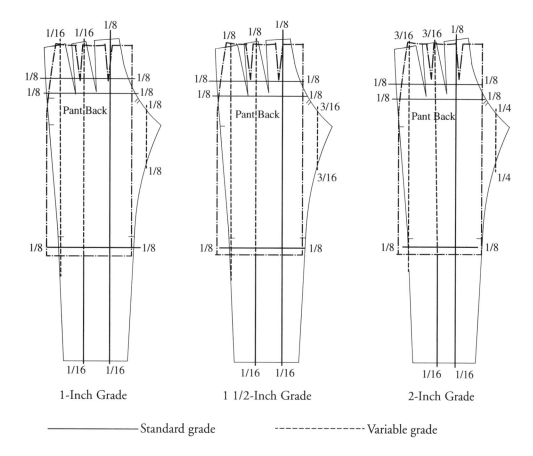

1-Inch Grade   1 1/2-Inch Grade   2-Inch Grade

——————— Standard grade   - - - - - - - - - - Variable grade

Figure A.16 Simplified Grade Distributions for Skirt/Pant Back

width grade, and the front crotch grade is one-fourth of the hip width grade (Figures A.15 and A16). The crotch width grade is variable because it is calculated from the variable hip width grade. The leg width grades are determined by the PS 42-70 Grade Guide, but they will vary with the style of the pant.

The length grades, which are taken directly from the PS 42-70 Grade Guide, are illustrated in Figures A.15 and A.16. Part of the waist to hip length grade on the pant back is placed above the ends of the darts for a better fit to the contour of the body. An additional 1/8 inch length grade is placed below the knee.

PATTERN GRADING
SUMMARY

The authors have simplified the complex grading system based on the PS 42-70 Grade Guide for misses sizes for use in this text. The system is not necessarily recommended, but it is developed from the only source of data available for misses sizes. The effects on fit, especially in the extreme sizes, can be analyzed by comparing the complex system developed from the PS 42-70 Grade Guide and the simplified system.

The exercises in the text include grading across the 6 to 22 size range in the PS 42-70 Size Specifications in order to give students experience in grading across a 1-inch, a 1 1/2-inch, and a 2-inch grade. However, the pattern grader should be cautioned that if a garment is produced in a wide size range, more than one master pattern should be used so that no more than two sizes are graded up and down from a master pattern size. Otherwise, fit may be compromised in the upper body areas of the smallest and largest sizes when grading by a simplified system.

REFERENCES

Armstrong, H. (1995). *Patternmaking for fashion design* (2nd ed.). New York: Harper Collins.

Cooklin, G. (1994). *Pattern grading for women's clothes*. London: Blackwell Scientific Publications.

Handford, J. (1980). *Professional pattern grading for women's, men's, and children's apparel*. Redondo Beach, CA: Plycon Press.

National Bureau of Standards. (1971). *Voluntary product standard: Body measurements for the sizing of women's patterns and apparel*. (NTIS No. PS 42-70) Washington, DC: Government Printing Office.

Price, J., & Zamkoff, B. (1996). *Grading techniques for modern design* (2nd ed.). New York: Fairchild Publications.

Scheier, M. (1974). *The ABC's of grading*. Bronxville, NY: Murray Scheier.

Taylor, P. J., & Shoben, M. M. (1986). *Grading for the fashion industry: The theory and practice*. London: Hutchinson.

Table A.1 PS 42-70 Sizing Specifications for Misses Sizes 6–22

Size	6	8	10	12	14	16	18	20	22
Girth Measurements (inches)									
Bust	31 1/2	32 1/2	33 1/2	35	36 1/2	38	40	42	44
Waist	22 1/2	23 1/2	24 1/2	26	27 1/2	29	31	33	35
Hip	33 1/2	34 1/2	35 1/2	37	38 1/2	40	42	44	46
Mid neck	13 1/8	13 3/8	13 5/8	14	14 3/8	14 3/4	15 1/4	15 3/4	16 1/4
Armscye	13 7/8	14 1/4	14 5/8	15 1/4	15 7/8	16 1/2	17 1/4	18	18 3/4
High hip	29 5/8	30 5/8	31 5/8	33 1/8	34 5/8	36 1/8	38 1/8	40 1/8	42 1/8
Sitting spread	33 1/2	34 1/2	35 1/2	37	38 1/2	40	42	44	46
Thigh, maximum	18 3/4	19 1/2	20 1/4	21 1/4	22 1/4	23 1/4	24 1/2	25 3/4	27
Thigh, mid	17	17 1/2	18	18 3/4	19 1/2	20 1/4	21 1/4	22 1/4	23 1/4
Knee	12	12 3/8	12 3/4	13 1/4	13 3/4	14 1/4	14 3/4	15 1/4	15 3/4
Calf	11 1/2	11 7/8	12 1/4	12 3/4	13 1/4	13 3/4	14 1/4	14 3/4	15 1/4
Ankle	8 1/8	8 3/8	8 5/8	8 7/8	9 1/8	9 3/8	9 5/8	9 7/8	10 1/8
Upper arm	9 5/8	9 7/8	10 1/8	10 1/2	10 7/8	11 1/4	11 7/8	12 1/2	13 1/8
Elbow	9 1/4	9 3/8	9 1/2	9 3/4	10	10 1/4	10 5/8	11	11 3/8
Wrist	5 1/4	5 3/8	5 1/2	5 5/8	5 3/4	5 7/8	6	6 1/8	6 1/4
Vertical trunk	55 1/2	57	58 1/2	60	61 1/2	63	64 1/2	66	67 1/2
Arc Measurements (inches)									
Bust, front	17 3/4	18 1/2	19 1/4	20 1/4	21 1/4	22 1/4	23 5/8	25	26 3/8
Waist, front	11 7/8	12 1/2	13 1/8	14	14 7/8	15 3/4	17	18 1/4	23 1/2
High hip, front	15 7/8	16 1/2	17 1/8	18	18 7/8	19 3/4	21	22 1/4	21 3/4
Hip, back	16 7/8	17 1/4	17 5/8	18 1/4	18 7/8	19 1/2	20 1/4	21	21 3/4
Vertical Measurements (inches)									
Stature (total height)	62 1/2	63	63 1/2	64	64 1/2	65	65 1/2	66	66 1/2
Cervical height	53 1/2	54	54 1/2	55	55 1/2	56	56 1/2	57	57 1/2
Waist height	38 3/4	39 1/8	39 1/2	39 7/8	40 1/4	40 5/8	41	41 3/8	41 3/4
High hip height	35 3/4	36	36 1/4	36 1/2	36 3/4	37	37 1/4	37 1/2	37 3/4
Hip height	31 1/2	31 5/8	31 3/4	31 7/8	32	32 1/8	32 1/4	32 3/8	32 1/2
Crotch height	28 3/8	28 1/2	28 5/8	28 3/4	28 7/8	29	29 1/8	29 1/4	29 3/8
Knee height	16 7/8	17	17 1/8	17 1/4	17 3/8	17 1/2	17 5/8	17 3/4	17 7/8
Ankle height	2 3/4	2 3/4	2 3/4	2 3/4	2 3/4	2 3/4	2 3/4	2 3/4	2 3/4
Width and Length Measurements (inches)									
Cross-back width	12	12 1/4	12 1/2	12 7/8	13 1/4	13 5/8	14 1/8	14 5/8	15 1/8
Cross-chest width	11 7/8	12	12 1/8	12 3/8	12 5/8	12 7/8	13 1/4	13 5/8	14
Bust point to bust point	6 3/4	7	7 1/4	7 1/2	7 3/4	8	8 1/4	8 1/2	8 3/4
Neck to bust point	8 1/2	8 3/4	9	9 3/8	9 3/4	10 1/8	10 5/8	11 1/8	11 5/8
Armscye depth	7	7 1/8	7 1/4	7 3/8	7 1/2	7 5/8	7 3/4	7 7/8	8
Armscye to waist	8	8 1/8	8 1/4	8 3/8	8 1/2	8 5/8	8 3/4	8 7/8	9

■Table A.1 *(continued)*

Size	6	8	10	12	14	16	18	20	22
Width and Length Measurements (inches)									
Waist to hips	7 3/4	8	8 1/4	8 1/2	8 3/4	9	9 1/4	9 1/2	9 3/4
Shoulder length	4 3/16	4 1/4	4 5/16	4 3/8	4 7/16	4 1/2	4 9/16	4 5/8	4 11/16
Shoulder slope (degrees)	23	23	23	23	23	23	23	23	23
Arm length, shoulder to wrist	22 11/16	22 7/8	23 1/16	23 1/4	23 7/16	23 5/8	23 13/16	24	24 13/16
Arm length, shoulder to elbow	13	13 1/8	13 1/4	13 3/8	13 1/2	13 5/8	13 3/4	13 7/8	14
Underarm length	16 9/16	16 5/8	16 11/16	16 3/4	16 13/16	16 7/8	16 15/16	17	17 1/16
Crotch length, total	26 3/8	27 1/8	27 7/8	28 5/8	29 3/8	30 1/8	30 7/8	31 5/8	32 3/8
Cervical to center front at waist	18 5/8	18 7/8	19 1/8	19 1/2	19 7/8	20 1/4	20 3/4	21 1/4	21 3/4
Waist length, front	12 3/4	13	13 1/4	13 1/2	13 3/4	14	14 1/4	14 1/2	14 3/4
Waist length, back	14 3/4	15	15 1/4	15 1/2	15 3/4	16	16 1/4	16 1/2	16 3/4

Source: Reprinted from *Voluntary Product Standard: Body Measurement for the Sizing of Women's Patterns and Apparel.*

Table A.2 PS 42-70 Grade Guide for Misses Sizes 6–22

Grade between Sizes	6–8	8–10	10–12	12–14	14–16	16–18	18–20	20–22
Girth Measurements (inches)								
Bust	1	1	1 1/2	1 1/2	1 1/2	2	2	2
Waist	1	1	1 1/2	1 1/2	1 1/2	2	2	2
Hips	1	1	1 1/2	1 1/2	1 1/2	2	2	2
Mid neck	1/4	1/4	3/8	3/8	3/8	1/2	1/2	1/2
Armscye	3/8	3/8	5/8	5/8	5/8	3/4	3/4	3/4
High hip	1	1	1 1/2	1 1/2	1 1/2	2	2	2
Sitting spread	1	1	1 1/2	1 1/2	1 1/2	2	2	2
Thigh, maximum	3/4	3/4	1	1	1	1 1/4	1 1/4	1 1/4
Thigh, mid	1/2	1/2	3/4	3/4	3/4	1	1	1
Knee	3/8	3/8	1/2	1/2	1/2	1/2	1/2	1/2
Calf	3/8	3/8	1/2	1/2	1/2	1/2	1/2	1/2
Ankle	1/4	1/4	1/4	1/4	1/4	1/4	1/4	1/4
Upper arm	1/4	1/4	3/8	3/8	3/8	5/8	5/8	5/8
Elbow	1/8	1/8	1/4	1/4	1/4	3/8	3/8	3/8
Wrist	1/8	1/8	1/8	1/8	1/8	1/8	1/8	1/8
Vertical trunk	1 1/2	1 1/2	1 1/2	1 1/2	1 1/2	1 1/2	1 1/2	1 1/2
Arc Measurements (inches)								
Bust, front	3/4	3/4	1	1	1	1 3/8	1 3/8	1 3/8
Waist, front	5/8	5/8	7/8	7/8	7/8	1 1/4	1 1/4	1 1/4
High hip, front	5/8	5/8	7/8	7/8	7/8	1 1/4	1 1/4	1 1/4
Hip, back	3/8	3/8	5/8	5/8	5/8	3/4	3/4	3/4
Vertical Measurements (inches)								
Stature (total height)	1/2	1/2	1/2	1/2	1/2	1/2	1/2	1/2
Cervical height	1/2	1/2	1/2	1/2	1/2	1/2	1/2	1/2
Waist height	3/8	3/8	3/8	3/8	3/8	3/8	3/8	3/8
High hip height	1/4	1/4	1/4	1/4	1/4	1/4	1/4	1/4
Hip height	1/8	1/8	1/8	1/8	1/8	1/8	1/8	1/8
Crotch height	1/8	1/8	1/8	1/8	1/8	1/8	1/8	1/8
Knee height	1/8	1/8	1/8	1/8	1/8	1/8	1/8	1/8
Ankle height	0	0	0	0	0	0	0	0
Width and Length Measurements (inches)								
Cross-back width	1/4	1/4	3/8	3/8	3/8	1/2	1/2	1/2
Cross-chest width	1/8	1/8	1/4	1/4	1/4	3/8	3/8	3/8
Bust point to bust point	1/4	1/4	1/4	1/4	1/4	1/4	1/4	1/4
Neck to bust point	1/4	1/4	3/8	3/8	3/8	1/2	1/2	1/2
Armscye depth	1/8	1/8	1/8	1/8	1/8	1/8	1/8	1/8
Armscye to waist	1/8	1/8	1/8	1/8	1/8	1/8	1/8	1/8

Table A.2 *(continued)*

Grade between Sizes	6–8	8–10	10–12	12–14	14–16	16–18	18–20	20–22
Width and Length Measurements (inches)								
Waist to hip	1/4	1/4	1/4	1/4	1/4	1/4	1/4	1/4
Shoulder length	1/16	1/16	1/16	1/16	1/16	1/16	1/16	1/16
Shoulder slope (degrees)	0	0	0	0	0	0	0	0
Arm length, shoulder to wrist	3/16	3/16	3/16	3/16	3/16	3/16	3/16	3/16
Arm length, shoulder to elbow	1/8	1/8	1/8	1/8	1/8	1/8	1/8	1/8
Underarm length	1/16	1/16	1/16	1/16	1/16	1/16	1/16	1/16
Crotch length, total	3/4	3/4	3/4	3/4	3/4	3/4	3/4	3/4
Cervical to center front at waist	1/4	1/4	3/8	3/8	3/8	1/2	1/2	1/2
Waist length, front	1/4	1/4	1/4	1/4	1/4	1/4	1/4	1/4
Waist length, back	1/4	1/4	1/4	1/4	1/4	1/4	1/4	1/4

Source: Reprinted from *Voluntary Product Standard: Body Measurement for the Sizing of Women's Patterns and Apparel.*

Table A.3 Bodice and Sleeve Grades From PS 42-70 Grades Guide

Size	6–8	8–10	10–12	12–14	14–16	16–18	18–20	20–22
Bodice Girth Measurements (inches)								
1. Bust	1	1	1 1/2	1 1/2	1 1/2	2	2	2
2. Waist	1	1	1 1/2	1 1/2	1 1/2	2	2	2
3. Mid neck	1/4	1/4	3/8	3/8	3/8	1/2	1/2	1/2
4. Armscye	3/8	3/8	5/8	5/8	5/8	3/4	3/4	3/4
Bodice Arc Measurements (inches)								
5. Bust, front	3/4	3/4	1	1	1	1 3/8	1 3/8	1 3/8
6. Waist, front		5/8	5/8	7/8	7/8	7/8	1 1/4	1 1/4
Bodice Width and Length Measurements (inches)								
7. Back width	1/4	1/4	3/8	3/8	3/8	1/2	1/2	1/2
8. Chest width	1/8	1/8	1/4	1/4	1/4	3/8	3/8	3/8
9. Bust point to point	1/4	1/4	1/4	1/4	1/4	1/4	1/4	1/4
10. Neck to bust point	1/4	1/4	3/8	3/8	3/8	1/2	1/2	1/2
11. Armscye depth	1/8	1/8	1/8	1/8	1/8	1/8	1/8	1/8
12. Armscye to waist	1/8	1/8	1/8	1/8	1/8	1/8	1/8	1/8
13. Shoulder length	1/16	1/16	1/16	1/16	1/16	1/16	1/16	1/16
14. Waist length, front	1/4	1/4	1/4	1/4	1/4	1/4	1/4	1/4
15. Waist length, back	1/4	1/4	1/4	1/4	1/4	1/4	1/4	1/4
16. Shoulder slope (degrees)	0	0	0	0	0	0	0	0
Sleeve Girth Measurements (inches)								
17. Upper arm	1/4	1/4	3/8	3/8	3/8	5/8	5/8	5/8
18. Wrist	1/8	1/8	1/8	1/8	1/8	1/8	1/8	1/8
Sleeve Length Measurements (inches)								
19. Arm length, shoulder to wrist	3/16	3/16	3/16	3/16	3/16	3/16	3/16	3/16
20. Shoulder to elbow	1/8	1/8	1/8	1/8	1/8	1/8	1/8	1/8
21. Underarm length	1/16	1/16	1/16	1/16	1/16	1/16	1/16	1/16

Table A.4 Skirt and Pant Grades From PS 42-70 Grade Guide

Size	6–8	8–10	10–12	12–14	14–16	16–18	18–20	20–22
Girth Measurements (inches)								
2. Waist	1	1	1 1/2	1 1/2	1 1/2	2	2	2
22. Hip	1	1	1 1/2	1 1/2	1 1/2	2	2	2
23. High hip	1	1	1 1/2	1 1/2	1 1/2	2	2	2
24. Thigh, mid	1/2	1/2	3/4	3/4	3/4	1	1	1
25. Knee	3/8	3/8	1/2	1/2	1/2	1/2	1/2	1/2
26. Ankle	1/4	1/4	1/4	1/4	1/4	1/4	1/4	1/4
Arc Measurements (inches)								
6. Waist, front	5/8	5/8	7/8	7/8	7/8	1 1/4	1 1/4	1 1/4
27. High hip, front	5/8	5/8	7/8	7/8	7/8	1 1/4	1 1/4	1 1/4
28. Hip, back	3/8	3/8	5/8	5/8	5/8	3/4	3/4	3/4
Vertical Measurements (inches)								
29. Waist height	3/8	3/8	3/8	3/8	3/8	3/8	3/8	3/8
30. Hip height	1/8	1/8	1/8	1/8	1/8	1/8	1/8	1/8
31. Crotch height	1/8	1/8	1/8	1/8	1/8	1/8	1/8	1/8
32. Knee height	1/8	1/8	1/8	1/8	1/8	1/8	1/8	1/8
33. Ankle height	0	0	0	0	0	0	0	0
34. Waist to hip	1/4	1/4	1/4	1/4	1/4	1/4	1/4	1/4

Appendix A 227

Table A.5 Comparison of PS 42-70 Size Specifications With Simplified Grading System Specifications for Bodice

Size	6	8	10	12	14	16	18	20	22
Mid neck	13 1/8 (13)	13 3/8 (13 1/4)	13 5/8 (13 1/2)	14	14 3/8 (14 1/2)	14 3/4 (15)	15 1/4 (15 3/4)	15 3/4 (16 1/2)	16 1/4 (17 1/4)
Bust front	17 3/4 (18 3/4)	18 1/2 (19 1/4)	19 1/4 (19 3/4)	20 1/4	21 1/4 (21)	22 1/4 (21 3/4)	23 5/8 (22 3/4)	25 (23 3/4)	26 3/8 (24 3/4)
Bust level on back[a]	13 3/4 (13)	14 (13 1/2)	14 1/4 (14)	14 3/4	15 1/4 (15 1/2)	15 3/4 (16 1/4)	16 3/8 (17 1/4)	17 (18 1/4)	17 5/8 (19 1/4)
Waist front	11 7/8 (12 1/4)	12 1/2 (12 3/4)	13 1/8 (13 1/4)	14	14 7/8 (14 3/4)	15 3/4 (14 1/2)	17 (16 1/2)	18 1/4 (17 1/2)	19 1/2 (18 1/2)
Waist back[a]	10 5/8 (10 1/4)	11 (10 3/4)	11 3/8 (11 1/4)	12	12 5/8 (12 3/4)	13 1/4 (13 1/2)	14 (14 1/2)	14 3/4 (15 1/2)	15 1/2 (16 1/2)
Cross back width	12 (12)	12 1/4 (12 1/4)	12 1/2 (12 1/2)	12 7/8	13 1/4 (13 1/4)	13 5/8 (13 5/8)	14 1/8 (14 1/8)	14 5/8 (14 5/8)	15 1/8 (15 1/8)
Cross chest width	11 7/8 (11 1/2)	12 (11 3/4)	12 1/8 (12)	12 3/8	12 5/8 (12 3/4)	12 7/8 (13 1/8)	13 1/4 (13 5/8)	13 5/8 (14 1/8)	14 (14 5/8)
Neck to bust point	8 1/2 (8 9/16)	8 3/4 (8 13/16)	9 (9 1/16)	9 3/8	9 3/4 (10 1/16)	10 1/8 (10 3/8)	10 5/8 (10 11/16)	11 1/8 (11)	11 5/8 (11 5/16)
Shoulder length	4 3/16 (4 1/8)	4 1/4 (4 3/16)	4 5/16 (4 1/4)	4 3/8	4 7/16 (4 9/16)	4 1/2 (4 5/8)	4 9/16 (4 3/4)	4 5/8 (4 7/8)	4 11/16 (5)
Armscye	13 7/8 (13 5/8)	14 1/4 (14 1/8)	14 5/8	15 1/4	15 7/8	16 1/2	17 1/4	18	18 3/4
Upper arm	9 5/8	9 7/8	10 1/8	10 1/2	10 7/8	11 1/4	11 7/8 (11 3/4)	12 1/2 12 1/4	13 1/8 (12 3/4)

Note: Numbers in parentheses are the specifications when the simplified grading system is used. Measurements are in inches.

[a] Bust level on back and waist back are not on PS 42 -70 specifications but can be calculated by subtracting front measurements from total girth specifications.

Table A.6 Comparison of PS 42 -70 and Simplified Grade Guides in Affected Areas

Size	6–8	8–10	10–12	12–14	14–16	16–18	18–20	20–22
Mid neck	1/4 (1/4)	1/4 (1/4)	3/8 (1/2)	3/8 (1/2)	3/8 (1/2)	1/2 (3/4)	1/2 (3/4)	1/2 (3/4)
Bust front	3/4 (1/2)	3/4 (1/2)	1 (3/4)	1 (3/4)	1 (3/4)	1 3/8 (1)	1 3/8 (1)	1 3/8 (1)
Bust level on back [a]	1/4 (1/2)	1/4 (1/2)	1/2 (3/4)	1/2 (3/4)	1/2 (3/4)	5/8 (1)	5/8 (1)	5/8 (1)
Waist front	5/8 (1/2)	5/8 (1/2)	7/8 (3/4)	7/8 (3/4)	7/8 (3/4)	1 1/4 (1)	1 1/4 (1)	1 1/4 (1)
Waist back [a]	3/8 (1/2)	3/8 (1/2)	5/8 (3/4)	5/8 (3/4)	5/8 (3/4)	3/4 (1)	3/4 (1)	3/4 (1)
Back width	1/4 (1/4)	1/4 (1/4)	3/8 (3/8)	3/8 (3/8)	3/8 (1/2)	1/2 (1/2)	1/2 (1/2)	1/2 (1/2)
Chest width	1/8 (1/4)	1/8 (1/4)	1/4 (3/8)	1/4 (3/8)	1/4 (3/8)	3/8 (1/2)	3/8 (1/2)	3/8 (1/2)
Neck to bust point	1/4 (1/4)	1/4 (1/4)	3/8 (5/16)	3/8 (5/16)	3/8 (5/16)	1/2 (5/16)	1/2 (5/16)	1/2 (5/16)
Shoulder length	1/16 (1/16)	1/16 (1/16)	1/16 (1/8)	1/16 (1/8)	1/16 (1/8)	1/16 (1/8)	1/16 (1/8)	1/16 (1/8)
Armscye	3/8 (1/2)	3/8 (1/2)	5/8	5/8	5/8	(3/4)	(3/4)	(3/4)
Upper arm	1/4	1/4	3/8	3/8	3/8	5/8 (1/2)	5/8 (1/2)	5/8 (1/2)

Note: Numbers in parentheses are the simplified grade. Measurements are in inches.

[a]Bust level on back and waist back were not on PS 42 -70 Grade Guide but were calculated by subtracting front arc measurements from girth measurements.

Appendix B

ASTM D 5586-95 Standard Table for Body Measurements for Women Aged 55 and Older, Misses Figure Type

INTRODUCTION

ASTM D 5586-95 Standard Table of Body Measurements for Women Aged 55 and Older Misses Figure contains averages for sizes 6 through 22 derived from data collected in an ASTM survey of women aged 55 and older (*Annual Book of ASTM Standards*, 1997). The table cannot be used as it is for sizing specifications or a grade guide because the differences between the sizes are not systematic increments. Procedures for converting the data into systematic incremental differences between sizes are presented in this appendix. Sizing specifications were established based on the systematic incremental differences so that the total difference between size 6 and size 22 is similar to the total difference in the ASTM D 5586 data. The grade guide developed from the data results in a complex grading system. A simplified incremental grade guide is also presented.

DEVELOPMENT OF SYSTEMATIC SIZING STANDARD AND INCREMENTAL GRADE GUIDE

Table B.1 contains the average body measurements in the ASTM D 5586 Standard Table plus four calculated measurements. Numbers 3, 6, 9, and 12 represent the differences between girth and arc measurements. The body areas in the table have been numbered to correspond with the body areas illustrated in Figures B.1, B.2, and B.3.

Table B.2 shows the incremental differences in the averages of the ASTM D 5586 data between adjacent sizes for each body area. The difference is shown in decimals and in fractions of an inch rounded to the nearest 32nd inch. The last column contains the total difference between sizes 6 and 22. There are several areas in which measurements for size 8 are smaller than size 6. In these cases, the size 8 was used for the calculation, but a plus (+) sign is added to the total difference.

Step 1: Systematic Incremental Differences Between Sizes
Length Grades

Length grades are generally the same (standard grades) for the 1-inch, the 1 1/2-inch, and the 2-inch grades, whereas width grades tend to be variable for these grades. Length grades were determined by calculating an average of the total differences in the vertical body specifications between sizes 6 and 22 (Table B.3). The length measurements for the lower body represent the distance from the floor to the specific body area, except for the waist to hip length measurement. This table illustrates how the length is distributed in pants. Shoulder length is included in Table B.3 even though that grade may be variable.

Total Circumference Grades and Width Grades

The bust, waist, and hip circumference data were analyzed to determine the sizes that required a 1-inch, a 1 1/2-inch, or a 2-inch grade. The front and back width measurements between armscyes and other body width measurements determined the cross grades. The average of the total differences between sizes 6 and 20 and the average of differences within the 1-inch, the 1 1/2-inch, and the 2-inch grades were the premises upon which the grade guide was developed.

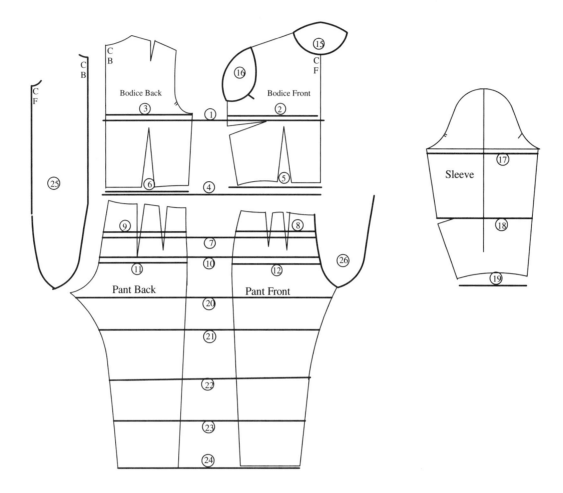

Figure B.1 Girth and Arc Measurements

Step 2. Development of Complex Grade Guide and Sizing Specifications

Table B.4 is the completed grade guide with systematic incremental differences between sizes. From this table of data a systematic table of size specifications was developed (Table B.5). The size specification table was developed by using size 12 as the reference size and calculating the remaining sizes by adding the grade between sizes for sizes 14 through 22 and subtracting the grade between sizes for sizes 10 through 6.

COMPLEX GRADING SYSTEM

Taylor and Shoben (1986) and Cooklin (1994) point out that the front and back of the body in the bust,

waist, and hip areas do not change the same between sizes, and the closer the anthropometric data are followed in developing a grade guide, the more complex the grade guide will be. The ASTM D 5586 Standard Table data show the difference between the front and back of the body, therefore, the grade guide developed from the data results in a complex grading system. Taylor and Shoben, and Cooklin also state that the more the grade guide is simplified, the less proficient it is. Fit problems will occur in extreme sizes in a wide range of sizes.

Step 1: Grade Distribution in a Complex System

The complex grading system grade distributions are illustrated in Figures B.4 through B.8. Following is an

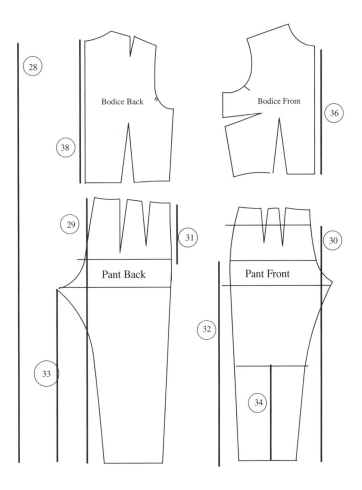

■Figure B.2 Vertical Measurements

explanation of how the distributions were determined. (For a more detailed procedure for determining the distribution, see Chapter 10 and Appendix A).

Chapter 10 and Appendix A illustrate the procedure for developing a grading system from size specifications that have systematic differences between sizes. Incremental differences for ASTM D 5586-95 (Table B.4) had to be established before size specifications could be determined (Table B.5). Only body measurements that are required to develop an incremental grade guide are included in Table B.5. The systematic incremental differences between sizes in Table B.4 were interpolated from the actual differences found in Table B.2. Numbers 3, 6, 9 and 12 are included in the measurement table so that the differences in the front

and back are apparent. Figures B.4 and B.5 show the distribution of the complex grade in the bodice front and back. The dash-dots indicate cross body grades and neck to bust point grades; the broken lines represent variable grades, and the solid lines represent the standard grades for the 1-inch, the 1 1/2-inch, and the 2-inch grades.

The total girth difference for the hip is less than the bust and waist, resulting in a mixed grade. The hip area changes from a 1-inch to a 1 1/2-inch grade between sizes 14 and 16, whereas, the bust and waist change between sizes 10 and 12. The 2-inch grade at the hip begins with size 20, but the 2-inch grade for the bust and the waist begins at size 18 (Table B.4).

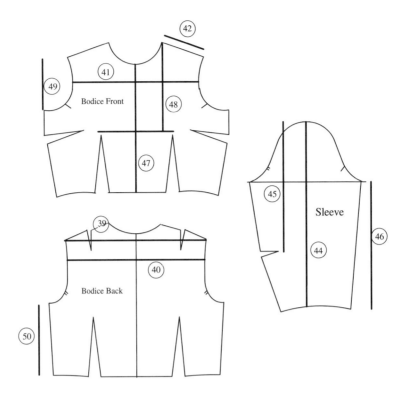

Figure B.3 Width and Length Measurements

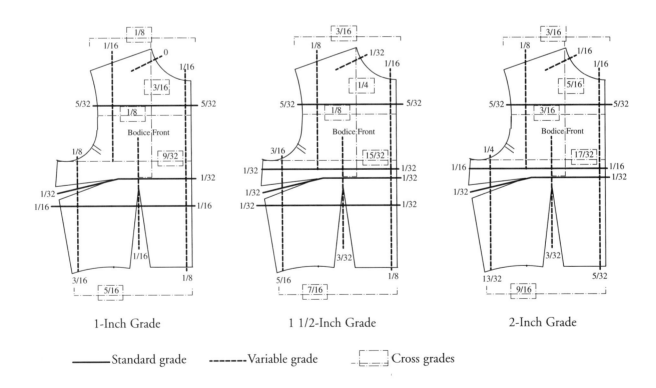

1-Inch Grade   1 1/2-Inch Grade   2-Inch Grade

———— Standard grade   - - - - - Variable grade   ⌐ ¬ Cross grades

Figure B.4 Misses 55+ Complex Grade System for Bodice Front

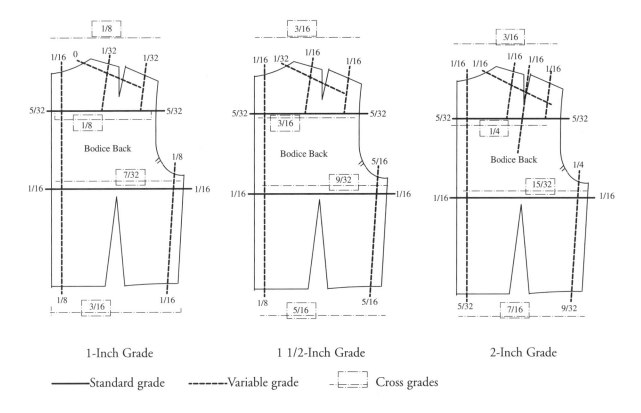

1-Inch Grade   1 1/2-Inch Grade   2-Inch Grade

———Standard grade   - - - - - -Variable grade   - -⌐-⌐- Cross grades

Figure B.5 Misses 55+ Complex Grade System for Bodice Back

Step 2: Grade Distributions for the Bodice Front and Back

Some grade distributions were taken directly from the incremental grade guide (Table B.4) and some were calculated based upon data given in that grade guide. The cross back shoulder and the shoulder length grades were given in the grade guide. The neck width grade was calculated; it is equal to the difference between one-half of the cross back grade and the shoulder length grade. The cross chest grade (cross shoulder grade on front) is the same as the cross back shoulder; but because the back width is greater in the 2 inch grade, the back shoulder dart was graded to allow more width on the back.

The cross bust grade and the armscye depth grade were given in the grade guide, but not the armscye width grade. In a simplified system, the armscye width can be calculated by subtracting the cross shoulder grade from the cross bust grade. However, for this data, that would result in the armscye girth being much greater than indicated in the data. To allow enough grade for the bust width (9/32 inch for a 1-inch grade, 15/32 inch for the 1 1/2-inch grade, and 17/32 inch for a 2-inch grade), the waistline bust dart take-up was graded by 1/16 inch for the 1-inch grade, and by 3/32 inch for the 1 1/2-inch and the 2 inch grades. Half the cross shoulder grade was calculated and used in the armscye width. Although this gives a systematic increase, it is important to be aware that the total girth of the armscye in the grade guide (a 5 5/8-inch difference between sizes 6 and 22) is still greater than the data (4 1/8 inches between sizes 6 and 22).

The armscye depth averaged out to 5/32 inch between sizes (Table B.3). This is greater than the PS 42-70. However, insufficient room in the armscye was a complaint of this population, so the greater depth seems logical. The total difference in armscye girth between sizes 6 and 22 in the complex grade guide is greater than the data indicate (Table B.1).

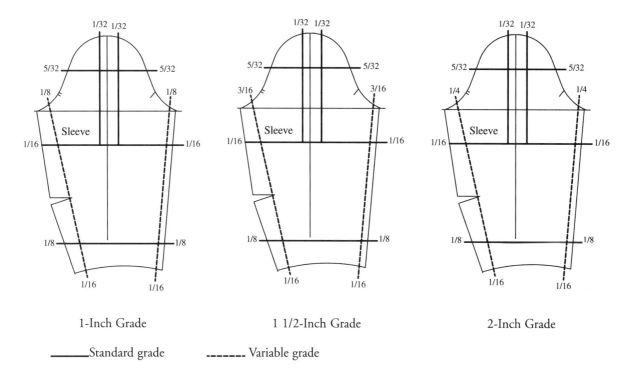

1-Inch Grade   1 1/2-Inch Grade   2-Inch Grade

——— Standard grade   - - - - - Variable grade

■Figure B.6 Misses 55+ Complex and Simplified Grade System for Sleeve

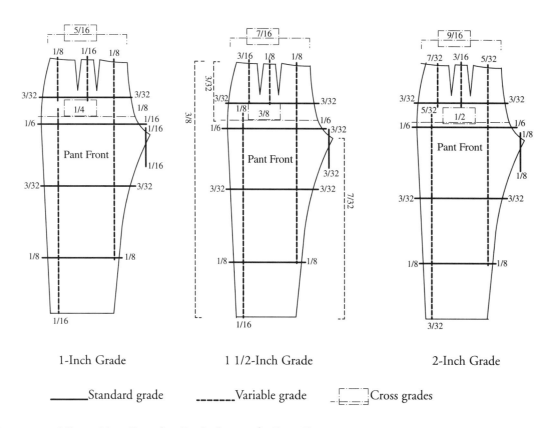

1-Inch Grade   1 1/2-Inch Grade   2-Inch Grade

——— Standard grade   - - - - - Variable grade   ⌐ ⌐ Cross grades

■Figure B.7 Misses 55+ Complex Grade System for Pant Front

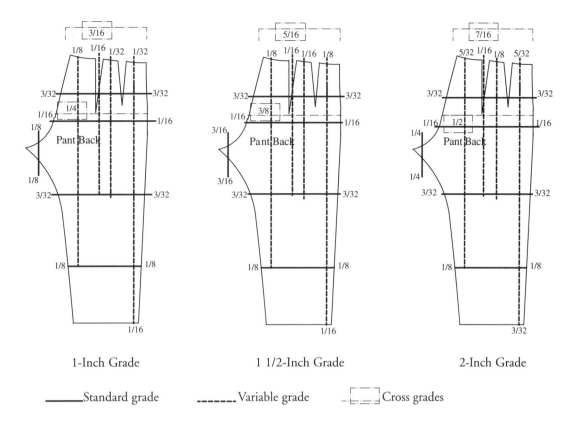

1-Inch Grade   1 1/2-Inch Grade   2-Inch Grade

———— Standard grade   - - - - - Variable grade   ⌐-⌐-⌐ Cross grades

Figure B.8 Misses 55+ Complex Grade System for Pant Back

There was a difference in waist length between the front and the back in the data. The average difference for the front was 1/4 inch, and 7/32 inch for the back (Table B.3). In order for the side seams to be graded the same and still have adequate length in waist front, the side bust dart take-up was graded. Also, because 5/32 inch was needed in the armhole, the armhole to waist was graded only 1/16 inch. The underarm to waist grade is placed between the underarm and the bust dart to accommodate the amount needed between the neck and bust point.

Step 3: Grade Distributions for the Sleeve

Figure B.6 shows the distribution for the sleeve grades. The sleeve length grades are standard for the 1-inch, the 1 1/2-inch, and the 2-inch grades. The grade in the sleeve cap plus the underarm grade equals the arm-

scye width grade in the bodice. The cap length grade is the same as the armscye depth grade in the bodice.

Step 4: Grade Distributions for the Skirt and Pant

Figures B.7 and B.8 are complex grade guide distributions for the pant front and back. The waist front and back of the skirt and pant are graded the same as the bodice waist between center front/back and the first dart. The remainder of the skirt/pant waist grade is divided with a portion of the grade placed between the two darts and the balance of the grade between the second dart and the side seam (Figures B.7 and B.8). **Note where the hip grade changes, because the change is not the same as in the waist.**

Distributions of the length grades are based primarily on the floor to waist height, floor to knee height, and the inseam length for pants. The length grade from the waist to hip is a standard 3/32 inch. The average length grade from the floor to the waist is 3/8 inch, and from the floor to inseam it is 7/32 inch (Table B.3). The difference between these grades is 5/32 inch, which indicates that a total grade of 5/32 inch is needed between the waist and crotch level. The knee height in the data is 3/16 inch, but because the fit at knee height is not critical, only 1/8-inch length is placed below the knee and the remainder of the inseam length is placed above the knee.

Length grades for the skirt can be simplified because no crotch area is involved. A length grade of 5/32 inch is placed between the waist and hip on the skirt. An additional 3/32-inch length grade is placed in the lower skirt.

The grade of 3/32 inch goes into the pant between the waist and hip. An additional 1/16-inch grade is placed between the hip and crotch level, and another 3/32 inch between the crotch level and the knee. The remaining 1/8-inch grade is placed below the knee.

There is no measurement in the data to determine the crotch width grade. Price and Zamkoff (1996) and Handford (1980) both use a standard 1/8-inch grade in the pant front and back. Scheier (1974) uses one-fourth of the hip grade (half-pattern) for the crotch width grade, and Taylor and Shoben use one-half the hip grade. Instructions for drafting pants specify one-half the width of pant back hip for the crotch back width and one-fourth of the pant front hip width for the crotch front width (Armstrong, 1995). The authors have used this last ratio for the width grades in

this grading system: the crotch width grade for the back is one-half of the back hip grade and the crotch width grade for the front is one-fourth the front hip grade (Figures B.7 and B.8).

The total of the front and back bodice waist lengths, the waist to hip lengths, and the crotch widths is greater than the vertical trunk grade in the data. However, the vertical trunk measurement is made over the shoulder, and it should be longer instead of shorter than the total of the specified measurements.

PART III: SIMPLIFIED GRADE GUIDE

Table B.6 is a simplified grade guide, in which the front and back of the body are graded the same. The last column contains the total difference between sizes 6 and 22 in each body area.

Figure B.9 illustrates the simplified grade distribution for the bodice front and back and Figure B.10 shows the distribution for pant front and back. The sleeve distribution is the same for both the complex and simplified systems (Figure B.6).

Comparison of Complex and Simplified Grade Guides

Table B.7 is a comparison of the total differences between all sizes for the ASTM D 5586 Standard Table, the complex grade guide, and the simplified grade guide. The areas in the simplified grade guide that differ the most from the data in ASTM D 5586 are the bodice front and back arc measurements, chest front width, shoulder back width, neck base girth, armscye girth, vertical trunk, and total crotch length.

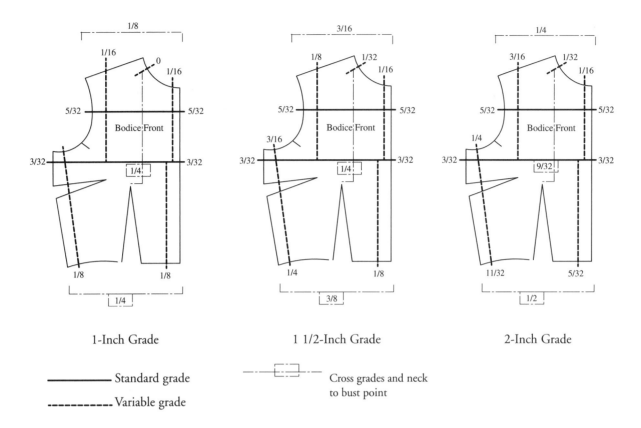

1-Inch Grade

1 1/2-Inch Grade

2-Inch Grade

—————— Standard grade

- - - - - - - Variable grade

- · - · - · - Cross grades and neck to bust point

■Figure B.9 Misses 55+ Simplified Grade System for Bodice Front and Back

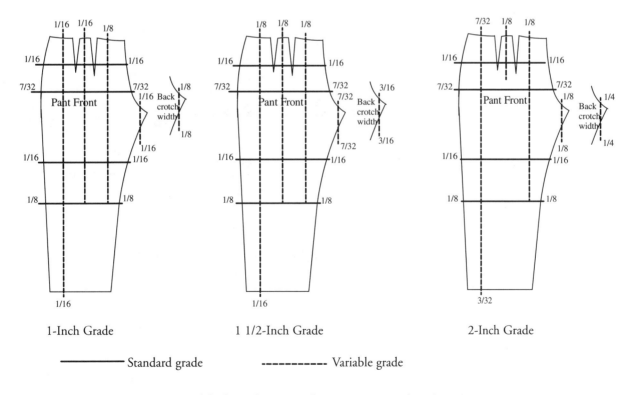

1-Inch Grade

1 1/2-Inch Grade

2-Inch Grade

—————— Standard grade

- - - - - - - Variable grade

■Figure B.10 Misses 55+ Simplified Grade System for Pant Front and Back

PATTERN GRADING
SUMMARY

These incremental grade guides have not been tested to determine their accuracy. Note should be made of the mixed grading system in which the hip is graded differently than the bust and waist. It appears as though the simplified system would produce fit problems with too much room in the neck/shoulder area in the largest sizes.

Computer technology may soon be available to employ the more complex grade guides in the pattern grading phase of apparel production to improve garment fit in all sizes.

REFERENCES

American National Standards Institute. (1997). Designation D 5586-95, standard table for body measurements for women aged 55 and older, misses figure type. In *Annual book of ASTM Standards* (Vol. 07.01). New York: Authors.

Armstrong, H. (1995). *Patternmaking for fashion design* (2nd ed.). New York: Harper Collins.

Cooklin, G. (1994). *Pattern grading for women's clothes*. London: Blackwell Scientific Publications.

Handford, J. (1980). *Professional pattern grading for women's, men's, and children's apparel*. Redondo Beach, CA: Plycon Press.

Price, J., & Zamkoff, B. (1996). *Grading techniques for modern design* (2nd ed.). New York: Fairchild Publications.

Scheier, M. (1974). *The ABC's of grading*. Bronxville, NY: Murray Scheier.

Taylor, P. J., & Shoben, M. M. (1986). *Grading for the fashion industry: The theory and practice*. London: Hutchinson.

Table B.1 ASTM D 5586 Standard Table of Body Measurements for Women Aged 55+ Misses Figure Type

Size	6	8	10	12	14	16	18	20	22
Girth Measurements in Inches									
1. Bust	30.66	31.45	32.60	34.18	35.68	37.22	39.13	41.01	43.23
2. Bust arc	16.38	17.11	17.31	18.32	19.34	20.14	21.14	21.93	23.00
3. *Back width at bust level*[a]	14.28	14.34	15.29	15.86	16.34	17.08	17.99	19.08	20.23
4. Waist	26.64	27.22	28.40	29.81	31.06	32.57	34.48	36.97	39.32
5. Waist arc	14.12	14.47	15.06	15.83	16.54	17.42	18.58	20.05	21.10
6. *Back waist width*[a]	12.52	12.75	13.34	13.98	14.52	15.15	15.90	16.92	18.22
7. Abdomen extension	33.78	33.83	34.75	36.43	37.62	39.07	41.21	43.49	45.54
8. Abdominal arc	17.69	17.74	18.29	19.15	19.91	20.71	21.91	23.08	23.96
9. *Back width abdominal level*[a]	16.09	16.09	16.46	17.28	17.71	18.36	19.30	20.41	21.58
10. Hip	35.67	35.51	36.40	37.79	38.92	40.03	41.61	43.46	44.82
11. Hip arc back	18.18	17.88	18.46	19.09	19.58	20.02	20.79	21.55	22.57
12. *Hip width across front*[a]	17.49	17.63	17.94	18.70	19.34	12.01	20.82	21.91	22.25
13. Sitting spread	37.14	36.82	38.02	39.68	40.83	41.96	43.79	45.86	47.77
14. Midneck	11.99	12.27	12.40	12.82	13.16	13.50	13.83	14.50	14.80
15. Neck base[b]	14.96	15.13	15.33	15.49	15.88	16.30	16.53	17.17	17.22
16. Armscye	15.43	15.85	16.43	16.58	17.22	17.65	18.23	18.87	19.53
17. Upper arm	10.08	10.26	10.66	11.27	11.73	12.27	12.85	13.64	14.08
18. Elbow	9.51	9.53	9.93	10.18	10.51	10.70	11.08	11.60	11.79
19. Wrist	5.92	5.90	5.98	6.12	6.24	6.36	6.52	6.70	6.85
20. Thigh, max	20.17	20.21	21.01	21.99	22.52	23.10	23.92	25.05	25.64
21. Thigh, mid	17.51	17.66	18.68	19.34	19.82	20.36	20.93	21.87	22.42
22. Knee	13.43	13.43	13.86	14.28	14.56	14.94	15.44	15.98	16.37
23. Calf	12.32	12.62	12.76	13.25	13.58	13.84	14.43	14.86	15.23
24. Ankle	9.09	9.15	9.18	9.25	9.50	9.52	9.75	10.01	10.18
25. Vertical trunk	57.94	57.61	58.59	59.54	61.17	62.07	63.53	65.14	66.64
26. Total crotch length	27.72	27.17	27.34	28.02	29.04	29.38	30.55	30.20	31.85
Vertical Measurements in Inches									
27. Height	62.70	63.42	64.00	64.42	65.00	65.59	66.10	66.42	67.08
28. Cervical height	55.11	55.26	55.79	56.37	57.09	57.64	58.28	58.76	59.42
29. Waist height back	39.38	39.54	39.80	40.43	40.84	41.17	41.53	41.96	42.45
30. Abdominal height	36.22	36.48	36.99	37.66	37.82	38.25	38.48	38.49	39.00
31. Waist to hip height	7.40	7.07	6.85	7.02	7.16	7.33	7.76	7.75	8.13
32. Hip height	32.57	33.27	33.70	34.15	34.34	34.63	34.61	34.78	34.96
33. Inseam	28.91	29.19	29.52	29.76	29.82	30.19	30.18	30.23	30.65

■Table B.1 (*continued*)

Size	6	8	10	12	14	16	18	20	22
Vertical Measurements in Inches									
34. Knee height	16.88	17.18	17.31	17.59	17.76	17.99	18.09	18.10	18.48
35. Ankle height	2.49	2.55	2.58	2.59	2.68	2.73	2.71	2.72	2.84
36. Waist length, front	12.94	13.09	13.28	13.44	13.69	13.96	14.17	14.56	14.88
37. Cervical to center front waist	19.15	19.20	19.52	19.83	20.27	20.67	20.97	21.56	22.11
38. Waist length, back	15.72	15.71	15.98	15.95	16.24	16.47	16.57	16.80	16.98
Width and Length Measurements Inches									
39. Cross back shoulder [b]	14.62	14.80	15.18	15.45	15.84	16.01	16.28	16.66	17.19
40. Back width	14.21	14.20	14.28	14.57	14.86	15.44	14.95	16.62	17.32
41. Chest width	13.54	13.53	13.52	14.00	14.23	14.56	15.02	15.75	16.00
42. Shoulder length	4.78	5.09	5.08	5.25	5.15	5.31	5.31	5.39	5.47
43. Shoulder slope (degrees)	21.40	22.02	22.34	21.98	22.54	22.51	21.76	20.51	20.86
44. Shoulder to wrist	22.41	22.70	23.02	23.23	23.54	23.86	24.08	24.24	24.73
45. Shoulder to elbow	12.68	12.84	13.42	13.46	13.59	13.71	13.87	13.99	14.21
46. Underarm to wrist	17.03	17.05	17.09	17.19	17.24	17.59	17.54	17.71	17.75
47. Bust point to bust point	6.67	6.82	7.03	7.29	7.51	7.73	8.24	8.64	8.84
48. Neck to bust point	10.43	10.62	10.68	11.02	11.40	11.68	11.92	12.09	12.34
49. Armscye depth	6.86	7.09	6.98	7.09	7.22	7.47	7.68	8.06	8.12
50. Armscye to waist	7.22	7.12	7.30	7.47	7.59	7.71	7.64	7.81	7.77

Note: Subjects; measurements are listed as comparison to PS 42-70 numbered sizes. Hang tag numbers currently used in U.S. Apparel Sizing range from two to four sizes smaller than the original PS 42-70 database.

[a] Differences between arc and girth measurements. Not included in original ASTM D 5586-95 chart.

[b] Measurements. not in original PS 42-70 data.

Source: Reprinted from *Annual Book of ASTM Standards.* Copyright ASTM. Reprinted with permission.

Table B.2 Incremental Difference Between Sizes: Women Aged 55+ Misses Figure Type

Size	6–8	8–10	10–12	12–14	14–16	16–18	18–20	20–22	Total Dif. Sizes 6–22
Difference Between Sizes for Girth Measurements in Inches (Decimals and Fractions to 32nd Inch)									
1. Bust	.79 25/32	1.15 1 5/32	1.58 1 9/16	1.50 1 1/2	1.54 1 17/32	1.91 1 29/32	1.88 1 7/8	2.22 2 7/32	12.57 12 9/16
2. Bust arc	.73 3/4	.20 7/32	1.01 1	1.02 1	.80 13/16	1.00 1	.79 25/32	1.07 1 1/16	6.62 6 5/8
3. *Back width at bust level* [a]	.06 1/16	.95 15/16	.57 9/16	.48 1/2	.74 3/4	.91 29/32	1.09 1 3/32	1.15 1 5/32	5.95 5 15/16
4. Waist	.58 9/16	1.18 1 3/16	1.41 1 7/16	1.25 1 1/4	1.51 1 1/2	1.91 1 29/32	2.49 2 1/2	2.35 2 11/32	12.68 12 11/16
5. Waist arc	.35 11/32	.59 19/32	.77 25/32	.71 23/32	.88 7/8	1.16 1 5/32	1.47 1 15/32	1.05 1 1/16	6.98 7
6. *Back width at waist*	.23 1/4	.59 19/32	.64 21/32	.54 17/32	.63 21/32	.75 3/4	1.02 1	1.30 1 5/16	5.70 5 23/32
7. Abdominal extension	.05 1/16	.92 9/16	1.68 7/8	1.19 3/4	1.45 13/16	2.14 1 7/32	2.28 1 3/16	2.05 7/8	11.76 6 9/32
8. Abdominal arc	.05 1/16	.55 9/16	.86 7/8	.76 3/4	.80 13/16	1.20 1 7/32	1.17 1 3/16	.88 7/8	6.27 6 9/32
9. Back width at high hip [a]	.00 3/8	.37 13/16	.82 7/16	.43 21/32	.65 15/16	.94 1 1/8	1.11 1 3/16	1.17 5 1/2	5.49
10. Hip	2.16 23/16	.89 29/32	1.39 1 13/32	1.13 1 1/8	1.11 1 1/8	1.58 1 19/32	1.85 1 27/32	1.36 1 3/8	9.15+ [b] 9 5/32
11. Hip back arc	2.30 5/16	.58 19/32	.63 5/8	.49 1/2	.44 7/16	.77 25/32	.76 3/4	1.02 1"	4.39+ [b] 4 13/32
12. *Front width at hip level* [a]	2.14 5/32	.31 5/16	.76 3/4	.64 21/32	.67 11/16	.81 13/16	1.09 1 3/32	.34 11/32	4.48+ [b] 4 1/2
13. Sitting spread	2.32 5/16	1.2 1 3/16	1.66 1 21/32	1.15 1 5/32	1.13 1 1/8	1.83 1 27/32	2.07 1 1/16	1.91 1 29/32	10.63+ [b] 10 21/32
14. Midneck	.28 9/32	.13 18	.42 7/16	.34 11/32	.34 11/32	.33 11/32	.67 21/32	.30 5/16	2.81 2 13/16
15. Neck base	.17 3/16	.20 7/32	.16 3/16	.39 13/32	.42 7/16	.23 1/4	.64 21/32	.05 1/16	2.26 2 1/4
16. Armscye	.42 7/16	.58 19/32	.15 3/16	.64 21/32	.43 7/16	.58 19/32	.64 21/32	.66 21/32	4.1 4 1/8
17. Upper arm	.18 3/16	.40 13/32	.61 19/32	.46 15/32	.54 17/32	.58 19/32	.79 25/32	.44 7/16	4.0 4
18. Elbow	.02 1/32	.40 13/32	.25 1/4	.33 11/32	.20 7/32	.38 3/8	.52 1/2	.19 7/32	2.28 2 9/32

■Table B.2 *(continued)*

Size	6–8	8–10	10–12	12–14	14–16	16–18	18–20	20–22	Total Dif. Sizes 6–22
Difference Between Sizes for Girth Measurements in Inches (Decimals and Fractions to 32nd Inch)									
19. Wrist	2.02 21/32	.08 3/32	.14 1/8	.12 1/8	.12 1/8	.16 5/32	.18 3/16	.15 5/32	.93+[b] 15/16
20. Thigh, max	.03 1/32	.80 13/16	.93 15/16	.53 17/32	.58 19/32	.82 13/16	1.13 1 1/8	.59 19/32	5.47 5 15/32
21. Thigh, mid	.15 3/16	1.02 1 1/32	.66 21/32	.48 1/2	.54 17/32	.57 9/16	.94 15/16	.55 9/16	4.91 4 29/32
22. Knee	.00	.43 7/16	.42 7/16	.28 9/32	.38 3/8	.50 1/2	.54 17/32	.39 13/32	2.94 2 15/16
23. Calf	.30 5/16	.14 1/8	.49 1/2	.33 11/32	.26 1/4	.59 19/32	.43 7/16	.37 3/8	2.91 2 29/32
24. Ankle	.06 1/16	.03 1/32	.07 1/16	.25 1/4	.02 1/32	.23 1/4	.26 1/4	.17 3/16	1.09 1 3/32
25. Vertical trunk	−.33 −11/32	.98 1"	.95 31/32	1.63 1 5/8	.90 29/32	1.46 1 5/32	1.61 1 5/8	1.50 1 1/2	8.70+[b] 8 23/32
26. Total crotch length	−.55 −9/16	.17 3/16	.68 11/16	1.02 1 1/32	.34 1 1/32	1.17 1 3/16	2.35 21 1/32	1.65 1 21/32	4.13+ 4 1/8
Difference Between Sizes for Vertical Measurements in Inches (Decimals and Fractions)									
27. Height	.72 23/32	.58 9/16	.42 7/16	.58 19/32	.59 19/32	.51 1/2	.32 11/32	.66 11/16	4.38 4 3/8
28. Cervical height	.15 5/32	.53 17/32	.58 19/32	.72 23/32	.55 9/16	.64 21/32	.48 1/2	.66 1 1/16	4.31 4 5/16
29. Waist height	.16 5/32	.26 1/4	.63 5/8	.41 13/32	.33 11/32	.36 11/32	.43 7/16	.49 1/2	3.07 3 1/16
30. Abdominal height	.21 1/4	.51 1/2	.67 11/16	.16 3/16	.43 7/16	.23 1/4	.01 0	.51 1/2	2.78 2 25/32
31. Waist to hip height	−.37 3/8	.22 7/32	.17 3/16	.14 5/32	.17 3/16	.43 7/16	2.01 0	.38 3/8	.73+[b] 3/4
32. Hip height	.70 23/32	.43 7/16	.40 13/32	.19 3/16	.29 9/32	2.02 21/32	.17 3/16	.18 3/16	2.39 2 13/32
33. Inseam	.28 9/32	.33 11/32	.24 1/4	.06 1/16	.37 3/8	2.01 0	.05 1 1/16	.42 7/16	1.74 1 3/4
34. Knee height	.30 5/16	.13 1/8	.28 9/32	.17 3/16	.23 1/4	.10 1/8	.01 0	.38 3/8	1.6 1 19/32
35. Ankle height	.06 1/16	.03 1/32	.01 0	.09 3/32	.05 1/16	2.01 0	.01 0	.12 1/8	.35 11/32

■ Table B.2 *(continued)*

Size	6–8	8–10	10–12	12–14	14–16	16–18	18–20	20–22	Total Dif. Sizes 6–22
Difference Between Sizes for Width and Length Measurements in Inches (Decimals and Fractions)									
36. Waist length, front	.15 5/32	.19 3/16	.16 5/32	.25 1/4	.27 9/32	.21 7/32	.39 13/32	.32 5/16	1.94 1 15/16
37. Cervical to center front waist	.05 1/16	.32 11/32	.31 11/32	.44 7/16	.40 13/32	.30 5/16	.59 19/32	.55 9/16	2.96 2 31/32
38. Waist length, back	−.01 0	.27 9/32	2.03 21/32	.29 9/32	.23 1/4	.10 1/8	.23 1/4	.18 3/16	1.26+ [b] 1 1/4
39. Cross back shoulder	.18 3/16	.38 13/32	.27 1/4	.39 3/8	.17 3/16	.27 1/4	.38 3/8	.53 17/32	2.57 2 9/16
40. Back bodice width	−.01 0	.08 3/32	.29 9/32	.29 9/32	.87 7/8	.51 1/2	1.18 1 3/16	.70 23/32	3.11+ [b] 3 1/8
41. Chest width	−.01 0	−.01 0	.48 1/2	.23 1/4	.33 11/32	.46 15/32	.73 3/4	.25 1/4	2.46+ [b] 2 15/32
42. Shoulder length	.31 5/16	2.01 0	.27 3/16	.39 1/8	.17 3/16	.27 0	.38 3/32	.53 3/32	2.57 11/16
43. Shoulder slope (degrees)	.62	.32	2.36	.56	2.03	2.75	21.25	.35	2.54
44. Shoulder to wrist	.29 9/32	.32 5/16	.21 7/32	.31 5/16	.32 5/16	.22 7/32	.16 3/16	.49 1/2	2.32 2 5/16
45. Shoulder to elbow	.16 3/16	.58 9/16	.04 1/32	.13 1/8	.12 1/8	.16 5/32	.12 1/8	.22 7/32	1.53 1 17/32
46. Underarm to wrist	.02 1/32	.04 1/32	.10 1/8	.05 1/16	.35 11/32	−.05 −1/16	.17 3/16	.04 1/32	.72 23/32
47. Bust point to bust point	.15 5/32	.21 7/32	.26 1/4	.22 7/32	.22 7/32	.51 1/2	.44 7/16	.20 7/32	2.17 2 3/16
48. Neck to bust point	.19 3/16	.06 1/16	.34 11/32	.38 3/8	.28 9/32	.24 1/4	.17 3/16	.25 1/4	1.91 1 29/32
49. Armscye depth	.23 1/4	−.11 −1/8	.11 1/8	.13 1/8	.25 1/4	.21 7/32	.38 3/8	.06 1/16	1.26 1 1/4
50. Armscye to waist	−.10 −1/8	.18 3/16	.17 3/16	.12 1/8	.12 1/8	−.07 1/16	.17 3/16	2.04 21/32	.55+ [b] 9/16
51. Weight (lbs)	3.87	7.92	10.62	9.00	9.93	14.81	14.68	15.55	86.28

[a] *Differences between arc and girth numbers.*

[b] *A plus sign (+) indicates that size 8 is smaller than size 6.*

Table B.3 Average Differences and Grades Between Sizes for Vertical Body Measurements From ASTM D 5586

Vertical Measurement	Total Difference Between Sizes 6 and 22	Average Difference Between Sizes	Standard Length Grade (Nearest 32nd Inch) Between Sizes
Waist height, back	3.07	0.38375	3/8
Abdominal height	2.78	0.3475	11/32
Waist to hip height	0.73	0.09125	3/32
Hip height	2.39	0.29875	5/16
Inseam height	1.74	0.2175	7/32
Knee height	1.6	0.2	3/16
Ankle height	0.35	0.04375	0
Waist length, front	1.94	0.2425	1/4
Waist length, back	1.26	0.161	5/32
Shoulder to wrist	2.32	0.29	9/32
Shoulder to elbow	1.53	0.19	3/16
Shoulder length[a]	0.69	0.0863	3/32
Armscye depth	1.25	0.15625	5/32

[a]Shoulder length may not be standard in 1–inch, 1 1/2–inch, and 2–inch grades.

Table B.4 Complex Incremental Grade Guide for Women Aged 55+ Misses Developed From ASTM D 5586 Standard Tables of Body Measurements

Size	6–8	8–10	10–12	12–14	14–16	16–18	18–20	20–22	Total Dif. Sizes 6–22
Girth Measurements in Inches									
1. Bust	1	1	1 1/2	1 1/2	1 1/2	2	2	2	12 1/2
2. Bust arc	9/16	9/16	15/16	15/16	1 1/16	1 1/16	1 1/16	1 1/16	7 1/8
3. Back width at *bust level*[a]	7/16	7/16	9/16	9/16	9/16	15/16	15/16	15/16	5 3/8
4. Waist	1	1	1 1/2	1 1/2	11/2	2	2	2	12 1/2
5. Waist arc	5/8	5/8	7/8	7/8	7/8	1 1/8	1 1/8	1 1/8	7 1/4
6. *Waist width across back*[a]	3/8	3/8	5/8	5/8	5/8	7/8	7/8	7/8	5 1/4
7. Abdominal extension	1	1	1 1/2	1 1/2	11/2	2	2	2	12 1/2
8. Abdominal arc	9/16	9/16	13/16	13/16	13/16	1 1/16	1 1/16	1 1/16	6 3/4
9. *Back width at high hip*[a]	7/16	7 1/16	11/16	11/16	11/16	15/16	15/16	15/16	5 3/4
10. Hip	1	1	1 1/2	1 1/2	11/2	2	2	2	11
11. Hip arc back	1/2	1/2	1/2	1/2	3/4	3/4	1	1	5 1/2
12. *Front width at hip level*[b]	1/2	1/2	1/2	1/2	3/4	3/4	1	1	5 1/2
13. Sitting spread	1	1	1	1	11/2	2	2	2	11
14. Midneck	1/4	1/4	3/8	3/8	3/8	3/8	3/8	3/8	2 3/4
15. Neck base	1/4	1/4	3/8	3/8	3/8	3/8	3/8	3/8	2 3/4
16. Armscye	9/16	9/16	11/16	11/16	13/16	13/16	13/16	13/16	5 5/8
17. Upper arm	5/16	5/16	7/16	7/16	7/16	9/16	9/16	9/16	3 5/8
18. Elbow	1/4	1/4	3/8	3/8	3/8	1/2	1/2	1/2	3 1/8
19. Wrist	1/8	1/8	1/8	1/8	1/8	1/8	1/8	1/8	1
20. Thigh, max	5/16	5/16	3/4	3/4	3/4	7/8	7/8	7/8	5 1/2
21. Thigh, mid	3/8	3/8	1/2	1/2	1/2	3/4	3/4	3/4	4 1/2
22. Knee	1/4	1/4	3/8	3/8	3/8	1/2	1/2	1/2	3 1/8
23. Calf	1/4	1/4	3/8	3/8	3/8	3/16	3/16	3/16	3 1/8
24. Ankle	1/8	1/8	1/8	1/8	1/8	1/8	1/8	1/8	1 3/16
25. Vertical trunk	1 1/4	1 1/4	1 1/4	1 1/4	1 1/4	1 1/4	1 1/4	1 1/4	10
26. Total crotch length	3/4	3/4	3/4	3/4	3/4	3/4	3/4	3/4	6
Vertical Measurements in Inches									
27. Height	1/2	1/2	1/2	1/2	1/2	1/2	1/2	1/2	4
28. Cervical height	1/2	1/2	1/2	1/2	1/2	1/2	1/2	1/2	4
29. Waist height, back	1/2	1/2	1/2	1/2	1/2	1/2	1/2	1/2	4
30. Abdominal height	3/8	3/8	3/8	3/8	3/8	3/8	3/8	3/8	3

■ **Table B.4** (*continued*)

Size	6–8	8–10	10–12	12–14	14–16	16–18	18–20	20–22	Total Dif. Sizes 6–22
Vertical Measurements in Inches									
31. Waist to hip height	1/8	1/8	1/8	1/8	1/8	1/8	1/8	1/8	1
32 . Hip height	1/4	1/4	1/4	1/4	1/4	1/4	1/4	1/4	2
33. Inseam	1/4	1/4	1/4	1/4	1/4	1/4	1/4	1/4	2
34. Knee height	1/8	1/8	1/8	1/8	1/8	1/8	1/8	1/8	1
35. Ankle height	0	0	0	0	0	0	0	0	0
36. Waist length, front	1/4	1/4	1/4	1/4	1/4	1/4	1/4	1/4	2
Width and Length Measurements in Inches									
37. Cervical to center front waist	3/8	3/8	3/8	3/8	3/8	3/8	3/8	3/8	3
38. Waist length, back	7/32	7/32	7/32	7/32	7/32	7/32	7/32	7/32	3
39. Center back shoulder	1/4	1/4	3/8	3/8	3/8	3/8	3/8	3/8	2 3/4
40. Back width	1/4	1/4	3/8	3/8	3/8	1/2	1/2	1/2	3 1/8
41. Chest width	1/4	1/4	3/8	3/8	3/8	3/8	3/8	3/8	2 3/4
42. Shoulder length	1/16	1/16	1/8	1/8	1/8	1/8	1/8	1/8	7/8
43. Shoulder slope (degrees)	0	0	0	0	0	0	0	0	0
44. Shoulder to wrist	5/16	5/16	5/16	5/16	5/16	5/16	5/16	5/16	2 1/2
45. Shoulder to elbow	3/16	3/16	3/16	3/16	3/16	3/16	3/16	3/16	1 1/2
46. Underarm to wrist	3/16	3/16	3/16	3/16	3/16	3/16	3/16	3/16	1 1/2
47. Bust point to bust point	1/4	1/4	1/4	1/4	1/4	5/16	5/16	5/16	2 3/16
48. Neck to bust point	3/16	3/16	1/4	1/4	1/4	5/16	5/16	5/16	2 1/16
49. Armhole depth	5/32	5/32	5/32	5/32	5/32	5/32	5/32	5/32	1 1/4
50. Armhole to waist	1/16	1/16	1/16	1/16	1/16	1/16	1/16	1/16	1/2
51. Weight (lbs)	11	11	11	11	11	11	11	11	88

[a]Differences between arc and girth numbers.

[b]Hip grade changes differently than bust and waist from 1 inch to 1 1/2 inches and from 1 1/2 inches to 2 inches.

▪ Table B.5 Sizing Specifications for Misses Women Aged 55+ Developed From ASTM D 5586-95 Standard Tables of Body Measurements Based on Incremental Differences Between Sizes

Size	6	8	10	12	14	16	18	20	22
Girth Measurements in Inches									
1. Bust	30 3/4	31 3/4	32 3/4	34 1/4	35 3/4	37 1/8	39 1/4	41 1/4	43 1/4
2. Bust arc	16 3/8	16 5/16	17 7/16	18 3/8	19 5/16	20 1/4	21 5/16	22 3/8	23 7/16
3. *Back width at bust level* [a]	14 7/16	14 7/8	15 5/16	17 7/8	16 7/16	17	17 15/16	18 7/8	19 13/16
4. Waist	26 1/2	27 1/2	28 1/2	30	31 1/2	33	35	37	39
5. Waist arc	13 3/4	14 3/8	15	15 7/8	16 3/4	17 5/8	18 3/4	19 7/8	21
6. *Waist width across back* [a]	12 3/4	13 1/8	13 1/2	14 1/8	14 3/4	15 3/8	16 1/4	17 1/8	18
7. Abdominal extension	33	34	35	36 1/2	38	39 1/2	41 1/2	43 1/2	45 1/2
8. Abdominal arc	17 1/16	17 5/8	18 3/16	19	19 13/16	20 5/8	21 7/8	22 3/4	23 13/16
9. *Back width at high hip* [a]	15 15/16	16 3/8	16 13/16	17 1/2	18 3/16	18 7/8	19 5/8	20 3/4	21 11/16
10. Hip	35	36	37	38	39	40 1/2	42	44	46
11. Hip arc back	17 1/2	18	18 1/2	19	19 1/2	20 1/4	21	22	23
12. *Front width at hip level* [a]	17 1/2	18	18 1/2	19	19 1/2	20 1/4	21	22	23
13. Sitting spread	39	39	40	41	42	43 1/2	45	47	49
14. Midneck	12	12 1/4	12 1/2	12 7/8	13 1/4	13 5/8	14	14 3/8	14 3/4
15. Neck base [b]	14 5/8	14 7/8	15 1/8	15 1/2	15 7/8	16 1/4	16 5/8	17	17 3/8
16. Armscye	15 7/16	16	16 9/16	17 1/4	17 15/16	18 5/8	19 7/16	20 1/4	21 1/16
17. Upper arm	10 3/16	10 1/2	10 13/16	11 1/4	11 11/16	12 1/8	12 11/16	13 1/4	13 13/16
18. Elbow	9 3/8	9 5/8	9 7/8	10 1/4	10 5/8	11	11 1/2	12	12 1/2
19. Wrist	5 3/4	5 7/8	6	6 1/8	6 1/4	6 3/8	6 1/2	6 5/8	6 3/4
20. Thigh, max	20 5/8	20 15/16	21 1/4	22	22 3/4	23 1/2	24 3/8	25 1/4	26 1/8
21. Thigh, mid	18 1/8	18 1/2	18 7/8	19 3/8	19 7/8	20 3/8	21 1/8	21 1/8	22 5/8
22. Knee	13 3/8	13 5/8	13 7/8	14 1/4	14 5/8	15	15 1/2	16	16 1/2
23. Calf	12 3/8	12 5/8	12 7/8	13 1/4	13 5/8	14	14 1/2	15	15 1/2
24. Ankle	8 3/8	8 5/8	8 7/8	9 1/4	9 3/8	9 3/4	10 1/4	10 3/4	11 1/4
25. Vertical trunk	55 3/4	57	58 1/4	59 1/2	60 3/4	62	63 1/4	64 1/2	65 3/4
26. Total crotch length	26 1/4	27	27 3/4	28 1/2	29 1/4	30	30 3/4	31 1/2	32 1/4
Vertical Measurements in Inches									
27. Height	63	63 1/2	64	64 1/2	65	65 1/2	66	66 1/2	67
28. Cervical height	55	55 1/2	56	56 1/2	57	57 1/2	58	58 1/2	59
29. Waist height, back	38 15/16	39 7/16	39 15/16	40 7/16	40 15/16	41 7/16	41 15/16	42 7/16	42 15/16
30. Abdominal height	36 5/8	37	37 3/8	37 3/4	38 1/8	38 1/2	38 7/8	39 1/4	39 5/8
31. Waist to hip height	6 5/8	6 3/4	6 7/8	7	7 1/8	7 1/4	7 3/8	7 1/2	7 5/8
32. Hip height	33 1/4	33 1/2	33 3/4	34	34 1/4	34 1/2	34 3/4	35	35 1/4

Table B.5 *(continued)*

Size	6	8	10	12	14	16	18	20	22
Vertical Measurements in Inches									
33. Inseam	28 3/4	29	29 1/4	29 1/2	29 3/4	30	30 1/4	30 1/2	30 3/4
34. Knee height	17 1/4	17 3/8	17 1/2	17 5/8	17 3/4	17 7/8	18	18 1/8	18 1/4
35. Ankle height	2 5/8	2 5/8	2 5/8	2 5/8	2 5/8	2 5/8	2 5/8	2 5/8	2 5/8
36. Waist length, front	12 3/4	13	13 1/4	13 1/2	13 3/4	14	14 1/4	14 1/2	14 3/4
37. Cervical to center front waist	19	19 1/8	19 7/8	20 1/4	20 5/8	21	21 3/8	21 3/4	22 1/8
38. Waist length, back	15 11/32	15 9/16	15 25/32	16	16 7/32	16 7/16	16 21/32	16 7/8	17 3/32
Width and Length Measurements Inches									
39. Center back shoulder	14 5/8	14 7/8	15 1/8	15 1/2	15 7/8	16 1/4	16 5/8	17	17 3/8
40. Back width	13 7/8	14 1/8	14 3/8	14 3/4	15 1/8	15 1/2	16	16 1/2	17
41. Chest width	13 1/8	13 3/8	13 5/8	14	14 3/8	14 3/4	15 1/8	15 1/2	15 7/8
42. Shoulder length	4 7/8	4 15/16	5	5 1/8	5 1/4	5 3/8	5 1/2	5 5/8	5 3/4
43. Shoulder slope (degrees)	0	0	0	0	0	0	0	0	0
44. Shoulder to waist	22 5/16	22 5/8	22 15/16	23 1/4	23 9/16	23 7/8	24 3/16	24 1/2	24 13/16
45. Shoulder to elbow	12 15/16	13 1/8	13 5/16	13 1/2	13 11/16	13 7/8	14 1/16	14 1/14	14 7/16
46. Underarm to waist	16 13/16	17	17 3/16	17 3/8	17 9/16	17 3/4	17 15/16	18 1/8	18 5/16
47. Bust point to bust point	6 1/2	6 3/4	7	7 1/4	7 1/2	7 3/4	8 1/16	8 3/8	8 11/16
48. Neck to bust point	10 3/8	10 9/16	10 3/4	11	11 1/4	11 1/2	11 13/16	12 1/8	12 7/16
49. Armscye depth	6 5/8	6 25/32	6 31/32	7 1/8	7 9/32	7 7/8	8 1/32	8 3/16	8 11/32
50. Armscye to waist	7 5/16	7 3/8	7 7/16	7 1/2	7 9/16	7 5/16	7 11/16	7 3/4	7 13/16
51. Weight (lbs)	97	108	119	130	141	152	163	174	185

[a]Differences between arc and girth measurements.

[b]Hip grade changes differently than bust and waist from 1 inch to 1 1/2 inches to 2 inches.

■Table B.6 Simplified Incremental Grade Guide for Women Aged 55+ Developed From ASTM D 5586 Standard Tables of Body Measurements

Size	6–8	8–10	10–12	12–14	14–16	16–18	18–20	20–22	Total Dif.Sizes 6–22
Girth Measurements in Inches									
1. Bust	1	1	1 1/2	1 1/2	1 1/2	2	2	2	12 1/2
4. Waist	1	1	1 1/2	1 1/2	1 1/2	2	2	2	12 1/2
7. Abdominal extension	1	1	1 1/2	1 1/2	1 1/2	2	2	2	12 1/2
10. Hip [a]	1	1	1	1	1 1/2	1 1/2	2	2	11
13. Sitting spread [a]	1	1	1 1/2	1 1/2	1 1/2	1 1/2	2	2	11
15. Neck Base	1/4	1/4	3/8	3/8	3/8	3/8	3/8	3/8	2 3/4
16. Armscye	9/16	9/16	11/16	11/16	13/16	13/16	13/16	13/16	6 7/16
17. Upper arm	5/16	5/16	7/16	7/16	7/16	9/16	9/16	9/16	3 5/8
18. Elbow	1/4	1/4	3/8	3/8	3/8	1/2	1/2	1/2	3 1/8
19. Wrist	1/8	1/8	1/8	1/8	1/8	1/8	1/8	1/8	1
20. Thigh, max	5/16	5/16	3/4	3/4	3/4	7/8	7/8	7/8	5 1/2
21. Thigh, mid	3/8	3/8	1/2	1/2	1/2	3/4	3/4	3/4	4 1/2
22. Knee	1/4	1/4	3/8	3/8	3/8	1/2	1/2	1/2	3 1/8
23. Calf	1/4	1/4	3/8	3/8	3/8	1/2	1/2	1/2	3 1/8
24. Ankle	1/8	1/8	1/8	1/8	1/8	3/16	3/16	3/16	1 3/16
25. Vertical trunk	1 1/4	1 1/4	1 1/4	1 1/4	1 1/4	1 1/4	1 1/4	1 1/4	10
26. Total crotch length	3/4	3/4	3/4	3/4	3/4	3/4	3/4	3/4	6
Vertical Measurements in Inches									
28. Cervical height	1/2	1/2	1/2	1/2	1/2	1/2	1/2	1/2	4
29. Waist height, back	1/2	1/2	1/2	1/2	1/2	1/2	1/2	1/2	4
30. Abdominal height	3/8	3/8	3/8	3/8	3/8	3/8	3/8	3/8	3
31. Waist to hip height	1/8	1/8	1/8	1/8	1/8	1/8	1/8	1/8	1
32 . Hip height	1/4	1/4	1/4	1/4	1/4	1/4	1/4	1/4	2
33. Inseam	1/4	1/4	1/4	1/4	1/4	1/4	1/4	1/4	2
34. Knee height	1/8	1/8	1/8	1/8	1/8	1/8	1/8	1/8	1
35. Ankle height	0	0	0	0	0	0	0	0	0
36. Waist length, front	1/4	1/4	1/4	1/4	1/4	1/4	1/4	1/4	2
38. Waist length, back	1/4	1/4	1/4	1/4	1/4	1/4	1/4	1/4	2
Width and Length Measurements in Inches									
39. Center back, shoulder	1/4	1/4	3/8	3/8	3/8	1/2	1/2	1/2	3 1/8
40. Back width	1/4	1/4	3/8	3/8	3/8	1/2	1/2	1/2	3 1/8
41. Chest width	1/4	1/4	3/8	3/8	3/8	1/2	1/2	1/2	3 1/8
42. Shoulder length	1/16	1/16	1/8	1/8	1/8	3/16	3/16	3/16	1 1/16
43. Shoulder slope (degrees)	0	0	0	0	0	0	0	0	0

Table B.6 (continued)

Size	6–8	8–10	10–12	12–14	14–16	16–18	18–20	20–22	Total Dif. Sizes 6–22
Width and Length Measurements in Inches									
44. Shoulder to waist	5/16	5/16	5/16	5/16	5/16	5/16	5/16	5/16	2 1/2
45. Shoulder to elbow	3/16	3/16	3/16	3/16	3/16	3/16	3/16	3/16	1 1/2
46. Underarm to waist	3/16	3/16	3/16	3/16	3/16	3/16	3/16	3/16	1 1/2
47. Bust point to bust point	1/4	1/4	1/4	1/4	1/4	5/16	5/16	5/16	2 3/16
48. Neck to bust point	3/16	3/16	9/32	9/32	9/32	9/32	9/32	9/32	2 1/16
49. Armhole depth	5/32	5/32	5/32	5/32	5/32	5/32	5/32	5/32	1 1/4
50. Armhole to waist	3/32	3/32	3/32	3/32	3/32	3/32	3/32	3/32	3/4

Note: Measurements were omitted that were not needed for simplified grading system.

[a]Hip grade changes differently than bust and waist from 1 inch to 1 1/2 inches and from 1 1/2 inches to 2 inches.

Table B.7 Comparison of Total Differences Between Sizes 6 and 22 in ASTM D 5586 Data in the Complex Grade Guide and in the Simplified Grade Guide

	ASTM D 5586	Complex Grade Guide	Simplified Grade
Differences Between Size 6 and Size 20 for Girth Measurements Inches			
1. Bust	12 9/16	12 1/2	12 1/2
2. Bust arc	6 5/8	**7 1/8**	**6 1/4**
3. *Back width at bust level*	*5 15/16*	*5 3/8*	*6 1/4*
4. Waist	12 11/16	12 1/2	12 1/2
5. Waist arc	7	**7 1/4**	**6 1/4**
6. *Back width at waist*	5 23/32	*5 1/4*	*6 1/4*
7. Abdominal extension	11 3/4	12 1/2	12 1/2
8. Abdominal arc	6 9/32	6 3/4	6 1/4
9. *Back width at abdominal level*	*5 1/2*	*5 3/4*	*6 1/4*
10. Hip	9 5/32	11	11
11. Hip arc back	4 13/32	5 1/2	5 1/2
12. *Front width at hip level*	*4 1/2*	*5 1/2*	*5 1/2*
13. Sitting spread	10 21/32	11	11
14. Midneck	2 13/16	2 3/4	2 3/4
15. Neck base [b]	**2 1/4**	**2 3/4**	**2 3/4**
16. Armscye	**4 1/8**	**5 5/8**	**5 5/8**
17. Upper arm	4	3 5/8	3 5/8
18. Elbow	2 9/32	3 1/8	3 1/8
19. Wrist	1 5/16	1	1
20. Thigh, max	5 15/32	5 1/2	5 1/2
21. Thigh, mid	4 29/32	4 1/2	4 1/2
22. Knee	2 15/16	3 1/8	3 1/8
23. Calf	2 29/32	3 1/8	3 1/8
24. Ankle	1 3/32	1 3/16	1 3/16
25. Vertical trunk	**8 23/32**	**9**	**9**
Differences Between Size 6 and Size 20 for Vertical Measurements in Inches			
26. Total crotch length	**4 1/8**	**5**	**5**
28. Cervical height	4 5/16	4	4
29. Waist height	3 1/16	4	4
30. Abdominal height	2 25/32	3	3
31. Waist hip, back	3/4	1	1
32. Hip height	2 13/32	2	2
33. Inseam	1 3/4	2	2

■ **Table B.7** *(continued)*

	ASTM D 5586	Complex Grade Guide	Simplified Grade
Differences Between Size 6 and Size 20 for Length Measurements in Inches			
34. Knee height	1 19/32	1	1
35. Ankle height	11/32	0	0
36. Waist length, front	1 15/16	2	2
37. Cervical to center front waist	2 31/32	3	3
38. Waist length, back	1 1/4	1 3/4	1 3/4
39. Center back shoulder	2 9/16	**2 3/4**	**3 1/8**
40. Back bodice width	3 1/2	3 1/8	3 1/8
41. Chest width	2 15/32	**2 3/4**	**3 1/8**
42. Shoulder length	1 1/16	1 1/16	1 1/16
43. Shoulder slope (degrees)	−1/2	0	0
44. Shoulder to waist	2 5/16	2 1/2	2 1/2
45. Shoulder to elbow	1 17/32	1 1/2	1 1/2
46. Underarm to waist	23/32	1 1/2	1 1/2
47. Bust point to bust point	2 3/16	2 3/16	2 3/16
48. Neck to bust point	1 29/32	2 1/16	2 1/16
49. Armscye depth	1 1/4	1 1/4	1 1/4
50. Armscye to waist	9/16	3/4	3/4

Note: Bold numbers indicate differences between the grade guides that might affect the fit of the garment in extreme sizes.

Appendix C

ASTM D 5585-95 Standard Table of Body Measurements for Adult Female Misses Figure Type, Sizes 2 to 20

INTRODUCTION

Data in the ASTM D 5585-95 Standard Table of Body Measurements for Adult Female Misses Figure Type, Sizes 2–20 are based on measurements in PS 42-70, on military survey data, and on industry and designer information (*Annual Book of ASTM Standards*, 1997). The major difference between this standard and the PS 42-70 standard is the size nomenclature. ASTM D 5585-95 is closer to industry ready-to-wear size designation.

DEVELOPMENT OF A GRADE GUIDE AND GRADING SYSTEM FROM ASTM D 5585-95

Table C.1 contains body measurements published in the *Annual Book of ASTM Standards* for misses figure type for sizes 2–20. (Measurements for the six other figure types in PS 42-70 were not included.) A grade guide for the standard was not published. However, Table C.2 contains a grade guide that consists of the incremental differences between adjacent sizes derived from the Standard Table of Body Measurements in Table C.1. There are no arc measurements included in the standard, so there is not enough information to develop a complex grading system. Therefore, only a simplified system, in which grades for the garment front and back are the same, is included in this Appendix.

Step 1: Bodice Front and Back Grades From the Grade Guide

Length Grades From Grade Guide

Grade distributions for the bodice front and back are illustrated in Figures C.1 and C.2. Length grades for the bodice front and back are indicated in Table C.2, except for the neck length grade, which is calculated from the neck girth information (Figure C.1). All of the bodice length is included above the waistline bust dart to accommodate the neck to bust length grade given in Table C.2. (Further discussion on the neck to bust length grades follows.) Except for the neck to bust point and shoulder length grades, the length grades are standard, so they are the same for the 1-inch, the 1 1/2-inch, and the 2-inch grades.

Width Grades From Grade Guide

Width grades for bodice front and back are indicated in Table C.2. Grades calculated from the chart information are identified by asterisks in Figures C.1 and C.2. Width grades from the grade guide were divided by 2 for half-pattern grades.

Calculation of Grades

The neck width grade was calculated by subtracting the shoulder length grade from one-half of the chest width (which is the same as the back width).

The armscye width grade was calculated by subtracting one-half the chest width grade from one-half of the cross bust grade. This calculation results in a discrepancy with the incremental differences in the armhole girth of 3/8 inch for the 1-inch grade listed in the Standard Table of Body Measurements. The armscye length is 1/8 inch for the front bodice and 1/8 inch for back bodice, which equals 1/4 inch of the total armscye girth. To provide for the total of a 1/4-inch cross

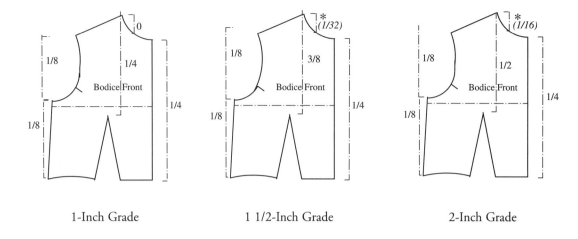

1-Inch Grade   1 1/2-Inch Grade   2-Inch Grade

*Calculated from grade guide data

Figure C.1 Length Grades for Bodice Front and Back

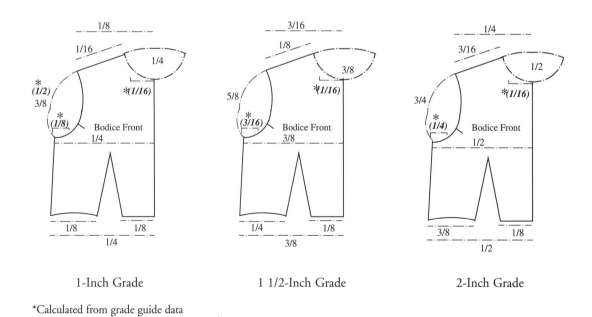

1-Inch Grade   1 1/2-Inch Grade   2-Inch Grade

*Calculated from grade guide data

Figure C.2 Width Grades and Neck/Armscye Girth Grades for Bodice Front and Back

bust grade, 1/8 inch must go into both the front and back armscye width. **The total length and width equals 1/2 inch for armscye girth instead of 3/8 inch in the 1-inch grade.** The measurements in the grade guide derived from the ASTM D 5585 standard for armscye girth is the same as in PS 42-70 Grade Guide, in which the same problem exists with the simplified grading system. However, the measurements in PS 42-70 can be used in the complex system.

Neck to Bust Grade

The neck to bust grade is 1/4 inch for a 1-inch grade, 3/8 inch for a 1 1/2-inch grade, and 1/2 inch for a 2-inch grade (Figure C.1). The neck girth grade is divided between neck width and neck length. The neck width was calculated previously, so the remainder is the neck length. This works for the 1-inch grade because the neck to bust length is the same as the front length, and all the neck girth must go in the neck width. But for the 1 1/2-inch and 2-inch grades, the neck length plus the center front length is not adequate to allow for the neck to bust grade of 3/8 inch for 1 1/2-inch grade and 1/2 inch for the 2-inch grade. Either the neck girth must be increased to accommodate the neck length or the bust dart point must be lowered. Again, this same problem exists in the PS 42-70 Grade Guide, and the authors adjusted the bust dart as the solution.

Step 2: Sleeve Length and Width Grades From the Grade Guide

Figure C.3 gives the sleeve grade distributions for the 1-inch, the 1 1/2-inch, and the 2-inch grades. Calculated grades are identified by asterisks. The sleeve width distributions must equal the total grade distributions in the armscye. The length grade in the sleeve cap is the same as the armscye length grade. The sleeve underarm and capline grades are equivalent to a bodice armscye width grade. In the 1-inch grade, the sleeve would not fit the armscye without the adjustment in the underarm grade in the armscye discussed earlier. A similar problem occurs in the 2-inch grade. The grade guide gives the upper arm girth (sleeve

width) as 5/8 inch and the armscye girth as 3/4 inch. The sleeve cap length grade of 1/4 inch (1/8 inch on each side of the sleeve cap) increases the total capline grade to 7/8 inch, which is 1/8 inch longer than the armscye. These sleeve and armscye grade measurements are the same as in the PS 42-70 Grade Guide. **The authors simplified the grading system by reducing the upper arm girth grade to 1/2 inch for the 2-inch grade.**

Step 3: Skirt/Pant Length and Width Grades

Figures C.4 and C.5 illustrate the grade distributions for the skirt and pant. The length grades are standard for the 1-inch, the 1 1/2-inch, and the 2-inch grades (Figure C.4). Because the hip, high hip, and waist heights are all 1/4 inch, it would appear that the pant increases in length a total of 1/4 inch and all the length is put in below the hip line. The rise grade is 1/4 inch, so the grade must be between the crotch level and the hipline. However, 1/8 inch is specified as knee height in the grade guide, which increases the total pant length to 3/8 inch instead of 1/4 inch, as the waist height indicates. The crotch height is 0, so that means the crotch would be lowered (or raised for smaller sizes) 1/8 inch between sizes to compensate for the 1/8-inch length below the knee. Grading pants in this manner produces an inseam that remains the same length throughout the size run. Although this method may be used in the industry, it is different from methods found in most grading text books. Individual size specifications will indicate if this method is satisfactory.

Width grades are illustrated for both the pant front and back, because the variable grade in the crotch width is different for the front and back. The width grades are the same for the skirt front and back. The waist of the skirt and pant grade the same as the bodice waist unless the garment has two darts in the half-pattern, which is illustrated in Figure C.5. The waist, hip, and skirt sweep total grades are the same. Pant style dictates the width grade for the leg opening. A straight-leg pant is illustrated.

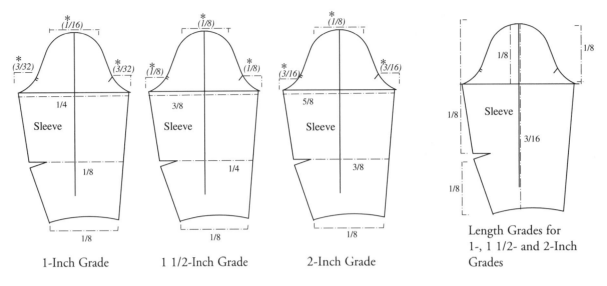

1-Inch Grade   1 1/2-Inch Grade   2-Inch Grade   Length Grades for
                                                                       1-, 1 1/2- and 2-Inch
                                                                       Grades

*Calculated from grade guide data.

■**Figure C.3** Sleeve Width and Length Grades

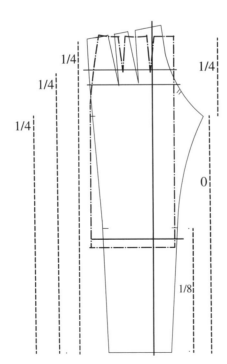

Standard grades for
1-, 1 1/2-, and 2-Inch
Grades

■**Figure C.4** Length Grades for Pant Front and Back

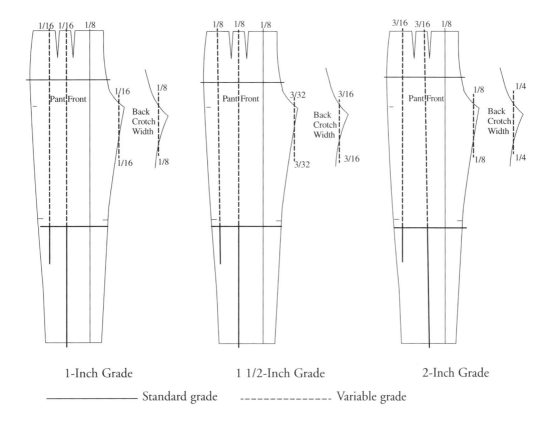

1-Inch Grade   1 1/2-Inch Grade   2-Inch Grade

———————— Standard grade   - - - - - - - - - - Variable grade

■Figure C.5 Width Grades for Pant Front and Back

There is no information given in the grade guide to determine the crotch width grade. Most pattern grading text books specify a standard 1/8 inch in both the front and back crotch width, which does simplify the grading system. The authors of this text book calculated crotch width based upon the hip width as cited by Scheier (1974) and Taylor and Shoben (1986), but used the drafting principle presented by Armstrong (1995) as the basis for the calculation. (See Appendix A.) The width distributions are presented in Figures C.5.

Figures C.6 and C.7 illustrate the amount of distribution in the upper and lower body for the 1-inch, the 1 1/2-inch, and the 2-inch grades. The simplified grading system developed from ASTM D 5585-95 is similar to the simplified system based on the PS 42-70 Grade Guide because they are essentially derived from the same database. A size run of garments graded by any grading system should be made before using the grading system for production runs of garments.

REFERENCES

American National Standards Institute. (1997). Designation D 5585-95, standard table of body measurements for adult female misses figure typw, sizes 2–20. In *Annual book of ASTM Standards* (Vol. 07.02). New York: Author.

Armstrong, H. (1995). *Patternmaking for fashion design* (2nd ed.). New York: Harper Collins.

Handford, J. (1980). *Professional pattern frading for women's, men's, and children's apparel*. Redondo Beach, CA: Plycon Press.

Scheier, M. (1974). *The ABC's of grading*. Bronxville, NY: Murray Scheier.

Taylor, P. J., & Shoben, M. M. (1986). *Grading for the fashion industry*. The theory and practice. London: Hutchinson.

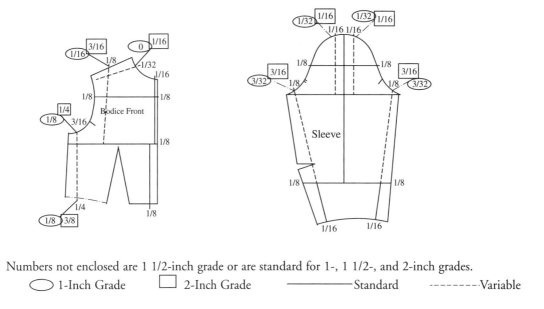

Numbers not enclosed are 1 1/2-inch grade or are standard for 1-, 1 1/2-, and 2-inch grades.

◯ 1-Inch Grade   ▢ 2-Inch Grade   ————Standard   - - - - - - -Variable

■ **Figure C.6** Distributions of 1-, 1 1/2-, and 2-Inch Grades for Bodice and Sleeve Basic Blocks

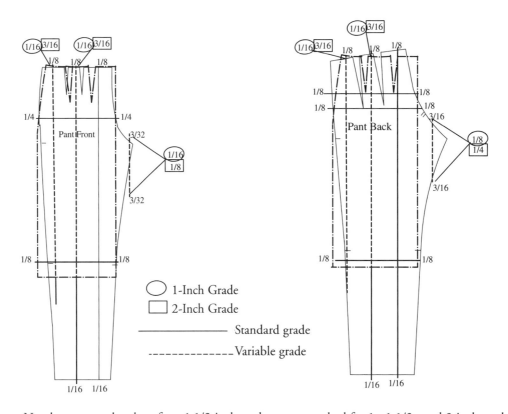

◯ 1-Inch Grade
▢ 2-Inch Grade
———— Standard grade
- - - - - - - Variable grade

Numbers not enclosed are for a 1 1/2-inch grade or are standard for 1-, 1 1/2-, and 2-inch grades.

■ **Figure C.7** Distributions of 1-, 1 1/2-, and 2-Inch Grades for Skirt and Pant Basic Blocks

Table C.1 ASTM D 5585-95 Standard Table of Body Measurements for Adult Female
Misses Figure Type, Sizes 2–20

Size	2	4	6	8	10	12	14	16	18	20
Girth Measurements in Inches										
1. Bust	32	33	34	35	36	37 1/2	39	40 1/2	42 1/2	44 1/2
2. Waist	24	25	26	27	28	29 1/2	31	32 1/2	34 1/2	36 1/2
3. High hip	31 1/2	32 1/2	33 1/2	34 1/2	35 1/2	37	38 1/2	40	42	44
4. Hip	34 1/2	35 1/2	36 1/2	37 1/2	38 1/2	40	41 1/2	43	45	47
5. Mid neck	13	13 1/4	13 1/2	13 3/4	14	14 3/8	14 3/4	15 1/8	15 5/8	16 1/8
6. Neck base	13 1/2	13 3/4	14	14 1/4	14 1/2	14 7/8	15 1/4	15 5/8	16 1/8	16 5/8
7. Armscye	14 1/4	14 5/8	15	15 3/8	15 3/4	16 3/8	17	17 5/8	18 3/8	19 1/8
8. Upper arm	10	10 1/4	10 1/2	10 3/4	11	11 3/8	11 3/4	12 1/8	12 3/4	13 3/8
9. Elbow	9 3/8	9 1/2	9 5/8	9 3/4	9 7/8	10 1/8	10 3/8	10 5/8	11	11 3/8
10. Wrist	5 5/8	5 3/4	5 7/8	6	6 1/8	6 1/4	6 3/8	6 1/2	6 5/8	6 3/4
11. Thigh, max	19 1/2	20 1/4	21	21 3/4	22 1/2	23 1/2	24 1/2	25 1/2	26 3/4	28
12. Thigh, mid	18 1/4	18 3/4	19 1/4	19 3/4	20 1/4	21	21 3/4	22 1/2	23 1/2	24 1/2
13. Knee	13	13 3/8	13 3/4	14 1/8	14 1/2	15	15 1/2	16	16 1/2	17
14. Calf	12 1/2	12 7/8	13 1/4	13 5/8	14	14 1/2	15	15 1/2	16	16 1/2
15. Ankle	8 3/8	8 5/8	8 7/8	9 1/8	9 3/8	9 5/8	9 7/8	10 1/8	10 3/8	10 5/8
16. Vertical trunk	56	57 1/2	59	60 1/2	62	63 1/2	65	66 1/2	68	69 1/2
17. Total crotch	25	25 3/4	26 1/2	27 1/4	28	28 3/4	29 1/2	30 1/4	31	31 3/4
Vertical Measurements in Inches										
18. Stature	63 1/2	64	64 1/2	65	65 1/2	66	66 1/2	67	67 1/2	68
19. Cervical height	54 1/2	55	55 1/2	56	56 1/2	57	57 1/2	58	58 1/2	59
20. Waist height	39 1/4	39 1/2	39 3/4	40	40 1/4	40 1/2	40 3/4	41	41 1/4	41 1/2
21. High hip height	35 1/4	35 1/2	35 3/4	36	36 1/4	36 1/2	36 3/4	37	37 1/4	37 1/2
22. Hip height	31 1/4	31 1/2	31 3/4	32	32 1/4	32 1/2	32 3/4	33	33 1/4	33 1/2
23. Crotch height	29 1/2	29 1/2	29 1/2	29 1/2	29 1/2	29 1/2	29 1/2	29 1/2	29 1/2	29 1/2
24. Knee height	17 5/8	17 3/4	17 7/8	18	18 1/8	18 1/4	18 3/8	18 1/2	18 5/8	18 3/4
25. Ankle height	2 3/4	2 3/4	2 3/4	2 3/4	2 3/4	2 3/4	2 3/4	2 3/4	2 3/4	2 3/4
26. Waist length front	13 1/2	13 3/4	14	14 1/4	14 1/2	14 3/4	15	15 1/4	15 1/2	15 3/4
27. Waist length back	15 1/2	15 3/4	16	16 1/4	16 1/2	16 3/4	17	17 1/4	17 1/2	17 3/4
28. True rise	9 3/4	10	10 1/4	10 1/2	10 3/4	11	11 1/4	11 1/2	11 3/4	12

■Table C.1 (*continued*)

Size	2	4	6	8	10	12	14	16	18	20
Width and Length Measurements in Inches										
29. Across shoulders	14 3/8	14 5/8	14 7/8	15 1/8	15 3/8	15 3/4	16 1/8	16 1/2	17	17 1/2
30. Cross back width	13 7/8	14 1/8	14 3/8	14 5/8	14 7/8	15 1/4	15 5/8	16	16 1/2	17
31. Cross chest width	12 7/8	13 1/8	13 3/8	13 5/8	13 7/8	14 1/4	14 5/8	15	151/2	16
Girth Measurements in Inches										
32. Shoulder length	4 15/16	5	5 1/16	5 1/8	5 3/16	5 5/16	5 7/16	5 9/16	5 3/4	5 15/16
33. Shoulder slope (degrees)	23	23	23	23	23	23	23	23	23	23
34. Arm length shoulder to wrist	22 15/16	23 1/8	23 5/16	23 1/2	23 11/16	23 7/8	24 1/16	24 1/4	24 7/16	24 5/8
35. Arm length shoulder to elbow	13 1/4	13 3/8	13 1/2	13 5/8	13 3/4	13 7/8	14	14 1/8	14 1/4	14 3/8
36. Arm length center back neck–wrist	30 1/8	30 7/16	30 3/4	31 1/16	31 3/8	31 3/4	32 1/8	32 1/2	32 15/16	33 3/8
37. Bust point to bust point	7	7 1/4	7 1/2	7 3/4	8	8 1/4	8 1/2	8 3/4	9	9 1/4
38. Neck to bust point	9 1/4	9 1/2	9 3/4	10	10 1/4	10 5/8	11	11 3/8	11 7/8	12 3/8
39. Scye depth	7 1/8	7 1/4	7 3/8	7 1/2	7 5/8	7 3/4	7 7/8	8	8 1/8	8 1/4

Source: Reprinted from *Annual Book of ASTM Standards.* Copyright ASTM. Reprinted with permission.

■Table C.2 Incremental Grade Guide Derived From ASTM D 5585-95 Standard Table of Body Measurements for Misses Sizes 2–20

Size	2–4	4–6	6–8	8–10	10–12	12–14	14–16	16–18	18–20
Girth Measurement Differences Between Sizes in Inches									
1. Bust	1	1	1	1	1 1/2	1 1/2	1 1/2	2	2
2. Waist	1	1	1	1	1 1/2	1 1/2	1 1/2	2	2
3. High hip	1	1	1	1	1 1/2	1 1/2	1 1/2	2	2
4. Hip	1	1	1	1	1 1/2	1 1/2	1 1/2	2	2
5. Mid neck	1/4	1/4	1/4	1/4	3/8	3/8	3/8	1/2	1/2
6. Neck base	1/4	1/4	1/4	1/4	3/8	3/8	3/8	1/2	1/2
7. Armscye[a]	3/8	3/8	3/8	3/8	5/8	5/8	5/8	3/4	3/4
8. Upper arm	1/4	1/4	1/4	1/4	3/8	3/8	3/8	5/8	5/8
9. Elbow	1/8	1/8	1/8	1/8	1/4	1/4	1/4	3/8	3/8
10. Wrist	1/8	1/8	1/8	1/8	1/8	1/8	1/8	1/8	1/8
11. Thigh, max	3/4	3/4	3/4	3/4	1	1	1	1 1/4	1 1/4
12. Thigh, mid	1/2	1/2	1/2	1/2	3/4	3/4	3/4	1	1
13. Knee	3/8	3/8	3/8	3/8	1/2	1/2	1/2	1/2	1/2
14. Calf	3/8	3/8	3/8	3/8	1/2	1/2	1/2	1/2	1/2
15. Ankle	1/4	1/4	1/4	1/4	1/4	1/4	1/4	1/4	1/4
16. Vertical trunk	1 1/2	1 1/2	1 1/2	1 1/2	1 1/2	1 1/2	1 1/2	1 1/2	1 1/2
17. Total crotch	3/4	3/4	3/4	3/4	3/4	3/4	3/4	3/4	3/4
Vertical Measurement Differences Between Sizes in Inches									
18. Stature	1/2	1/2	1/2	1/2	1/2	1/2	1/2	1/2	1/2
19. Cervical height	1/2	1/2	1/2	1/2	1/2	1/2	1/2	1/2	1/2
20. Waist height	1/4	1/4	1/4	1/4	1/4	1/4	1/4	1/4	1/4
21. Hip height	1/4	1/4	1/4	1/4	1/4	1/4	1/4	1/4	1/4
22. Hip	1/4	1/4	1/4	1/4	1/4	1/4	1/4	1/4	1/4
23. Crotch height	0	0	0	0	0	0	0	0	0
24. Knee	1/8	1/8	1/8	1/8	1/8	1/8	1/8	1/8	1/8
25. Ankle	0	0	0	0	0	0	0	0	0
26. Waist front length	1/4	1/4	1/4	1/4	1/4	1/4	1/4	1/4	1/4
27. Waist back length	1/4	1/4	1/4	1/4	1/4	1/4	1/4	1/4	1/4
28. True rise	1/4	1/4	1/4	1/4	1/4	1/4	1/4	1/4	1/4
Width and Length Measurement Differences Between Sizes in Inches									
29. Across shoulders	1/4	1/4	1/4	1/4	3/8	3/8	3/8	1/2	1/2
30. Back width	1/4	1/4	1/4	1/4	3/8	3/8	3/8	1/2	1/2
31. Chest width	1/4	1/4	1/4	1/4	3/8	3/8	3/8	1/2	1/2
32. Shoulder length	1/16	1/16	1/16	1/16	1/8	1/8	1/8	3/16	3/16
33. Shoulder slope (degree)	0	0	0	0	0	0	0	0	0
34. Shoulder to wrist	3/16	3/16	3/16	3/16	3/16	3/16	3/16	3/16	3/16

■**Table C.2** (*continued*)

Size	2–4	4–6	6–8	8–10	10–12	12–14	14–16	16–18	18–20
Width and Length Measurement Differences Between Sizes in Inches									
35. Shoulder to elbow	1/8	1/8	1/8	1/8	1/8	1/8	1/8	1/8	1/8
36. Center back neck to wrist	5/16	5/16	5/16	5/16	3/8	3/8	3/8	7/16	7/16
37. Bust point to bust point	1/4	1/4	1/4	1/4	1/4	1/4	1/4	1/4	1/4
38. Neck to bust point	1/4	1/4	1/4	1/4	3/8	3/8	3/8	1/2	1/2
39. Scye depth	1/8	1/8	1/8	1/8	1/8	1/8	1/8	1/8	1/8

[a] Armscye girth 1-inch grade must be 1/2 inch instead of 3/8 inch to allow for distribution of total width grade.

Appendix D

Pattern Grading Aids

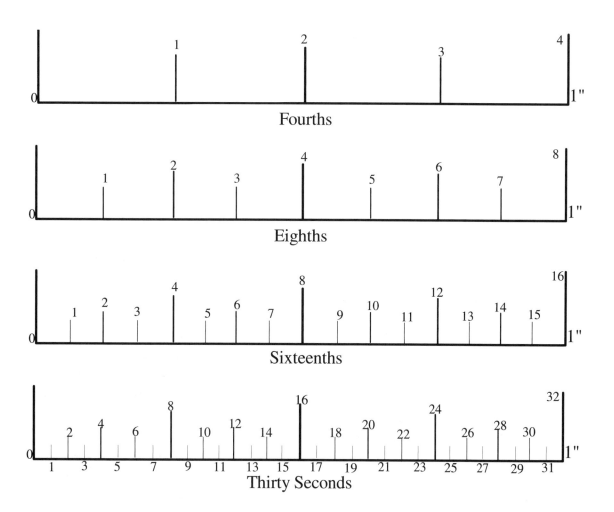

Figure D.1 Fractions of an Inch

Table D.1 Conversion Chart for Decimals and Common Fractions

Decimal	X/32th	X/16th	X/8th	X/4th	X/2th
.03125	1/32				
.0625	2/32	1/16			
.09375	3/32				
.125	4/32	2/16	1/8		
.15625	5/32				
.1875	6/32	3/16			
.21875	7/32				
.25	8/32	4/16	2/8	1/4	
.28125	9/32				
.3125	10/32	5/16			
.34375	11/32				
.375	12/32	6/16	3/8		
.40625	13/32				
.4375	14/32	7/16			
.46875	15/32				
.5	16/32	8/16	4/8	2/4	1/2
.53125	17/32				
.5625	18/32	9/16			
.59375	19/32				
.625	20/32	10/16	5/8		
.65625	21/32				
.6875	22/32	11/16			
.71875	23/32				
.75	24/32	12/16	6/8	3/4	
.78125	25/32				
.8125	26/32	13/16			
.84375	27/32				
.875	28/32	14/16	7/8		
.90625	29/32				
.9375	30/32	15/16			
.96875	31/32				
1.00	32/32	16/16	8/8	4/4	2/2

■Table D.2 Grade Rule Table: Misses

Pattern Piece:	
Unit: Denominator:	
Size Range:	
Master Size:	
Grade Rules:	
Notes:	

Size	Rule		Rule		Rule		Rule		Rule		Rule	
	X	Y	X	Y	X	Y	X	Y	X	Y	X	Y
6												
8												
10												
12	0	0	0	0	0	0	0	0	0	0	0	0
14												
16												
18												
20												
22												
Size	Rule		Rule		Rule		Rule		Rule		Rule	
	X	Y	X	Y	X	Y	X	Y	X	Y	X	Y
6												
8												
10												
12	0	0	0	0	0	0	0	0	0	0	0	0
14												
16												
18												
20												
22												

■Table D.3 Grade Rule Table

Pattern Piece:
Grade Rule Table:
Unit: Denominator:
Size Range:
Master Size:
Grade Rules:

Size	Rule		Rule		Rule		Rule		Rule		Rule	
	X	Y	X	Y	X	Y	X	Y	X	Y	X	Y

Size	Rule		Rule		Rule		Rule		Rule		Rule	
	X	Y	X	Y	X	Y	X	Y	X	Y	X	Y

Glossary

Additive grades — See *cumulative grades*.

Alpha sizes — Sizes designated by alphabetical classification rather than numerical classification. *Small, medium,* and *large* are examples of alpha sizing. Alpha sizing usually represents a greater amount of increase or decrease in garment dimensions between each size than does numerical sizing. Most alpha sizing collapses at least two numeric sizes into one alpha size.

Alphanumeric sizes — Sizing nomenclature that designates sizes by alphabetical classification followed by the numeric sizes that are incorporated into each of the alpha sizes. Example: small (8–10), medium (12–14), large (16–18).

Alternate grade reference axes — Additional *x,y* axes that do not intersect at the original 0,0 point of reference on the Cartesian graph, and are used to avoid distortion of graded designs.

Anthropometric data — Measurement data on the dimensions of specified areas of the human body collected by using scientific methods.

Anthropometric survey — The process of measuring specified body areas of a large sample of the population being studied.

Arc measurements — Measurements of a portion of a circumference. In anthropometry, arc measurements include areas such as the front waist and back waist.

Armscye — An armhole with a curved area between the mid-armhole and the underarm and side seam intersection.

American Society for Testing and Materials (ASTM) — ASTM is a government and trade supported organization that develops and publishes voluntary standards for many types of products including textiles and apparel.

ASTM D-5585: The Standard Table of Body Measurements for Adult Female Misses Figure Type, Sizes 2–20 — This voluntary standard is based on body measurements currently in use by apparel manufacturers and retail organizations and from previously conducted anthropometric surveys. New nationwide anthropometric research was not conducted for this standard.

ASTM D-5586: The Standard Table for Body Measurements for Women Aged 55 and Older, Misses Figure Type — This voluntary standard is based on body measurements taken in a nationwide anthropometric research study conducted on women aged 55 and older.

Axes — The straight lines on a graph that are used as a reference for the measurement of an object. The *x* axis is horizontal and the *y* axis is vertical. These *x* and *y* axes are at right angles to one another.

Basic blocks — A set of pattern pieces that form the basis of a style category such as skirts, bodices, and pants. Basic blocks are free of fashion details and have the minimum number of seams and darts that are required to fit the corresponding body type. Basic blocks usually contain major pattern pieces but not finishing details such as facings and pockets. They generally do not have seam allowances. An individual pattern piece is referred to as a block.

Basic slopers — Basic slopers are used for flat pattern design and consist of the minimum number of pattern pieces for a basic fitted garment. They do not have seam allowances and all darts extend to their respective pivot points. Basic slopers are used for flat pattern design.

Blending — The process of joining two separate lines with the resulting line creating a smooth transition between the two original lines.

Body dimensions — The actual measurements of the human body. Anthropometric surveys designate the specific areas of the body that are measured.

Body types — Classifications of the specified population that are based on key length and circumference body measurements. Body type classifications are made to improve the fit for a greater number of segments of the general population. Examples include *juniors*, *misses*, and *women's* classifications.

Cardinal points — The grade points that control the change in the perimeter of a pattern piece when it is graded. Most seam intersections and some curved areas have designated cardinal points.

Cartesian graph — A graph consisting of two perpendicular lines that divide an area into four quadrants. The horizontal line is the *x* axis and the vertical line is the *y* axis. The area to the left of the *y* axis and the area below the *x* axis is negative. The area to the right of the *y* axis and the area above the *x* axis is positive. The locations of specific points are identified by their *x* and *y* locations.

Circumference measurements — Measurements that completely encircle the body at the designated location. They are also called girth measurements.

Comfort stretch — Utilization of stretch in a fabric for comfort only, with stretch not incorporated into the fit of the garment.

Complex grading system — A grading system that distributes circumferential changes in size within the pattern pieces corresponding to the way they occur on the body. This system requires the back of garments to be graded differently than the front.

Computer grading — Computerized system that performs the task of grading patterns from a master size into a range of sizes. The changes in the dimensions of each pattern piece are based on grade rules entered into the computer system.

Conversion Factor — The percentage of the body dimension that is used when grading a stretch garment.

Cross grades — Grades for areas that represent width on the body. Each one-quarter basic block pattern piece contains one-half of a cross grade. Cross grades are variable grades.

Cumulative grades — The sum of all grade distributions between a cardinal point and the 0,0 point of reference as well as the sum of all sizes graded from the master pattern at each cardinal point.

Denominator — The term for the number below the line in a fraction. It designates the number of equal portions the whole number is divided into.

Design — The identifying characteristics of a garment that differentiate it from other garments of the same style. For example, a princess dress is a style, but a specific garment with princess seams curving into the armhole and a specific type neckline, sleeve, and collar is a design.

Digitizing — The process of entering the pattern piece, along with its identifying information, into the computer. The information is translated into the format required by the specific computer so that the shape and size of each pattern piece can be worked with and manipulated as necessary.

Fabric face — The side of the fabric that is worn on the outside of a garment.

Face-up and **Face-down** — Terms used when cutting garments to designate whether the pattern is placed on the right side (face-up) of the fabric or on the wrong side (face-down) of the fabric.

Fit model — An individual whose body measurements reflect those of the sample size for the target market for which a manufacturer produces. The fit of garments is tested and perfected on the fit model.

Fitting ease — The amount of ease in a garment necessary to allow the wearer to move freely.

Garment specifications — Tables listing the dimensions of specified garment areas for each size in a size range.

Girth — Circumference body measurement.

Girth measurements — Measurements that incorporate the total circumference of the body at the position where the measurement is taken.

Grade (noun) — **1.** The total increase or decrease in body girth between each size within a given size range. **2.** The incremental size change at each cardinal point on a pattern piece.

Grade (verb) — To systematically decrease and increase the dimensions of a sample-size master pattern to create a range of sizes for production.

Grade distribution — The method of distributing the total change in body dimension within each individual pattern piece.

Grade guide — A table that is developed from sizing specifications that dictates the system of grade distribution in order to determine the dimensional changes for each pattern piece across a size range.

Grade point — The points on a pattern piece that require a grade rule to control their movement during the grading process. All cardinal points are grade points.

Grade rule — The written record of the designated movement required to grade a pattern for a range of sizes. Each grade point on a pattern piece requires a grade rule.

Grade rule table — A set of grade rules that designate the amount of change in the dimensions of a pattern piece as it is graded into a range of sizes. Each individual grade rule controls the movement of a specific point on the pattern piece.

Graded nest — An illustration of a set of pattern pieces showing all sizes within a size range stacked along a common reference line. The nest illustrates the differences in each successive size.

Grading system — An aggregate of grade rules that specifies how the increase or decrease in size is distributed throughout the pattern piece.

Incremental grade — The amount of dimensional change from any one size to the next size in the size range. Incremental grade rules designate the dimensional changes from the adjacent size for each pattern piece across a size range.

Length grades — Grades for areas that represent length on the body. Each one-quarter basic block pattern piece usually contains the entire length grade. Length grades are standard grades.

Machine grading — The process of using a grading machine to grade a pattern. Machine grading entails clamping the pattern piece in the grading machine and turning a knob to mechanically move the pattern as specified for each grade point.

Manual grading — The process of grading patterns using only rulers and paper.

Master pattern — The complete set of pattern pieces for a specific design with all seamlines trued and balanced. Seam allowances are optional. The master pattern usually exists in the sample size.

Measurement method — Method of marking a new grade point by using a transparent ruler when each cardinal point on the master pattern is considered to be 0,0.

Mixed grades — Grading systems in which the dimensional changes in bust, waist, and hip are not equal for each size in the range. For example, the bust and hip grade may be 1 1/2 inch, whereas the waist grade is 1 inch when grading from one size to the next.

Numerator — The term for the number above the line in a fraction. It designates the number of equal portions of the whole number that the fraction represents.

Numeric sizes — Sizes designated by numerical classification rather than alphabetic classification. Numeric sizes are appropriate for garments designed to fit close to the body.

Pattern — A diagram of each of the component pieces required to construct a garment.

Pattern dimensions — The length and width of perimeter seamlines on a pattern.

Pattern grading — The process of systematically increasing and decreasing the dimensions of a master pattern into a range of pattern sizes for a specific design.

Pattern orientation — The direction in which the pattern piece is laid on a table or digitize before any pattern grading system is employed.

Point of reference — The point on the master pattern that is used as a reference when designating the amount of movement a grade point requires to be graded to other sizes in a size range.

Production pattern — A master pattern that has been graded to all sizes in a size run. The seam allowances and any dart take-up are included. Seams are trued and balanced on all sizes.

PS 42-70 — Voluntary Product Standard: Body Measurements for the Sizing of Women's Patterns and Apparel. This is a standard classification of body types, size designation, and body measurements for each size. It was updated in 1968 and published by the Department of Commerce National Bureau of Standards in 1970.

Quadrant — One of the four areas formed by the x and y axes on a Cartesian graph.

Relative grade — The amount of dimensional change from the sample size to a designated size in the size range. Relative grade rules designate the dimensional changes for each pattern piece from the sample size to each size across the size range. Relative grading is additive of all changes for all sizes between the sample size and graded size. For example, grading from size 12 to size 16 involves adding the grades from size 12 to 14 and from size 14 to size 16 together.

Rigid fabric — Fabrics used for garment construction that do not utilize any inherent give or stretch in the basic fit of the garment. All woven fabric and some knits fall into this category.

Rise — The difference between the crotch level and the waistline. The rise is a perpendicular measurement between the two body areas.

Sample-size pattern — The starting reference for grading. Master patterns are developed and trued for the sample size and then graded to other sizes within the given size range.

Scye — A curved seamline for the purpose of fitting body areas such as the curved armscye or the crotch curve in pants.

Simplified grading system — A grading system that distributes the circumferential changes in size equally between the back and the front pattern pieces.

Size nomenclature — The descriptive name of each size in a size range. These numerical or alpha designations identify garment size.

Size run — A group of garments incorporating one of each size within a size range for a specific style.

Size specifications — Tables listing the dimensions of specified body areas for each size in a designated size range. A set of specifications may contain body dimensions or garment dimensions.

Sizing standards — Classifications of body types, size designation, and body measurements that are developed from anthropometric studies.

Sloper — Any pattern that has all seam allowances removed so that it may be used as a basis for flat pattern design.

Standard grade — Grade increments that remain constant regardless of whether a 1-inch, 1 1/2-inch, or 2-inch grade is required for the specified size.

Stretch fabric — Fabrics used in garment construction where the inherent stretch of the fabric structure and/or fiber are an integral part of the garment design. The pattern dimensions are smaller than the body it is designed to fit. Some knit fabrics with elastomer yarns fall into this category.

Stretch Factor — The maximum stretch in any given direction that a fabric will stretch and still recover to the original dimension.

Stretch Garments — Apparel items that utilize fabric stretch for both fit and function. These garments are cut smaller than the actual body dimensions.

Style — A general category or classification of garments, such as straight skirt, princess dress, or cardigan.

Styling ease — Additional ease beyond that required for function (fitting ease). Styling ease contributes to the uniqueness of the design.

Style sense — The proportion and balance of the design lines within a specified garment.

Sweep — The width of the lower edge of a skirt or pant.

Three-dimensional grading system — A complex grading system in which arc measurements require different analyses than width and length measurements. Circumferential changes in size are distributed within the pattern pieces as they occur on the body instead of being equally distributed. This system requires the back of a garment to be graded differently from the front.

True — To blend and adjust seamlines between graded cardinal points so that the line character of the sample-size pattern is retained, and seams and notches on corresponding pieces match.

Two-dimensional grading system — A simplified grading system that distributes the circumferential changes in size equally between the back and the front pattern pieces. Loose-fitting garments are more successfully graded with a two-dimensional system than are close-fitting garments.

Uniform grades — Grading systems in which the dimensional changes in the bust, waist, and hip are equal for each size in the range. For example, if the bust grade is 1 inch, then the waist and hip grades are also 1 inch.

Vanity sizing — Assigning a smaller number to a garment to designate size that had previously carried a larger number.

Variable grade — Grade increments that vary depending upon whether a 1-inch, 1 1/2-inch, or 2-inch grade is required for the specified size.

Voluntary sizing standard — Sizing standards published by governments and trade-supported organizations for use as a guide to garment sizing for apparel manufacturing. The purpose of these standards is to aid in the consistency of sizing of apparel, although the use of these standards is voluntary. Manufacturers may deviate from the size definitions in order to develop a fit appropriate for their designated target market.

Width grades — Grades that are determined by the vertical grade distribution lines across the pattern. They are applied to increase or decrease the width dimensions of a pattern.

***x,y* axes** — See *Cartesian graph.*

***x,y* point** — The specific location of a point relative to the 0,0 point on a Cartesian graph. The negative and positive sign of each *x* and *y* number designates the quadrant in which the point is located.

Zero, zero (0,0) point — The intersection of the *x* axis and *y* axis on a Cartesian graph.

Index